DATE DUE

~~MR 29 '99~~		
AG ~~5 '99~~		
~~MY 15 '01~~		
~~JA 24 '03~~		

DEMCO 38-296

AFRICAN POLITICAL ECONOMY

AFRICAN
POLITICAL
ECONOMY

Contemporary
Issues in
Development

Kempe Ronald Hope, Sr.

M.E. Sharpe
Armonk, New York
London, England

Copyright © 1997 by M. E. Sharpe, Inc.

book may be reproduced in any form
n the publisher, M. E. Sharpe, Inc.,
Armonk, New York 10504.

aloging-in-Publication Data

Hope, Kempe R.
African political economy: contemporary issues
in development / Kempe Ronald Hope, Sr.
p.   cm.
Includes bibliographical references and index.
ISBN 1-56324-941-3 (hardcover : alk. paper). —
ISBN 1-56324-942-1 (pbk. : alk. paper)
1. Botswana—Economic conditions—1966–
2. Botswana—Economic policy.   3. Africa—Economic
conditions—1960–   4. Africa—Economic policy.   I. Title.
HC930.H67   1996
338.96—dc20   96-24893
CIP
Printed in the United States of America

The paper used in this publication meets the minimum requirements of
American National Standard for Information Sciences—
Permanence of Paper for Printed Library Materials,
ANSI Z 39.48-1984.

∞

BM (c)   10   9   8   7   6   5   4   3   2   1
BM (p)   10   9   8   7   6   5   4   3   2   1

To the Peoples of Africa

Contents

List of Tables

Preface

Beginning in the 1970s and worsening in the 1980s, Africa has been a continent in rapid decline. That tragic situation has resulted in the 1980s' being declared as Africa's lost decade.

Using an interdisciplinary political economy approach, this book captures the issues and factors related to the African development dilemma by delineating the main components of the continent's socioeconomic crisis and analyzing the requirements and elements of the challenge of policy reform and change for the twenty-first century.

Africa, particularly sub-Saharan Africa, with its undiversified economic structure and undeveloped policy infrastructure, has been immobilized by its inability to adjust to the external and internal shocks it has experienced. The continent is now the poorest region in the world and it is the only region where poverty is expected to increase in the future. In short, the peoples of Africa are in despair.

This book catalogues the factors contributing to such despair. They include a crippling total external debt; a weakening balance of payments; intensification of the brain drain; deepening capital flight; declining agricultural productivity and foreign direct investment; deteriorating physical infrastructure; escalating unemployment and crime; pronounced famine and malnutrition; soaring budget deficits; rapid urbanization; expanding environmental degradation; worsening political and civil strife; rampant corruption; and increasing poverty, socioeconomic inequalities, population growth rates, and incidence of AIDS.

However, in this sea of despair there are African countries, such as Botswana, that are models of success (depicted in good governance and prudent and successful economic management) for the rest to emulate. Also, several other countries have begun to make the transition from the lost decade of the 1980s to the promise of the twenty-first century. Some countries have even made significant progress toward political and economic liberalization. The task facing the continent, therefore, is to spread and sustain these gains throughout the region, which requires a much more indigenous vision and long-term perspective thinking.

It is undisputed that Africa needs to develop a new shared vision of its future that embraces economic and political liberalization as well as regional cooperation and integration. Improving policies alone can boost growth substantially, but if neighboring countries adopt a policy change together, the effects on growth would be more than double what they would be with one country acting alone.

Policy reform and change are of crucial importance in Africa. But so also are the political processes from which the choices of policy reform and change emerge, are implemented, and are sustained. Undoubtedly, politics has been an obstacle to development in postcolonial Africa. This book amply demonstrates that bad governance has been bad for the development process in Africa. Consequently, if the vision for the twenty-first century is to be realized, Africa's leaders must display a new political resolve both to disengage from authoritarian, nondemocratic systems of personal rule, and to dismantle the bureaucratic obstacles to policy reform and change. Then, and only then, can policy reform and change take hold to reverse the continent's tragic decline and marginalization.

In preparing this book, I received, as usual, generous advice and intellectual support from several colleagues. I would like to make particular mention of Dr. Derick A.C. Boyd of the University of East London; Professor Rudy Grant of York University; Mr. Gladson K. Kayira of the Ministry of Finance and Development Planning of the government of Botswana; and Dr. Laurence C. Clarke, Director of the Caribbean Center for Monetary Studies and a consummate Africanist. Of course, neither individually nor collectively do they bear any responsibility for the final output as contained herein. I also express here a debt of gratitude to Olivia for putting up with my demands for meeting the deadlines for word processing and editing.

The views expressed in this book are private and do not necessarily represent the views of the United Nations or any of its affiliated agencies, the government of Botswana, or any other institution with which I am currently affiliated.

KRH, Sr.
Gaborone, Botswana

Acknowledgments

Some of the chapters in this book have been adapted, revised, and/or expanded from some of my previous work. The following are the relevant acknowledgments:

Chapters 1 and 8, originally co-authored with Gladson Kayira, were derived from a paper presented to the Eighteenth Annual Southern African Universities Social Science Conference, Swaziland, December 4–7, 1995; chapter 2 was originally published in the *Journal of Contemporary African Studies*, vol. 14, no. 1 (1996), pp. 53–67, published by Carfax Publishing Company, P.O. Box 25, Abingdon, Oxfordshire OX14 3UE, UK; chapter 5 originally appeared in the *Journal of Asian and African Studies*, vol. 30, nos. 1–2 (1995), pp. 80–89, published by E.J. Brill, P.O. Box 9000, 2300 PA, Leiden, The Netherlands; chapters 6 and 10 were derived from a paper prepared for the Seventh International Anti-Corruption Conference, Beijing, China, October 6–10, 1995; chapter 9 was first published in *Public Administration and Development*, vol. 15, no. 1 (1995), pp. 41–52, published by John Wiley and Sons, Baffins Lane, Chichester, West Sussex PO19 1UD, UK; and chapter 11 was adapted from a paper commissioned for the 1996 Biennial Conference of the Commonwealth Association for Public Administration and Management, Malta, April 21–24, 1996.

Part I

Development Problems and Issues

1

The Economic Crisis in Africa: An Analytical Perspective on Its Origins and Nature

The majority of African countries are experiencing a serious economic crisis. That crisis, though showing signs of moderation in some countries, has resulted in development eluding most of the others, with far-reaching negative consequences on their populaces. When there is no development, there is hopelessness; and where there is hopelessness, there is no effort to work toward development. The circle becomes complete and reinforcing.

Unfortunately, in most of Africa, the economic crisis has made life an endless series of vicious circles that are now spreading economic suffering in a concentrated fashion. The economic crisis in Africa represents a historical tragedy, and the historical evidence now suggests that such a crisis need not have occurred. Despite some views to the contrary, the overwhelming opinion is that this economic crisis is primarily the inevitable outcome of the failure of postindependence development policy formulation and implementation in the majority of the African countries.

In most of Africa, postindependence development policy was formulated through a statist ideological framework, which was then implemented by experimentation. Moreover, some, if not all, of the countries had to contend with an adverse international economic environment. That combination produced disastrous results. Among other things, poverty and socioeconomic inequalities increased, the external debt burden became heavier, the brain drain intensified, capital flight deepened, the balance of payments weakened, the physical infrastructure deteriorated, unemployment and crime escalated, famine and malnutrition became more pronounced, budget deficits soared, agricultural

productivity declined, urbanization burgeoned, environmental degradation expanded, political and civil strife worsened, and corruption became more rampant.

These disastrous development results were, in turn, the catalyst behind
the deepening economic crisis in Africa, and consequently provided
the imperative for policy reform in those countries. Policy reform can
be defined as changes in government policy, institutional structure, or
administrative procedures that are designed to alter economic activity
and improve performance (Roemer and Radelet 1991). Put more suc-
cinctly, it is policy change, across the board, to effect sustained economic progress that will lead to a more desirable economic outcome
than current practice permits.

The policy reform that emerged in the 1980s as a response to the
ensuing economic crisis in Africa was dominated by donor-sponsored
structural adjustment programmes (SAPs), primarily the World Bank
and the International Monetary Fund.[1] The SAPs have triggered a
fierce debate over their effectiveness as an antidote to the economic
crisis in Africa, and a significant body of literature that is very critical
of SAPs has emerged.[2] However, most of the critics of SAPs, although
making a convincing case in some of their criticisms, on the other hand
have failed to provide convincing and implementable alternatives for
economic recovery in the African countries.

This chapter, which is structured as a comparative analytical review,
examines the origins and nature of the economic crisis in Africa and
the policy framework giving rise to it, drawing on Southern African
country examples to illuminate and illustrate the analytical perspective.

The Origins and Nature of the Economic Crisis in Africa

The economic crisis in Africa emerged in the 1970s following the
achievement of independence in most of the countries in the 1960s.
During the 1980s the crisis worsened. Basically, after an initial period
of growth immediately after independence, most of the African economies began to decline. In the 1980s, the decline became more rapid
and had reached crisis proportions before donor-supported policy reforms were implemented.

There is little doubt that the magnitude of the economic crisis in
Africa has brought considerable agony to the citizens of those coun-

tries, and perhaps the best indicator of that is the rates of poverty. Although the data series are incomplete for some of the countries, based on the available data as shown in Table 1.1, only in Botswana and Zimbabwe is the percentage of the population below the absolute poverty line less than 50 percent. There are more poor people now than there were in 1985 in most of the African countries (World Bank 1994a). Poverty in Africa is exacerbated by high rates of population growth. At current rates of growth, most of the African countries will double their population within the first two decades of the twenty-first century (UNDP 1995).

Contributing to poverty, in relation to population growth, is the dismal economic performance of most of the African countries when measured in terms of national income accounts. In most of the countries, the annual growth rate of gross national product (GNP) per capita declined between the periods 1965–80 and 1980–93. During the period 1980–93, only two of the Southern African countries (Botswana with 6.2 percent and Swaziland with 3 percent) had statistically significant positive growth rates in GNP per capita while during the period 1965–80 only one country (Zambia with –1.2 percent) had a negative growth rate.

Declining growth rates in per capita income would also suggest an association with income inequality, which can be measured by the Gini index, estimated from the Lorenz curve describing the income or expenditure distribution for a given population. The movement in the Gini closely follows the movement in poverty. Where there is an increase in poverty levels, as measured by the head count, there is usually a parallel increase in the level of inequality, and vice versa (World Bank 1994a). Currently, there are estimates of the Gini index for several countries for varying periods ranging from 1981–82 to 1993–94. In the majority of countries the Gini index is very high, ranging from 43.5 percent in Zambia to 59.2 percent in Tanzania, and thereby indicating considerable income inequality (World Bank 1994a).

In Africa, the poor are mostly rural. There are more poor rural households than poor urban households and the incidence of rural and urban poverty among countries provides some stark contrasts. The data for 1991, for example, indicate that Malawi has the largest disparity in rural and urban poverty, with 85 percent of the population in the rural areas below the absolute poverty line compared to 8 percent in the urban areas, while Zambia has the smallest disparity with 42 percent of

6

Table 1.1

Basic Indicators for Selected Countries

Country	Annual population growth rate (percentage) 1960–92	GNP per capita (US$)		GNP per capita (avg. annual growth) (percentage)		Annual inflation rate (percentage)		Population in poverty (percentage) MRE[a]
		1980	1993	1965–80	1980–93	1965–80	1980–93	
Angola	2.3	N/A[b]	1,670[d]	0.6	-1.0[c]	N/A	12.3[c]	N/A
Botswana	3.3	940	2,790	9.9	6.2	8.1	12.3	43.0
Lesotho	2.5	450	650	6.8	-0.5	8.0	13.8	55.6
Malawi	3.4	190	200	3.2	-1.2	7.0	15.5	82.0
Mozambique	2.1	190[e]	90	0.6	-1.5	9.9	42.3	N/A
Namibia	2.6	1,500[e]	1,820	0.6	0.7	N/A	11.9	N/A
South Africa	2.5	1,840	2,980	3.2	-0.2	10.0	14.7	N/A
Swaziland	2.8	880	1,050	3.7	3.0	N/A	1.6	50.2
Tanzania	3.1	290	90	0.8	0.1	9.9	24.3	57.6
Zambia	3.2	650	380	-1.2	-3.1	6.4	58.9	64.3
Zimbabwe	3.2	760	520	1.7	-0.3	6.4	14.4	25.5

Sources: UNDP, *Human Development Report* (New York: Oxford University Press, several years); World Bank, *World Development Report* (New York: Oxford University Press, several years); World Bank, *African Development Indicators 1994–95* (Washington, DC: World Bank, 1995); World Bank, *Trends in Developing Economies Extracts: Volume 3: Sub-Saharan Africa* (Washington, DC: World Bank, 1994); United Nations, *Africa Recovery* (New York: United Nations, several issues); and World Bank, *World Tables 1994* (Baltimore: Johns Hopkins University Press, 1994).

Notes:

[a]Most recent estimate.

[b]Not Available.

[c]1980–92.

[d]1992.

[e]1982.

the rural population being poor compared to 31 percent of the urban population (World Bank 1995a).

However, despite the fact that most of the poor in Africa live in the rural areas, urban poverty has been increasing as urbanization has become much more rapid.[3] With the exception of South Africa, all of the Southern African countries had urban population growth rates that exceeded 3.5 percent during the period 1980–93, with Mozambique having the highest rate at 8.4 percent (World Bank 1995b). This rapid urbanization in Africa can be attributed primarily to rural-to-urban migration. Migration to urban areas is a rational economic decision for those in search of economic betterment. It is therefore a survival strategy for the rural poor. In Tanzania, for example, the percentage share of net migration in urban growth was 85 percent for the period 1975–90 (Findley 1993).

However, when coupled with the other elements of the economic crisis in Africa, rapid urbanization has some very serious consequences. Most of those consequences are related to insufficient capacity for labor absorption in the urban areas, resulting in increasing rates of urban unemployment, and the lack of government capacity to provide the requisite social services (Hope 1995a).

With respect to capacity to absorb labor, with the exception of Lesotho (1.96 percent) and Mozambique (1.79 percent), all of the Southern African countries had average annual labor-force growth rates that exceeded 2 percent during 1965–95, and it is projected that during 1995–2005 the majority of the countries will have labor-force growth rates exceeding 2.5 percent, with some countries surpassing the 3 percent mark (World Bank 1995b).

However, this growth in the labor supply has not been matched by a similar growth in formal-sector employment. As a matter of fact, in most of the countries, formal-sector employment has been declining since the 1980s (World Bank 1995c). In Zambia, for example, formal-sector employment as a proportion of the labor force has been declining so rapidly that it is now the primary contributor to urban poverty and income inequality in the country (Seshamani 1992). In addition, real wages in the formal sector have also been declining (Vandemoortele 1991).

Much of the decline in formal-sector employment can be attributed to the decline in manufacturing employment. In South Africa, for example, the growth rate of manufacturing employment declined from

2.9 percent in 1970–80 to 0.9 percent in 1980–90, while in Zimbabwe the decline was less dramatic for the same two periods, moving from 3.48 percent to 3.14 percent (Khan 1994). In terms of formal-sector wage rates, not only has the ratio of nonagricultural to agricultural wage rates been declining but so also has been the ratio of nonagricultural wages to per capita income.

Since 1980, real wages have declined more rapidly than per capita income. This suggests that the wage earners have borne a heavy burden of the economic crisis (Vandemoortele 1991). In Tanzania, for example, employees in the nonagricultural sector earned about seven times the country's per capita income in 1975 compared to only two and one-half times in 1986, while in Zambia similar employees earned approximately five times the country's per capita income in 1975 compared to a little more than one and one-half times in 1984 (Vandemoortele 1991).

With the decline in formal-sector employment, there has been an increase in subterranean- (informal) sector employment and activities.[4] The expansion of subterranean-sector employment in Africa is, ironically, one of the few positive things to have emerged from the ensuing economic crisis in the region. The phenomenal expansion of the subterranean sector has been documented in numerous studies and reports in recent years. The great majority of that documentation suggests that the evolution of the subterranean sector has taken place because of the failure of the developing countries to formally make the kind of economic progress that would have allowed for, among other benefits, low urban unemployment rates, a reduction in national poverty rates, wages and salaries that kept pace with inflation, the ready availability of basic goods and services, a functioning infrastructure, and a relatively honest and efficient bureaucracy (Hope 1993a; Hope 1993b).

The subterranean sector now absorbs the majority of labor-force entrants in Africa, and government attitudes in the region have changed in favor of its role as a labor sponge and center of self-reliance and private initiative. In Botswana, for example, the government has given prominence to the subterranean sector for its increasingly important role in providing income-earning opportunities and meeting demands for goods and services, particularly for the low-income population (Republic of Botswana 1991a). In Zambia, the subterranean sector now absorbs nearly 80 percent of urban workers (Kashambuzi 1995).

Based on the available evidence, women seem to be overrepresented in the subterranean sector in Africa. In Zambia, women now account for two-thirds of subterranean-sector production of services, and in the urban areas of Botswana in 1984–85, nearly half of employed women—but only 10 percent of employed men—were working in the subterranean sector (UNDP 1995). In Tanzania, in 1988, 95 percent of women workers and 84 percent of male workers were concentrated in the subterranean sector (World Bank 1995b). The involvement of women in the subterranean sector has grown as the economic crisis has reduced job opportunities in the formal sector and increased the need for an additional source of family income. In Zambia, for example, women's earnings from the subterranean sector increased considerably as a share of total household earnings in the 1980s (UNDP 1995).

Turning to social services, although access to these services has been increasing over the years, the budgetary constraints of the governments have resulted in a situation where there are still too many people without access to health care, safe water, sanitation facilities, and adequate housing, particularly in the rural areas. In some countries, such as Zambia, only 28 percent of the rural population, compared to 70 percent of the urban population, had access to safe water during 1988–93 (UNDP 1995). In other countries, such as Lesotho, only 23 percent of the rural population and 14 percent of the urban population had access to sanitation facilities during the same period (UNDP 1995).

One major area of concern, in terms of access to services, is housing. While some countries, such as Botswana, seem to have an oversupply of urban housing, there are several others where the housing situation has become environmentally hazardous as a result of overcrowding and the increasing concentration of squatter settlements. In Johannesburg, South Africa, for example, squatter housing was estimated to have reached 22 percent of the total housing stock by 1990, while in Dar es Salaam, Tanzania, by 1990 squatter housing was 51 percent of the total housing stock (*The Economist* 1995). This demonstrates a serious situation regarding lack of access to adequate shelter and a potential source of societal conflict.

Of all of the indicators reflecting the seriousness of the economic crisis in Africa, two of the most significant are the persistent budget deficits and the aggregate net resource flows. As seen in Table 1.2, with the exception of Botswana since 1983 and Swaziland (for some years), all of the countries recorded budget deficits throughout the 1980s. The budget deficit/surplus (excluding grants) is a measure of

Table 1.2

Government Deficit/Surplus (Excluding Grants) for Selected Countries, 1980–93 (percentage of GDP)

Country	1980	1984	1985	1986	1987	1988	1989	1990	1991	1992	1993	1986–MRY[a]
Angola	N/A[b]	N/A	-5.8	-7.8	-11.3	-19.6	-19.7	-23.7	N/A	N/A	N/A	-16.4
Botswana	-5.1	10.6	20.4	19.5	14.4	17.7	9.7	11.0	9.9	10.4	-5.0	10.9
Lesotho	N/A	-7.9	-5.8	-10.2	-29.6	-27.1	-19.7	-13.1	-8.8	-3.0	-0.5	-14.0
Malawi	-20.3	-7.6	-9.9	-12.3	-11.8	-8.4	-4.8	-5.6	-5.6	-13.0	-8.4	-8.7
Mozambique	-10.9	-20.7	-19.0	-24.6	-22.9	-26.8	-24.7	-29.2	-24.9	-28.6	-22.2	-25.5
Namibi	N/A	N/A	N/A	-9.0	-12.5	-7.0	0.8	-3.1	-4.1	-6.9	-5.7	-5.9
South Africa	-2.4	-4.7	-4.1	-5.5	-7.3	-5.6	-0.4	-4.7	-4.4	-4.9	-9.0	-5.2
Swaziland	4.4	-2.0	-4.7	-5.9	1.3	-3.4	4.4	-0.5	-2.0	-3.5	-7.8	-1.3
Tanzania	-11.4	-7.9	-6.2	-6.9	-7.1	-8.2	-5.4	-6.1	-2.7	-2.6	N/A	-5.6
Zambia	-19.4	-8.9	-15.4	-23.0	-13.3	-13.2	-7.4	-5.4	-5.6	-2.3	-1.2	-8.9
Zimbabwe	-10.9	-11.3	-9.4	-9.0	-11.8	-9.8	-9.1	-7.7	-7.5	-8.2	-6.4	-8.7

Sources: World Bank, *African Development Indicators 1994–95* (Washington, DC: World Bank, 1995), p. 187; and Vito Tanzi, "The Consistency Between Long-Term Development Objectives and Short-Term Policy Instruments in Fund Activities" in *From Adjustment to Development in Africa*, ed. G.A. Cornia and G.K. Helleiner (New York: St. Martin's Press, 1994), pp. 77–78.

Notes:

[a]Most recent available year.

[b]Not available.

the ability of a government to finance its activities from its own resources. For most of the countries, the deficit as a share of GDP had
reached unsustainable levels by the beginning of the 1980s. In both
Malawi and Zambia, for example, the deficit was equivalent to approximately one-fifth of GDP by 1980. Such budget deficits suggest that
the governments were consistently spending much more than they
were capable of raising as revenues from domestic activities despite
their high levels of taxation (Tanzi 1992). In Zambia and Zimbabwe,
for example, total expenditure as a percentage of GDP exceeded 35
percent during the period 1981–86, while total revenue as a percentage
of GDP during the same period was 30 percent in Zimbabwe and 23
percent in Zambia (World Bank 1994b).

Contributing significantly to these budget deficits has been the very
poor performance of the public enterprises, which in turn resulted in
the need for governments to inject substantial sums of money into
those enterprises to keep them afloat.[5] Basically, African public enterprises have failed to generate a sufficient amount of working capital
internally. Consequently, "they have demonstrated a limited ability to
finance new or replacement investments" (Nellis 1994). African public
enterprises have now gone from being a burden on the national treasury to being a major burden on the domestic banking system and
capital markets.

The budget deficit situation, in turn, led to a heavy reliance on
foreign financing primarily in the form of external borrowing and official grants. During the 1970s and 1980s, the external debt of all the
countries increased and some countries also relied heavily on official
grants. In Tanzania, for example, during 1974–80, the nominal value
of foreign aid per capita increased nearly fourfold and more than doubled in real terms (Hyden and Karlstrom 1993), while in Mozambique,
foreign aid as a percentage of GNP reached 59.2 percent in 1989 (Kyle
1994). Also, with the exception of Malawi, by 1993 the total external
debt burden per capita in all of the countries exceeded U.S.$250. In
Zambia, the total external debt burden per capita was U.S.$849 by
1986, the highest in the developing world, while its GNP per capita
was only U.S.$260 (World Bank 1995a; Fardi 1991). Clearly such a
state of affairs would be unsustainable.

Further evidence of the harsh realities of the debt problem as a
major contributor to the economic crisis in Africa can be gleaned from
an examination of the debt service ratios. From the available data for

Southern Africa, with the exception of Botswana, Swaziland, and Lesotho, all of the countries had double-digit (exceeding 15 percent) debt service ratios (debt service as a percentage of exports) by 1993, with both Zambia and Zimbabwe exceeding 30 percent. Furthermore, and again with the exception of Botswana, Lesotho, and Swaziland, all of the countries had external debt that exceeded 40 percent of GNP by 1993. In some countries, such as Mozambique, Zambia, and Tanzania, the net present value of external debt as a proportion of GNP had exceeded 100 percent by 1988, with Mozambique at the top with 376 percent (World Bank 1995b; World Bank 1990).

The economic crisis in Africa is also reflected in the inflation rates and the foreign reserves situation. The fiscal deficits and the resultant heavy borrowing have fueled inflation. During the period 1980–93, the average annual rate of inflation exceeded 10 percent in most of the countries. In some countries, such as Tanzania and Zambia, the inflation rate exceeded 25 percent during 1981–86 (World Bank 1994b). For Zimbabwe, it was also determined that the deficit was very responsive to changes in the rate of inflation, with a one percentage point change in domestic inflation increasing the deficit by 0.31 percentage points of GDP in the 1980s (Morandé and Schmidt-Hebbel 1994).

Due to poor balance-of-payments performance, as a result of deteriorating terms of trade, among other things, the import-coverage ratio of reserves declined in all of the countries during the 1980s except for Botswana. In Botswana, the balance of payments has been in surplus since 1982, primarily as a result of the outstanding export performance of the diamond industry (Hope 1996a). By the end of the 1980s, Botswana's import-coverage ratio of eighteen months was eighteen times that of Lesotho, South Africa, and Zambia; nine times that of Malawi, Mozambique, and Zimbabwe; and six times that of Swaziland. In contrast, by the end of the 1980s, Tanzania, for example, did not have enough foreign reserves to cover a full month of its imports and, in this regard, the country was worse off than it was in the 1960s (Sarris and Van den Brink 1994).

The final aspect of the economic crisis to be considered relates to savings and investment. It has been shown elsewhere that the presence of high and variable inflation lowers both investment and domestic savings, while large debt ratios tend to crowd out savings and investment (Hadjimichael et al. 1995). In the Southern African region, with the exception of Botswana, gross domestic savings as a proportion of

GDP declined during most of the 1980s. The worst performer was Lesotho, whose dependence on the South African economy cast it in the role of an exporter of labor and dependent on remittances and on receipts from the Southern African Customs Union (Petersson 1993). Lesotho had negative gross domestic savings during the 1980s, reaching a high of −93.7 percent of GDP in 1984 and declining to −46.4 percent of GDP by 1989 (World Bank 1995a).

Savings determine the rate at which productive capacity, and therefore income, can grow. On average, the more rapidly growing countries, such as Botswana, have had higher rates of savings than the slower-growing countries such as Tanzania. In addition, savings indicate the flow of real resources that are not consumed and therefore available for possible investment. Investment in Africa was uneven in the 1980s and was too low to support both a sustainable expansion in output and greater economic diversification.

During the 1980s, Angola had the lowest rate of gross domestic investment, measured as a proportion of GDP, in Southern Africa. By 1989, Angola's gross domestic investment was only 12 percent of GDP. On the other hand, Lesotho's gross domestic investment in the latter half of the 1980s was the highest in Southern Africa, averaging more than 50 percent of GDP during 1985–89 compared to 28 percent during 1975–79 and 24 percent during 1980–85 (World Bank 1995a). The average annual growth of gross domestic investment in Lesotho was 15.9 percent in 1985–95 compared to −1.7 percent in 1980–85 (World Bank 1994c). This performance was achieved primarily through improved rates of private investment.

Conclusions

The economic crisis in the majority of the African countries is rooted in the postindependence policy framework, which put considerable faith in the role of government to plan and allocate resources for economic development. Although such external factors as fluctuations in the terms of trade did also have some influence on the resultant economic crisis, it is the internal policy framework that played the much more crucial role in the birth and growth of the economic crisis in Africa.

In Africa, most of the countries embarked on development policies in the 1960s and 1970s that, among other things, distorted their price structures and removed their comparative advantage. Development

planning and other forms of state interventions in the economic process resulted in the diversion of resources from their socially most
productive uses (Rimmer 1995). As a result, economic growth and
development became elusive and the majority of the African countries
accelerated into a deep economic crisis.

The impact of that economic crisis has been so devastating that the
1980s are now correctly referred to in the literature as "Africa's Lost
Decade" (Ndegwa and Green 1994). Some authors, such as Landell-Mills
(1992), have gone even further by arguing that "the first three decades of
African independence have been an economic, political and social disaster." This economic deterioration at the national level, and the ensuing
economic deprivation at the human level, provided the imperative for
policy reform which emerged most dominantly in the form of structural adjustment programmes.

However, although this chapter is not concerned with the policy
response to the economic crisis in Africa, suffice to say here that the
SAPs have met with varying degrees of success. Nonetheless, to date,
there have been no real alternative policy frameworks that have been
adopted and implemented by the African governments. Consequently,
the SAPs retain their dominance as the preferred policy response to the
economic crisis in Africa.

This chapter has provided one analytical perspective on the economic
crisis in Africa. It does not claim to be exhaustive. Nevertheless, it provides considerable detail on the economic decline and human setbacks
that have gripped most of the African countries and which now present a
considerable development challenge for those countries as they approach
the twenty-first century and more particularly so for the poorer countries
such as Malawi, Sierra Leone, Ethiopia, Mozambique, Tanzania, and
Zambia, all of which have GNP per capita below U.S.$300 and a large
percentage of their population below the poverty line.

On the other hand, two countries—Botswana and South Africa—are
well poised to maintain and/or improve their economic performance.
Botswana has been a model of economic success with its sound development management and good governance (Hope 1995b). However,
the country needs to diversify its economy beyond dependence on
diamond exports to come to grips with its problems of unemployment
and income inequality (Hope 1996a). With respect to South Africa, the
transition to majority rule in 1994 created an internal environment for
increased domestic and foreign private investment and a receptive ex-

ternal environment for increased exports. Given its already substantial industrial base, South Africa has the potential to become a major economic power in the world economy.[6] Such a potential must be prudently tapped, particularly, among other things, to mitigate the estimated 30 to 40 percent unemployment rate among the Black population (Lundahl and Moritz 1993), and to accumulate resources for reconstruction and development projects.

Notes

1. The objectives and impact of structural adjustment programmes are discussed in chapter 8.
2. See, for example, Strydom and Fiser (1995) and Schatz (1994).
3. The causes and consequences of rapid urbanization are discussed in chapter 3.
4. See chapter 4 for a much more thorough analysis of the subterranean sector in Africa.
5. For a good analysis of the size, scope, and performance of the public enterprise sector in Africa, see Nellis (1994).
6. The current economic conditions for investment and growth in South Africa are regarded as the best they have ever been. See the *Sunday Times: Business Times* (1996): 2.

2

Growth, Unemployment, and Poverty in Botswana

Botswana is a very unusual country, both within Africa and among less developed countries as a whole, in terms of macroeconomic performance and development management. Although it was one of the poorest countries in the world when it achieved independence in 1966, Botswana has been transformed into one of the richest economies in Africa and is now one of the few African economies to be classified by the World Bank and the United Nations as an "upper-middle-income" country.

For much of the postindependence period, Botswana was one of the fastest growing economies in the world, in sharp contrast to the economic stagnation and deterioration of most of Africa and due, in large part, to the country's emergence as the world's second largest producer of diamonds, after the Russian Federation. Botswana has, therefore, been able to move from a pre-independence poverty-stricken economy, dependent primarily on the cattle industry and subsistence agriculture, to a rapidly growing economy with increases in export earnings and government revenues.

This rapid economic progress has been sustained by the country's internationally acclaimed good governance, which is taken here to mean sound development management and encompassing political accountability, bureaucratic transparency, the exercise of legitimate power, freedom of association and participation, freedom of information and expression, and capacity building. In other words, Botswana has been able to maintain the necessary administrative capacity for economic development and progress (Hope 1995b). This, in turn, has been achieved "through the supportive interrelations between an open market economy and a system of élite democracy, successfully blending some 'traditional' with modern elements, and offering a considerable range of fairly free and meaningful political choices" (Good 1992).

However, despite Botswana's rapid growth and considerable economic success, there is now concern that uneven development, as exhibited by rising unemployment, persistent poverty, and widening income inequality, is becoming a serious problem with the potential to affect the country's political economy and stability in the future, and thereby threaten an African success story (Curry 1987). This chapter discusses and analyzes the growth of the Botswana economy and the paradox of unemployment, poverty, and income inequality in relationship to that growth.

The Record of Growth and Economic Performance

The economy of Botswana, measured in terms of GDP, has been growing positively during the postindependence period, although not as spectacularly during 1992–93. The average annual growth, in real terms, during the entire postindependence period has been about 13 percent. Real GDP per capita was about nine times higher in 1991 than in 1966 when the country became independent (Republic of Botswana 1991a). Over the same period, growth in the mineral sector increased its share of GDP from 2 percent to 40 percent while the share of agriculture declined from 41 percent to 5 percent.

Although, since the mid-1970s, the mineral sector has been the engine of growth for the economy of Botswana, other sectors also contributed to the economic success of the country in the postindependence period. For example, there was a significant expansion of the national cattle stock and of beef exports in response to the favorable export prices offered by the European Community (Republic of Botswana 1991a).

Botswana has a very open economy, with imports and exports both exceeding 50 percent of GDP. The establishment and expansion of the diamond industry has led to a very rapid increase in export earnings, particularly during the latter half of the 1980s. Export earnings increased, on average, by 27 percent per year during the period 1981–1991. Diamonds currently account for about 71 percent of export earnings, vehicles and parts for 13 percent, copper-nickel and meat products for a further 8 percent, and other goods, such as textiles, the other 8 percent (Republic of Botswana 1996a).

During the same period, imports also grew rapidly, on average by 20 percent per year. However, the outstanding export performance, which more than doubled as a ratio to GDP, changed Botswana from having a large structural trade deficit in the 1960s to having a visible trade surplus by the mid-1980s (Harvey and Lewis 1990). With a surplus on the capital account in most years, combined with inflows of aid finance, the balance of payments has been in surplus since 1982.

The favorable balance-of-payments position of Botswana is reflected in the country's substantial reserves of foreign currency, which totaled 13,212 million pula (U.S.$4.6 billion) at the end of 1995 and were equivalent to around 23 months of import cover of goods and services (Republic of Botswana 1996b). In the short to medium term, it is quite obvious that Botswana would not face a foreign exchange constraint, and that state of affairs has enabled the country to maintain an increasingly liberal exchange-control regime.

Botswana's import pattern reflects both its proximity to South Africa and its membership in the Southern Africa Customs Union (SACU), which permits duty-free imports from the more industrialized South Africa. The SACU was originally established in 1910, creating a free-trade area that now includes South Africa, Botswana, Lesotho, Namibia, and Swaziland. In 1969, the government of Botswana renegotiated the Customs Union Agreement and derived more favorable treatment under the new terms.[1] In 1976, the 1969 agreement was amended, and agreed upon the following year, to allow for a stabilization factor equivalent to a lower limit of 17 percent and an upper limit of 23 percent as a proportion of imports, so as to guarantee a minimum rate of revenue to Botswana and the other smaller members of the SACU (Mayer and Zarenda 1994). This amendment was made retroactive to 1975.

However, the agreement gave South Africa both the right to determine the external tariffs applied by all members of the SACU and the responsibility for managing tariff receipts. That arrangement has now become a source of conflict because, although it reduces the administrative burden on the other countries, it confers powers on Pretoria to redistribute the receipts, for which there is now a two-year time lag. The primary effect of this two-year lag in the transfer of the SACU revenues to Botswana, as well as to the other members of the SACU, is that South Africa provides itself with an interest-free loan of the amount outstanding to Botswana and the other members of the SACU, for whom the real value of that sum is also further diminished by inflation.

In addition, while South African products freely enter the markets of Botswana, access in the other direction is much more limited. For example, in April 1995 the South African government banned the duty-free importation of semi-knocked-down Hyundai vehicles assembled in Botswana on the grounds that such importation threatened South Africa's employment market. This decision not only affects Hyundai Botswana but also some twenty to thirty semi-knocked-down operations in the SACU area (*Business Focus* 1995). Moreover, Botswana's membership in the SACU has fostered the development of largely import-competing industries, which have faced limited growth potential as a result of the rather small size of the Botswana domestic market (IMF 1995a). Consequently, Botswana's market has been quite important to the South African economy, particularly in providing a protected market for the latter's manufacturing exports. Nonetheless, the SACU is regarded as one of the more operational and properly functioning customs unions in Africa (*The Courier* 1992; AfDB 1993).

Also, Botswana's economy is fairly isolated from the major markets of Southern Africa, and this increases the costs of both importing inputs and getting manufactured exports to their destinations at competitive prices (AfDB 1993). The effect has been the emergence in Botswana of a very shallow industrial base comprised of manufacturing enterprises that primarily produce consumer-oriented products. Botswana's manufacturing enterprises are highly concentrated in urban areas and are primarily foreign owned despite comprehensive and commendable government policies for promoting local entrepreneurship (Republic of Botswana 1991a; Kaunda and Miti 1995).

Currently, approximately 78 percent of Botswana's imports originate from the SACU area while only about 6 percent come from other African countries, primarily Zimbabwe. Another 9 percent of imports come from Europe (of which 4 percent originate from the United Kingdom), and the balance originates from the United States, and the rest of the world, almost evenly. With respect to Botswana's exports, the primary destination is Europe with a 76 percent share (of which the United Kingdom gets 50 percent); the SACU area gets about 19 percent, and the rest goes to the United States and other African countries.

Since most consumption expenditure in Botswana is for goods and services that have to be imported, it is obvious that the country's rate of inflation would be considerably influenced by that of South Africa from which the majority of imports originate. The average annual rate of inflation is now showing a declining trend. In 1995, Botswana's average annual rate of inflation was 10.8 percent compared to 11.4 percent in 1990 and 12.7 percent in 1993, reflecting the declining prices in both South Africa and Botswana. This moderation of inflation in Botswana also depicts a pattern toward convergence with the rate prevailing in South Africa.

The increase in the production and export of diamonds has given a tremendous boost to government revenues in Botswana. The government of Botswana collects between 75 percent and 80 percent of the profits of the diamond industry through the combination of royalty payments, profits tax, withholding tax on remitted dividends, and dividends received by virtue of its 50 percent shareholding in the diamond mining company Debswana. The next most important source of government revenues is Botswana's entitlement from the revenue pool of the SACU. This is followed by the substantial profits earned by the Bank of Botswana through its management of the country's also substantial foreign exchange reserves. However, taxes, both direct and indirect, contribute only a relatively small proportion of government revenue.

Government revenues increased from U.S.$540 million in 1985 to an estimated U.S.$1.6 billion in 1994. In 1985, the shares of total revenues were 51.3 percent, 13.2 percent, and 17.3 percent, respectively, for mineral revenues, Customs Union Pool, and Bank of Botswana profits. After steadily holding second place, it is now expected that revenues from the Customs Union Pool will decline while profits from the Bank of Botswana will increase and replace the Customs Union Pool as the second largest source of government revenues. Their respective shares for 1993–94 were 43 percent for mineral revenues, 21 percent for Bank of Botswana profits, and 17 percent for the SACU Customs Pool. This trend is also expected to hold for the foreseeable future (Republic of Botswana 1995a).

As a consequence of good economic performance, the government of Botswana has also been able to increase its expenditures in all areas of social and economic infrastructure and services. In addition, there has recently been increased spending on the military. Defense spending as a percentage of total government spending increased from 8.3 percent in 1980, declined to 5.7 percent in 1985, and increased to 11 percent in 1994. Government expenditures (total of recurrent and development expenditure and net lending to the parastatals) increased from U.S.$397 million in 1983 to an estimated U.S.$1.5 billion in 1994. Since 1983 the government of Botswana has been running a budget surplus through prudent fiscal policy. This prudent fiscal policy is also reflected in Botswana's external debt structure. With a total outstanding government external debt of approximately U.S.$674 million and a debt service ratio of less than 7 percent in 1993, compared to the average debt service ratio of 25 percent and 21 percent in sub-Saharan Africa and all developing economies, respectively, Botswana's debt obligations are easily manageable.

The Unemployment Problem

Despite Botswana's considerable economic progress during the past twenty-five years, there are not enough jobs for those seeking employment and, consequently, unemployment has therefore become a serious problem. It is a serious problem because it may indicate a sluggish economy; it can contribute to states of idleness, which may in turn contribute to crime; it can result in poverty; and it may even lead to social chaos and instability, among other things.

Table 2.1 shows the actual and rising unemployment rates for the period 1981–1994. After declining steadily in the 1980s, the unemployment rate began to increase in 1991. Considerable unemployment has occurred despite the remarkable growth in formal-sector employment opportunities during the postindependence period. Formal-sector employment grew from 48,000 in 1972 to 228,900 in 1991. This represented an average annual growth rate of 8.6 percent over the nineteen-year period. Much of this growth occurred during the period 1985–1991, averaging 12.5 percent per year. By 1991, 49 percent of the labor force were employed in the formal sector.

However, in 1992 there was a temporary setback to employment growth as formal-sector employment declined during that year to 224,800, reflecting a negative growth (1.8 percent) for the first time since 1972. This resulted from a downturn in economic activity, which led in turn to widespread retrenchments, particularly in the construction and textile sectors. Between September 1991 and March 1993, private-sector employment declined from 144,600 to 131,800, a decrease of approximately 8.8 percent. However, over that same period,

Table 2.1

Unemployment Rates in Botswana, 1981–94 (percentage)

Year	Unemployment rate
1981	10.2
1984	25.3
1985	19.9
1986	16.0
1987	12.7
1991	13.9
1993	19.5
1994	21.0

Sources: Republic of Botswana, *Labor Statistics 1991/92* (Gaborone: Government Printer, 1993), p. 38; Republic of Botswana, *Report of the Presidential Commission on the Review of the Incomes Policy* (Gaborone: Government Printer, 1990), p. 19; and Republic of Botswana, *Household Income and Expenditure Survey: 1993/94* (Gaborone: Government Printer, 1995), p. 40.

the total growth in employment in the public sector, in absolute terms, was almost enough to compensate for those losses (Salkin 1994; Hope 1995b). By March 1995 formal-sector employment had increased to 234,500, reflecting a growth rate of 5.2 percent between March 1991 and March 1995. Most of that growth occurred in the government sector. In contrast, employment in the private and parastatal sectors declined over that period by 3 percent (Republic of Botswana 1996a).

Unemployment in Botswana tends to be high among the fifteen-to-twenty-four age group, approximately 44 percent of the total unemployed. Unemployment is also high (22 percent) among the twenty-five-to-thirty-four age group. When comparisons are made of the labor-force participation rates by sex in relation to the unemployment rate, there are some significant revelations. The female labor-force participation rate is now increasing. In 1991 it was 39 percent and in 1994 it was 46 percent. At the same time, however, female unemployment rates remain higher than those of men. In 1981, the female unemployment rate of 25.3 percent compared to 7.8 percent for men, three times higher. By the mid-1980s that gap had narrowed, with the female unemployment rate declining to 17.8 percent while that of men increased to 13.4 percent. In 1991, the female unemployment rate remained relatively the same as in the mid-1980s (17.3 percent) while the male unemployment rate declined to 11.3 percent (Republic of

Botswana 1993a). By 1994 the female unemployment rate was 23 percent compared to 20 percent for males (Republic of Botswana 1996a).

The disparity in the male/female labor-force participation rates, as they relate to unemployment, can best be explained by the educational attainment picture. For the economically active population, those who completed some secondary schooling through Form Three were fairly evenly split, by sex, as cash earners (employees or self-employed). In 1991, there were 29,551 males and 29,804 females falling into that category. Beyond Form Three, however, there are significant differences. In 1991, there were almost twice as many male as female cash earners who had achieved a complete secondary education or higher. There were 15,037 male cash earners in the economically active population who had completed secondary school, compared to 8,717 females. Similarly, there were 11,122 male cash earners who had attained a tertiary education compared to 5,485 females (Republic of Botswana 1993a).

Undoubtedly, the generally greater educational attainment of Botswana men influences their lower unemployment rates. Further, although the number of males and females actively seeking work in 1991 were almost statistically similar (31,852 male and 29,413 female), there were 56 percent more females than males in that group who had completed secondary schooling or higher. This suggests, on the one hand, that Botswana men find it easier to enter the labor force and, on the other hand, that Botswana women are perhaps encountering some barriers to labor-force entry. Also, compared to men, women who are employed have a much lower representation in the formal sector and a greater representation in the informal sector. Women comprise 36 percent of formal-sector employees and 75 percent of informal-sector employees (Jefferis 1993). This trend is, however, consistent with the findings for developing countries generally.[2]

Another factor in the unemployment puzzle relates to the role of migration from the traditional agricultural sector. There has been a massive exodus from traditional family agriculture, resulting in the decline of employment from 121,000 in 1984 to approximately 75,000 in 1991. Traditional family agriculture occupied 33 percent of the labor force in 1984 and only 15 percent in 1991. This indicates the deteriorating state of traditional agriculture in Botswana and its limited potential for generating income relative to other types of economic activity. Also, it has been suggested elsewhere that many people did not move back to agricultural activity after the end of the 1981–86 drought, particularly since the end of the drought occurred at the beginning of the period of rapid growth in other formal-sector employment opportunities (Jefferis 1993).

However, even in periods of rapid growth, there are no guarantees of finding employment and, consequently, some of those migrating are adding to the number of unemployed. As a matter of fact, had this migration not taken place and traditional agriculture employment stayed at around the same as in the mid-1980s, unemployment would now be virtually zero (Republic of Botswana 1993b). At the very least, the current double-digit rates of unemployment would not have prevailed.

The Dilemma of Poverty and Income Inequality

Botswana's impressive macroeconomic performance may have also concealed uneven development (Harvey 1992). In spite of the country's record of successful economic development and management, there is growing concern over what seems to be persistent poverty and deepening inequality in the distribution of income and wealth both between and within the urban and rural areas. More than half of the rural population, and a considerable proportion of the urban population, have incomes that are inadequate to meet basic needs. Since the majority of the population live in the rural areas, it is estimated that around 50 percent of the population are below the poverty line (Jefferis 1991).

A more recent and sophisticated analysis undertaken by the government of Botswana found that in the capital city, Gaborone, 21 percent of families lived below the poverty datum line (PDL) compared to 55 percent nationally. The comparable figures for the rural and urban areas are 64 percent and 30 percent of families, respectively, living below the poverty line (Republic of Botswana 1991b). The study used the incomes recorded in 1985–86 from a household income and expenditure survey (HIES) and inflated them to 1989 levels for correct comparison with the poverty datum line. For each of the households, in a sample of 2,077, a poverty datum line was calculated and compared with reported total income.

Also, there are twice as many households below the poverty line in the rural areas as in the urban areas. Furthermore, the average amount by which the households below the poverty datum line fall below that line is 17 percent in the urban areas, 33 percent in the rural areas, and 29 percent nationally.

However, an even more recent publication puts Botswana's absolute poverty rates at 43 percent nationally, 55 percent in the rural areas, and 30 percent in the urban areas for the period 1980–1990, compared to the sub-Saharan Africa regional aggregate poverty rates of 54 percent overall, 65 percent rural, and 23 percent urban for the same period (UNDP 1994).

A logical starting point for any discussion of income distribution is, obviously, to look at incomes. The 1985–86 HIES found that the median monthly income for urban households was a little more than twice that of rural households; the average male-headed household had a monthly income that was about two-thirds larger than that of female-headed households; and non-cash income was more important to rural households (exceeding 50 percent of total income) than to urban households (only 10 percent of total income) (Republic of Botswana 1988).

The 1989 PDL study, on the other hand, found that average monthly income of the urban households had grown to almost three times that of rural households. Moreover, while average incomes increased by 128 percent for rural households between 1985–86 and 1989, it increased by 201 percent for urban households.[3] The 1993–94 HIES also determined that the average monthly total disposable income of urban households was almost three times that of rural households, while the average monthly disposable cash income of urban households was almost four times that of the rural households (Republic of Botswana 1995b). This skewed distribution of urban and rural household incomes is further reflected in Botswana's income inequality index.

The income inequality index is measured by the ratio of the income share of the highest 20 percent of households to the lowest 20 percent of households. For the period 1980–1987, Botswana's income inequality index was 23.6 (UNDP 1991). However, for the period 1980–1991, the index rose to 47.4 (UNDP 1994). This earned Botswana the dubious distinction of having the highest degree of inequality in the distribution of income among all countries in the world for which statistics were available for that period. For regional comparative purposes the 1980–1991 index is 26.1 for Tanzania, 22.6 for Kenya, 13.6 for Lesotho, 4.9 for Uganda, 4.8 for Ethiopia, and 6.3 for Ghana. In simple terms, what the income inequality index suggests is that the top 20 percent income category in Botswana earns forty-seven times more than the lowest 20 percent income category. The 1993–94 HIES also indicates that there is no significant change in income distribution. The Gini coefficient in 1993–94 was 0.537 compared to 0.556 in the 1985–86 HIES (Republic of Botswana 1995b).

In addition to income inequality, persistent poverty in Botswana can also be explained by the grossly skewed distribution of wealth and the lack of potential for income generation. Poverty persists in Botswana for a number of reasons, primary among which is the fact that 32 percent of households have no family member in formal-sector employment; 49 percent of rural households do not own cattle, which is the principal agricultural asset in Botswana; 20 percent of the population live in accommodations with more than three persons per room; 17 percent of seven-to-thirteen-year-olds are not attending school; and educational access and quality are not uniform across the country (Republic of Botswana 1993b).

Moreover, there are institutional and sociocultural difficulties in the capacity of poor families to own or have access to land, water, and the credit facilities for acquiring cattle. This results in rural families being able to raise only between 25 percent and 40 percent of their basic income from their own production, with the remainder coming from nonagricultural and other sources, including as much as 40 percent in the form of transfers from government and relatives (Republic of Botswana 1993b).

Among the other factors that have contributed to persistent poverty in Botswana, and the widening gap between the rich and the poor, are droughts which have led to the ownership of livestock in fewer hands; alienation of communal land; and the curtailment of the facilities for hunting and gathering as part of environmental management (Peke 1994). Also, there is still the troubling existence of gender inequality in Botswana, which has a serious poverty impact, particularly on female-headed households in the rural areas.[4] Women are restricted in the acquisition of land, cattle, and credit and there are also problems related to their access to education in their early years.[5] This puts them at a greater disadvantage than men when seeking to become economically active. It also influences their literacy rates which, although improving, were 72 percent of the rate for men in 1992 (UNDP 1995).

In Botswana, land, cattle, and wealth go together in what can be regarded as the mainstay of the rural economy with a unique character which includes official support that coincides with the interests of the elite in government (Love 1994; Good 1993). However, that unique character is now dissipating as cattle ownership is becoming more and more unequally distributed and thereby contributing to the persistence of poverty among large numbers of households. Consider, for example, these further statistics. Commercial farms (mainly freehold and lease-hold) cover about 8 percent of the total land area and represent less than 1 percent of the total number of farms, but they hold 18 percent of all cattle. Traditional farms, on the other hand, cover a much larger share of Botswana's total land area and hold 82 percent of all cattle.[6] There is also a great disparity in performance between the two types of farms.

The commercial farms have annual calving rates and annual cattle mortality rates of 70 percent and 5 percent, respectively, while for the traditional farms the comparable rates are 50 percent for calving and 11 percent for annual mortality (Republic of Botswana 1991a). The commercial farms considerably outperform the traditional farms in the raising of cattle as well as in crop yield. The average crop yield of the commercial farms is 749 kg per hectare and for the traditional farms it is 241 kg per hectare, a little less than one-third (Republic of Botswana 1991a). Given such disparities in performance, it is understandable that the traditional farms can no longer sustain the levels of employment they once did and, as more people migrate out of the traditional agricultural sector, both income/wealth inequality and poverty deepen.

Conclusions

The economy of Botswana has entered a period of uncertainty where both economic and sociopolitical stability will be dependent on how well the government is able to mitigate the problems of unemployment, persistent poverty, and income/wealth inequality. This, of course, will also be influenced by some factors outside of the government's control such as international and regional market developments. However, it is possible to argue, as has been done elsewhere (Hope 1995b; Harvey 1992), that the necessary capacity exists to successfully manage the situation. Indeed, had it not been for sound development management in the past, Botswana's present growth with uneven development might have been more of a case of elusive development and rampant "Dutch Disease."[7] But, although Botswana seems more or less immune to "Dutch Disease," the country now needs to come to grips with its own disease, whose symptoms are expressed in uneven development and an undiversified economy (Norberg and Blomstrom 1993).

Much has already been put in place to adjust for the problems of unemployment, poverty, and inequality, but the government of Botswana recognizes that much more has to be done and has uttered a number of statements in that regard.[8] One area where policy needs to be enhanced is in the creation of income-earning opportunities to improve income distribution and reduce poverty through an emphasis on self-reliance. This can best be achieved by encouraging the growth of subterranean- (informal) sector activities.

As discussed in chapter 4, the subterranean sector has made a major difference between the ability to subsist and abject poverty for large numbers of people in the developing countries. Indeed, well-targeted programs of support for the subterranean sector can be far more cost-effective, in terms of employment promotion, poverty alleviation, and output, than certain large-scale programs of investment in and support for the formal sector (Hope 1993a). This has also been recognized by the government of Botswana in its development planning.[9] However, the enabling policy framework still needs to be elucidated and implemented. This needs to be done with some degree of urgency, given the imperative to plan for the consequences of the expected future decline of formal-sector activities in light of Botswana's narrow industrial base as previously discussed.

Further support for the above-discussed policy framework can be derived from the empirical studies of the subterranean sector around the world, most of which confirm that the sector contains a disproportionate number of the poor. Consequently, macroeconomic policies supporting assistance to subterranean-sector activities and workers could be a useful tool for both poverty alleviation and improving income distribution. Indeed, in the recent enlightened view of such international institutions as the World Bank (1995b), governments are urged to construct a framework for labor policy that, among other things, complements subterranean and rural labor markets and avoids biases that favor relatively privileged groups of workers at the expense of the poorest.

Finally, the government of Botswana must be commended for its early recognition of some of the problems and issues analyzed in this work and also for some of its attempts to develop policy to mitigate their impact. Finding lasting solutions to these concerns is never an easy task, especially since there are other (primarily external) influences beyond the government's control, as stated above. Nevertheless, as part of its commendable policy thrust, Botswana has decided to adopt a strategy for accumulated human development in the formulation of its Eighth National Development Plan (1997–2003), including a poverty alleviation framework with initiatives for the participation and partnership of institutions of civil society (UNDP 1995).

Notes

1. A more exhaustive analysis of this 1969 renegotiation and its outcomes can be found in Harvey and Lewis (1990).
2. See, for example, Hope (1993a; 1993b).
3. Calculated from data in Republic of Botswana (1991b).
4. For a good discussion of the causes and consequences of the low economic status of rural female-headed households in Botswana, see Kossoudji and Mueller (1983).
5. See Nyati-Ramahobo (1992).
6. This was the ownership and distribution structure in 1988 as reported in Republic of Botswana (1991a). The disparity is claimed to be much greater at present. See, for example, Hope and Edge (1996) and other sources cited therein.
7. For a good discussion of the theoretical and conceptual framework of "Dutch Disease," as well as its lack of practical application to Botswana, see Norberg and Blomstrom (1993).
8. A litany of statements on the need to give some priority to developing projects and programs to address poverty, unemployment, and inequality can be found, for example, in Republic of Botswana (1991a).
9. The National Development Plan 7 states, "It has been increasingly recognized that the informal sector plays an important role in providing income-earning opportunities and meeting demands for goods and services for the low income population. This sector produces a wide range of goods and services. However, its growth can be further developed." See Republic of Botswana (1991a).

3

Urbanization and Urban Management in Africa

During the past three decades, there has been rapid urbanization in Africa, due primarily to development strategies that emphasized urban growth at the expense of agricultural and rural development. Consequently, the rate of increase in the size of the nonagricultural population now exceeds the rate of increase in meaningful nonagricultural employment opportunities, leading to what has come to be known as "overurbanization."

The roots of rapid urbanization in Africa can be traced to the region's colonial past. The colonizers established centers of life (manifested in administrative, cultural, economic, and recreational activities) in those areas that gave them access to ports. Such access was vital because it allowed for the outward shipment of raw materials back to the colonizing countries and the inward shipment of manufactured goods. The European imperialist powers had viewed the colonies as a source of raw materials and as an outlet for selling their manufactures. Consequently, the spatial structures of most African economies became strongly focused on a small number of port cities. It was on these cities that newly established transport systems concentrated and it was toward these cities that the population drifted (Findlay and Findlay 1987).

Within these port cities, or in their immediate surroundings, there were usually extensive open spaces for the exclusive use of the Europeans. These polo fields, parks, cricket fields, golf courses, and so on also served as *cordons sanitaires* separating the colonizers from the colonized (Drakakis-Smith 1993). Remarkably, such areas still exist in some African cities where they still retain some or all of their degree of exclusiveness. This is especially true of the privately owned or leased spaces such as school playing fields or golf courses (Drakakis-Smith 1993).

With the end of the colonial era, population redistribution toward these cities did not cease. On the contrary, it increased as these cities retained and extended their dominance as the primary centers of economic activity and emerged to become the "primate" cities of the twentieth century (Gilbert and Gugler 1992). In many cases, the only change independence brought to these African cities was to substitute African citizens for European administrators and elites.

The legacies of colonialism for the cities of Africa are, however, not confined to spatial or environmental characteristics. They also relate to the regulation of social space. Many of the social and political problems experienced by contemporary African cities are also deeply rooted in their colonial past, associated to a considerable degree with the common practice where a minority ethnic group assumes responsibility for urban petty commerce. Most of the cities of East Africa, for example, have substantial East Indian business communities. This breeds resentment by the majority African populations, who consider themselves excluded from profitable urban economic activities. Such resentment has, from time to time, resulted in ethnic clashes (Drakakis-Smith 1993). This chapter focuses on the trends of urbanization in Africa, its contributory factors and consequences, and some aspects of policies to effectively manage it.

African Urbanization Trends

Since 1950, the urban proportion of the world's population has risen rapidly and this trend is expected to continue well into the foreseeable future. Nearly two-thirds of the urban dwellers in the world reside in the Third World. As seen in Table 3.1, the proportion of the population residing in urban areas in Africa is projected to increase from approximately 34 percent in 1990 to 57 percent by 2025, with significant variation in the level of urbanization among the regions. In 1990, approximately 22 percent of the East African population resided in urban areas compared to 33 percent, 38 percent, 45 percent, and 55 percent for West Africa, Middle Africa, North Africa, and Southern Africa, respectively. This range and rank order are projected to be maintained through 2025, although at a higher level. The percentage urban is projected to vary from 47 percent in Eastern Africa to 74 percent in Southern Africa.

Despite such overall rapid urbanization, the least developed African

Table 3.1

Percentage of African Population Residing in Urban Areas by Region, 1990–2025

Region	1990	1995	2000	2005	2010	2015	2020	2025
Africa	33.9	37.3	40.7	44.0	47.4	50.7	53.9	57.1
Eastern Africa	21.8	25.4	29.0	32.5	36.0	39.6	43.2	46.8
Middle Africa	37.8	41.6	45.6	49.5	53.4	57.0	60.4	63.6
Northern Africa	44.6	47.9	51.2	54.5	57.7	60.7	63.6	66.3
Southern Africa	54.9	58.2	61.3	64.2	66.8	69.3	71.6	73.8
Western Africa	32.5	36.1	39.8	43.6	47.3	51.0	54.6	58.0

Source: United Nations, *World Urbanization Prospects 1990* (New York: United Nations, 1991), pp. 106–9.

countries (Burkina Faso, Burundi, Ethiopia, Guinea-Bissau, Malawi, Mali, Niger, Rwanda, and Uganda) are characterized by particularly low levels of urbanization. All of these countries had fewer than 20 percent of their populations living in urban areas in 1990. In Burundi, for example, only 5.5 percent of the population is urban and it is projected that it will still be under 20 percent urban in 2025.

As seen in Table 3.2, current urban growth rates are high for every region in Africa but much more so in East Africa. These high growth rates will persist to the end of the century but with a monotonic decline. However, even during the period 2020–25, African urban populations are expected to be growing at 3 percent per year, a rate that would be six times the projected rate for the industrial countries. Similarly, the rate of urbanization is expected to decline in Africa from 1.9 percent in 1990–95 to 1.2 percent in 2020–25. The rate of urbanization can be defined as the average annual rate of change of the percentage living in urban areas. It is also the difference between the growth rate of the urban population and that of the total population.

Factors Contributing to Rapid Urbanization in Africa

The rapid growth of the urban population in Africa is the direct result of a shift in the balance between the urban and rural economies. This shift is closely linked to economic growth and to the changing patterns of employment; in other words, to the urban bias in development strat-

Table 3.2

Average Annual Growth Rate of Urban Population in Africa by Region, 1990–2025 (percentage)

Region	1990–95	1995–2000	2000–05	2005–10	2010–15	2015–20	2020–25
Africa	4.94	4.72	4.48	4.21	3.85	3.43	3.05
Eastern Africa	6.41	5.94	5.44	5.12	4.72	4.24	3.74
Middle Africa	5.07	4.98	4.83	4.56	4.21	3.75	3.24
Northern Africa	3.92	3.66	3.40	3.08	2.71	2.36	2.18
Southern Africa	3.49	3.29	3.04	2.79	2.53	2.26	1.97
Western Africa	5.32	5.12	4.90	4.59	4.12	3.62	3.16

Source: United Nations, *World Urbanization Prospects 1990* (New York: United Nations, 1991), pp. 154–55.

egies, which has resulted in the development of commerce and industry, and the growth of transportation, communication, education, and other types of infrastructure in the urban areas. Consequently, and as previously discussed, capital cities dominate in Africa for purely historical reasons. The primate city in Africa remains the focal point of both governmental and private sector activities and, as such, it is the rational settling place for the population.

Natural Population Increase

A natural population increase occurs when fertility rates exceed mortality rates. Demographers use the term "demographic transition" to refer to the broad pattern of secular change in birth and death rates that accompanies a population's development from a traditional agricultural base into a modern industrial society. Before and after the transition, the size of the population is nearly constant. However, in the intervening period, which can extend to well over a century, rapid growth occurs (Bongaarts 1995). Africa is regarded as lagging behind other regions in its demographic transition.

The primary factors in the decline in mortality around the world have been well documented and are better understood than the factors in the decline of fertility. The decrease in mortality was in large part the unanticipated and unplanned byproduct of social, technological, economic, and political change (Hope 1996b). Due mainly to the decline in mortality rates, population growth has accelerated in Africa from an average of 2.7 percent per year during 1965–80 to approximately 3.1 percent per year at present. Yet, despite the continued decline in mortality, there is alarming evidence that some causes of death, believed to have been eradicated or subjected to control, have reappeared. For example, deaths attributed to malaria and tuberculosis have increased as these diseases have again become a health problem in a number of African nations (World Bank 1993a). The main reason for this state of affairs can be traced to the persistent poverty of those nations, which has resulted in the reemergence of some diseases due to poor nutrition, poor sewage systems, and inadequate and polluted water supplies.

In addition to the reemergence of some diseases, there are also the problems associated with dealing with new health epidemics such as AIDS, for example, as discussed in chapter 5. Sub-Saharan Africa has

had the lowest life expectancy levels and the slowest rate of improvement. Consequently, life expectancy, which was fifty-one years during
the period 1990–95, is still considerably below that of the other developing-country regions (Bongaarts 1995). Sub-Saharan Africa will continue to lag in life expectancy partially because the continent is
severely impacted by the AIDS epidemic. As discussed in chapter 5,
there are various projections regarding the negative impact of the disease on life expectancy.

Although the AIDS epidemic can be said to have had a limited
impact in the 1980s, its impact will most certainly grow with the size
of the epidemic and, in the twenty-first century, mortality measures
will be substantially affected (Bongaarts 1995). Based on projections
for fifteen African countries, the average life expectancy during 2000–5,
with and without AIDS, is reduced by more than six years (57.7 minus
51.2) and the death rate is higher by 2.9 deaths per one thousand
people (13.7 minus 10.8). The population growth rate would also be
lowered but growth is expected to remain high as the birth rate would
be basically unaffected. Under this scenario, in sub-Saharan Africa as
whole, the population growth rate would be reduced by only 0.1 percent in 2000–5 (Bongaarts 1995).

Mortality is the result of the interaction of three sets of factors
affecting an individual's physical well-being. These are (a) public
health services, such as immunization, which affect mortality regardless of individual behavior; (b) health and environmental services (for
example, clean water), which reduce the costs of health to individuals
but require some individual response; and (c) an array of individual
characteristics, including both income, which affects health through
food consumption and housing, and education, which affects the speed
and efficiency with which individuals respond to health and environmental services (Birdsall 1980). Of these three sets of factors affecting
mortality, the benefits of the first have been more or less fully har-
vested. Further mortality declines depend, therefore, on changes in
individual behavior that are facilitated by increasing income and education and better access to health services.

Africa is the only region in the world that is yet to experience
significant reproductive change. The total fertility rate for sub-Saharan
Africa as a whole has remained virtually unchanged at about 6.3 to 6.6
for the past twenty-five years. This is significantly higher than in other
regions and countries with similar levels of income, life expectancy,

female education, and contraceptive prevalence. In a few countries in sub-Saharan Africa, fertility has, in fact, increased while it has been declining in the rest of the developing world (Cleaver and Schreiber 1994). Nonetheless, there are a few countries where there are encouraging signs of fertility decline. The currently available literature, though not necessarily agreeing on the reasons for such a change, demonstrates fertility declines in Zimbabwe, Botswana, Kenya, Nigeria, Côte d'Ivoire, Ghana, Mozambique, and Sudan,[1] for example.

In Africa, high fertility rates are influenced by such factors as marriage and reproductive and contraceptive behavior patterns. Childbearing tends to be encouraged, irrespective of economic circumstances. Consequently, women in Africa, both the educated and uneducated, want and have more children than their counterparts in the rest of the world (Cleaver and Schreiber 1994). However, educated African women want far fewer children than do the uneducated ones. In general, the average number of children per woman should decline as the woman's level of education increases. It has long since been determined that female education bears one of the strongest negative relationships to fertility (Cochrane 1979). The relationship between female education and fertility or its proximate determinants is negative in most settings, although curvilinear in some (Mason 1995). Education has a depressant effect on desired fertility, which is viewed to fall on a continuum that ranges from zero to a specific number (Mhloyi 1994). Fertility tends to decline monotonically as a mother's education increases above primary schooling. However, in sub-Saharan Africa, the effect of education on fertility has been less pronounced than elsewhere in the world (Cleaver and Schreiber 1994).

Apart from cultural factors that encourage childbearing, one other explanation for the high fertility rates in Africa relates to contraceptive prevalence. Contraceptive prevalence in sub-Saharan Africa is very low, to say the least. Data for the period 1986–93 indicate that the percentage of women in sub-Saharan Africa who used contraceptive methods was only 15 percent compared to 83 percent in East Asia, 41 percent in South Asia, and 58 percent in Latin America and the Caribbean (UNDP 1995). However, some countries, such as Botswana, Kenya, and Zimbabwe, had significantly higher contraceptive prevalence rates, ranging between twice the rate of sub-Saharan Africa as a whole for Botswana and Kenya and almost three times for Zimbabwe.

One of the negative consequences of the low rates of contraceptive prevalence is that of teenage pregnancy. Teenage pregnancy is wide-spread in Africa, with rates higher than in other regions of the world. The widespread pattern of adolescent childbearing has serious social, economic, and demographic effects. It contributes to the inequalities suffered by girls and women in educational and vocational training systems[2] as well as in employment (Oppong and Wéry 1994). High rates of teenage pregnancy also have implications for the proportion of births that are deemed to be at risk. High rates of maternal deaths, pregnancy wastage, and infant and child mortality are all recognized as being associated with risky births. Sub-Saharan Africa, for example, has the highest rates of maternal mortality in the world; they stood at 606 per 100,000 live births for 1980–92 compared to 92 for East Asia, 189 for Latin America and the Caribbean, 469 for South Asia, 10 for the industrial countries, and 295 for South East Asia and the Pacific during the same period (UNDP 1995).

The primary demographic factors that make for future natural urban population increase in Africa are threefold. First is the expected increase in population growth. The second factor is the very high proportion of children and youth in the general population; 44 percent of the population is fifteen years of age or younger. Thus, when those in this age group enter their reproductive period of life, their sheer numbers will represent an awesome potential for large population increases, regardless of the fact that the rate of increase is predicted to diminish in the future. The third and final factor is time itself. A lengthy period is needed for a population structure to mature and attain a balance. This occurs when the death rate has passed through its transition period (from high to low levels) and the birth rate has done likewise. In time, the age structure will also evolve so that a larger proportion of the population is adult.

Rural-Urban Migration

Rural to urban migration is the other important determinant of urban population growth. In Table 3.3, we see the migrant share of urban growth in selected countries. In sub-Saharan Africa, where most of the cities are relatively small but growing rapidly, migration from rural areas is a major influence on urban growth. For example, in the two major cities of Botswana, the capital city of Gaborone and Francis-town, net internal migration contributed 70 percent and 56 percent,

Table 3.3

Migrant Share of Urban Growth in Selected Countries, 1975–90
(percentages)

Country	Migrant share of urban growth
Kenya	64.2
Senegal	75.2
Tanzania	85.0
Tunisia	76.9

Source: Sally E. Findley, "The Third World City: Development Policy and Issues" in *Third World Cities: Problems, Policies, and Prospects*, ed. John D. Kasarda and Allan M. Parnell (London: Sage), p. 15.

respectively, to population growth between 1981 and 1991. Because the vast majority of migrants tend to be young adults in the peak reproductive age groups with higher fertility than the urban population as a whole, the long-term contribution of internal migration to urban population growth is actually much greater (Oberai 1993).

There are basically two models of the migration process. In the first, migration is regarded as a purposeful and rational search for a better place to live and work. In the second, migration is viewed as a response to conditions that push the migrant into moving, perhaps without a rational weighing of alternatives. The various theories on internal migration have stimulated a great deal of empirical activity and the results seem consistent. Although people migrate for a variety of reasons, the empirical evidence suggests very clearly that the primary factor determining migration is economic betterment. People migrate to urban areas mainly in response to better employment and income opportunities.

In the Third World countries, urban income per person can run as much as 50 to 100 percent higher than rural incomes and the differences are particularly large in Africa (Hope 1996b). As examples, in Botswana, the average urban household disposable cash income was almost four times that of rural households in 1993–94 as discussed in chapter 2; in Nigeria, the average urban family income in 1978–79 was five times that of the rural; in Sierra Leone, the average urban income was four times the agricultural income for 1978–79; while, in 1985, the ratio of nonagricultural to agricultural wage rates was 5.2 in Swaziland, 3.6 in Malawi, 3.5 in Zimbabwe, and 2.3 in Zambia (UNDP

1990). In addition to income and employment opportunities, the expectation of better education facilities for children is usually cited as a major reason for migration to urban areas.

Besides the predominant economic factors, there are also some demographic factors that tend to influence migration selectivity. Young adult men predominate among migrants in Africa. They are usually unmarried. However, an increasing number of married men are now migrating from the rural areas in search of the means to take care of their families. Also, in recent times there has been an increase in the number of unmarried, separated, divorced, and widowed women moving to the cities on their own (Gilbert and Gugler 1992). As discussed in chapter 4, many of these women engage themselves in meaningful economic activities, primarily in the subterranean sector.

Another factor in migration selectivity is that of education. A large proportion of the migrants tend to be well educated and highly motivated relative to the population at the point of origin. Individuals with formal education, especially at the secondary level or higher, can obtain good jobs in government or commerce. These jobs are located in major urban centers, and hence aspiring employees must migrate to these cities. Cities that receive migrants thus are not, on balance, burdened with a flood of uneducated, unskilled, and unmotivated individuals and households, although there is little doubt that rural-urban migration tends to keep urban wages below levels that would prevail in the absence of migration (Hope 1996b).

Migration is also multisectoral in nature and, with respect to rural sub-Saharan Africa, it is closely linked to the problems associated with rising population pressure, land tenure uncertainties, poor land use, and environmental resource degradation (Cleaver and Schreiber 1994). Undoubtedly, rural-urban migration will continue in Africa into the foreseeable future given rapid population growth, the limited developmental capacity of the majority of rural areas, and the seemingly permanent economic attraction of the cities.

The Consequences of Rapid Urbanization in Africa

Urbanization was once regarded as being positively associated with higher productivity and industrialization. Industries tend to locate in urban areas, particularly the large cities, to derive the benefits of ready access to large markets, capital, labor, legal services, social and economic infrastructure, and cross-border markets. This, in turn, tends to concentrate economic activities in the urban areas and maintain the urban bias in development policy. However, it is now persuasively clear that there are negative consequences associated with the concentration of economic activity and population in the urban areas. The "overurbanization" that results leads to unemployment, underemployment, inadequate housing and access to public services, traffic congestion, and environmental pollution, for example, not only in Africa but in the Third World in general (Hope 1996b).

The principal measurement of how well urban areas have absorbed the rapid population growth are estimates of urban unemployment. One of the major consequences of the rapid urbanization experienced by African nations in the past two decades has been the increasing supply of urban job seekers. In all African countries, the supply of urban job seekers far exceeds demand. In the region as a whole, the urban unemployment rate has doubled over the past two decades, rising from 10 percent in the mid-1970s to about 20 percent in the 1990s (Vandemoortele 1991). The youth unemployment rate is two to four times the unemployment rate for older workers (Khan 1994). In Kenya, for example, the urban unemployment rate increased from 11.2 percent to 16.2 percent between 1977–78 and 1986; in Zimbabwe the urban unemployment rate was 19 percent in 1987; in Botswana the urban unemployment rate was 17 percent in 1993–94; and in Ghana those with no schooling in the urban areas are only 20 percent of the unemployed and discouraged workers, in a country where 80 percent of those unemployed or discouraged are in urban areas.[3]

Some studies have shown that the migrant group of the urban population tends to have lower rates of unemployment than the natives, possibly because they accept jobs that natives are not interested in undertaking. Low unemployment rates among migrants may or may not lead to increased unemployment among natives. If the jobs are really ones that natives are not interested in, the unemployment levels of the natives may be unaffected (Hope 1996b). This is an important issue since it brings into question the popular assumption that migrants raise urban unemployment levels through either their own unemployment or their taking jobs away from urban natives. It is also of importance because of the increasing evidence that a large proportion of the migrants tend to find themselves employment in the subterranean sector rather than in the formal labor market.

Despite the fact that average household incomes in Africa tend to be systematically higher in urban than in rural areas and tend to be positively associated with city size, in the cities, underemployment and unemployment have a negative income impact on the family and often contribute to its instability. Since the mother and other family members leave home to work, children and young people lose some adult supervision. Often the children themselves must find work; and if they do, they also leave home at an early age, which in turn makes for the disintegration of the family unit. One effect of urbanization has too often been the abandonment of children as traditional value systems erode.

However, some research has observed that there is little evidence of a breakdown in family values among migrants. Migrants tend to remain firmly rooted in the rural community in which they grew up. Spouses and children who had to be left behind, members of the extended family, and other village relationships continue to define a rural place as home for these migrants (Gilbert and Gugler 1992). In Nigeria, for example, urban dwellers invariably stressed that they were strangers to the city. They tended to identify with their community of origin and their close family relationships there. They visited, contributed to development efforts, built houses there, and so on (Gugler 1991). These commitments to the extended family and the rural village are also not uncommon even among the permanent migrants.

The rapid process of urbanization in Africa has also given rise to concern regarding the costs of urbanization. The uncontrolled urban growth makes it difficult for cities to provide residents with the services they desire despite the current urban bias with respect to development expenditures and strategies (Rondinelli and Kasarda 1993). Indeed, in many African cities the overall quality and coverage of public services and facilities have steadily deteriorated during the past two decades. In fact, the capacity of national and urban governments to provide even minimal levels of basic services has been outpaced by the rapidity of urban growth not only in Africa but in the Third World as a whole (Rondinelli and Cheema 1988).

There is also evidence that air pollution, noise levels, congestion, health problems, and crime[4] tend to increase more than proportionately with the size of urban centers. Urban living has increased both the quantity and the quality of the economic needs and desires of the population. Such changes are very important since they raise individual expectations and impose added constraints on the economic policies of governments, thereby reinforcing the urban bias in the use of resources (Hope 1996b).

Urbanization in Africa has occurred at a very rapid pace and most cities have been unable to meet the growing demand for housing and urban services. Such urban growth is expected to continue into the foreseeable future even if national policy biases favoring urbanization are corrected. Consequently, the degree of efficiency with which African nations allocate their resources will increasingly determine their overall economic performance.

Currently, the urban bias in African development policy has resulted in the rural areas' lagging behind the urban areas in access to basic services, thereby reinforcing the concentration of poverty in those rural areas. For example, the population with access to health services in sub-Saharan Africa during the period 1985–93 was 49 percent in the rural areas compared to 78 percent in the urban areas; for safe water it was 35 percent in the rural areas and 73 percent in the urban areas; while for sanitation it was 29 percent in the rural areas and 59 percent in the urban areas for the same period (UNDP 1995). For all of these services, access in the urban areas was more than twice that in the rural areas, except for health services, which were one-and-one-half times greater. Similar patterns have been observed with respect to malnutrition in children.

In almost all African countries, the proportion of rural preschool children who are malnourished is greater than the respective proportion in the urban areas. On average, it is 1.6 times higher with respect to the underweightedness measure, 1.5 times higher with the stunting measure, and 1.2 times higher with the wasting measure. Generally, urban children tend to be taller and heavier than their rural counterparts (von Braun et al. 1993). Malnourished children have higher rates of morbidity and mortality than well-nourished children. Malnutrition is related to decreased cellular immunity and an increased incidence and/or duration of illness. High malnutrition rates are generally correlated with high infant and young child mortality rates (Huffman and Steel 1995).

One aspect of urbanization related to urban poverty in Africa has been the increase in the number of street children.[5] Not all street children are homeless or abandoned. However, one fundamental characteristic of street children is that they do not attend school but opt instead to try to subsist by banding together and hanging out in tne streets. Most male street children in Africa engage in casual work activities such as car washing or shoe shining while the female street children often have to resort to prostitution. Some street children also beg and steal. The street children phenomenon, which has been known in parts of Latin America for many years, is now appearing on a significant scale in Africa with devastating consequences on the health and education of such children (Gilbert and Gugler 1992). In Botswana, for example, more than one-fifth of the street children abuse drugs and more than one-third abuse alcohol despite their awareness of the health hazards associated with such drug and alcohol abuse (Campbell and Ntsabane, forthcoming).

In general, African countries are substantially more urbanized than is probably justified by their degree of economic development. Moreover, such urbanization is taking place in an environment of economic deterioration in many of those countries. Since the rate of increase in the size of the urban population exceeds the rate of increase in formal-sector employment opportunities, there is also increasing urban unemployment and urban poverty. This state of affairs, in turn, deepens the economic crisis being experienced in most of the countries in the region.

Managing Rapid Urbanization in Africa

As shown above, urban growth has taken place, more or less, quite spontaneously in Africa with considerable negative consequences for all of the countries. All of the data and other evidence suggest that urban populations will continue to grow much faster than rural populations even if the urban bias in development strategies is reversed. What is therefore needed is the development and implementation of appropriate national urbanization policies. Such policies will be influenced from country to country by the economic, social, political, and cultural characteristics within each. However, they must include elements that reduce urban unemployment and narrow the rural-urban wage gap; increase the relative disposition and access to public services; and foster agricultural and rural development.

Overcoming Urban Unemployment

The primary cause of urban poverty, as a consequence of rapid urbanization in Africa, is the severely limited income earned through gainful employment. Policies designed to increase urban employment and wages must therefore be given foremost attention. The basic issue to be dealt with, therefore, is how the urban labor supply can be absorbed at decent wages without further increasing the rural-urban wage differential and retarding economic activity by increasing production costs.

Perhaps the most powerful stimulus to job creation, and hence labor demand, is economic growth. Economic growth leads to rapid labor absorption throughout an entire economy in both urban and rural areas. Conversely, when economies stagnate, as is currently the case in Africa, unemployment is a much more pressing problem. Policies aimed at improving the economic growth of the African nations are therefore very important elements of any employment strategy. Such policies must be outward-looking. Among other things, they must promote trade and private investment and result in the growth of the manufacturing and service activities sectors. By 2025, 56 percent of the African labor force engaged in formal-sector employment will be in the manufacturing and services sectors (United Nations 1988).

One element of employment creation, which is thoroughly discussed in chapter 4 but must be mentioned here, is that related to the role of the subterranean sector. The subterranean sector is a dynamic and growing one which is expected to absorb the majority of new labor-force entrants in Africa. One of the distinguishing features of this sector is that its economic activities are concentrated on services and small- and medium-scale enterprises. The subterranean sector has a major role to play in alleviating the urban unemployment problem in Africa and, as such, must be allowed to flourish through a committed means of recognition of its positive role in the development process and the implementation of policies to promote it. Subterranean-sector employment also reduces poverty directly and provides safety nets in times of economic crisis. "Hawkers, microenterprises, artisans, and the like not only generate significant income, they are also efficient channels of marketing, distribution, and waste recycling" (Binswanger and Landell-Mills 1995).

African governments can promote the subterranean sector by removing regulatory constraints, by simplifying bureaucratic procedures, by eliminating police harassment of those engaged in activities in the sector, and also by providing tangible supports, such as technical assistance and low-interest credit (Bromley 1993). Moreover, with more specific reference to small- and medium-scale enterprises, African governments must also provide support and incentives to these enterprises to take advantage of their high levels of productivity and labor intensity so as to generate further employment opportunities. Bromley (1993) has identified fifteen major areas of support to small- and medium-scale enterprises, including imposing constraints on competing larger enterprises and sometimes reserving specific economic activities for small enterprises; the direct purchasing of goods and services from these enterprises by government agencies, export corporations, and marketing boards, for example; and the provision of assistance to create new small- and medium-scale enterprises by identifying potential business opportunities and entrepreneurs and providing seed capital and other forms of start-up assistance.

With respect to incentives, Ramachandran (1993) has identified three types—fiscal, financial, and physical. Fiscal incentives can be classified into capital, labor, outputs, and profits. South Africa, for example, provides incentives that cover investments on access roads to industrial premises and power supply; in Cameroon partial exemption from corporation taxes is offered; and in Zambia exemption from customs duties and sales tax on all machinery and equipment are offered if the investment meets certain requirements. In terms of financial incentives, they are primarily in the form of capital grants and subsidized loans for the acquisition of fixed assets and for expenditure on training, employment, research, and modernization. In South Africa, for example, incentives related to employment are offered as a flexible amount per job, while in Lesotho training grants are offered. In Botswana, there exists a financial-incentives package covering grants related to capital (the purchase of fixed assets or working capital), training, and unskilled labor. Physical incentives are usually provided with respect to subsidized land and buildings. However, they are not as popular as fiscal or financial incentives.

One final aspect of the quest to overcome urban unemployment pertains to the deconcentration of employment from the major urban centers. This can be achieved by providing incentives to encourage new economic activities to locate in secondary cities or other parts of a country. This type of employment deconcentration can reduce regional economic disparity and benefit the poor. On a larger scale, such employment deconcentration can benefit both national and regional interests and is compatible with national economic growth (Gilbert and Gugler 1992). Among African countries, Tanzania has made some attempts at achieving employment deconcentration and reducing urban bias.

Improving Access to Urban Public Services

Inefficiency, the economic crisis, and rapid urbanization have all contributed to African governments being unable to provide, in a timely and respectable manner, all the public services urban residents require. That, in turn, has generated considerable health, education, transportation, and housing problems in the African countries which need to be urgently addressed. The basic premise of this section is that, overall, African governments have failed miserably to satisfy the demand for urban public services in their countries and, that being the case, wherever possible there should be the private provision of such services.

Recognition of the link between education and development has led to considerable public expenditures on education in the Third World. In Africa, much of that expenditure is misdirected toward tertiary education, which benefits only a small portion of the population, as shown in chapter 7. With the possible exception of Botswana and South Africa, such a pattern of education expenditure is not only inefficient but also considerably wasteful in sub-Saharan Africa. Such a state of affairs is therefore unsustainable over the long term and expenditure needs to be redirected toward the more obvious benefit to be derived from investing in primary and secondary education as also discussed in chapter 7. Such expenditure must necessarily entail attempts to, among other things, improve the student-teacher ratio, improve student access to educational materials and textbooks, and improve the physical condition and other infrastructure related to schools. In addition, African governments should allow for private schools for those willing and able to pay for such schooling. This should result in much lower government expenditure on education than would otherwise be the case if such alternative schools did not exist.

Turning now to health care, African governments need to recognize that improving health requires efforts far beyond medical care. It is also very closely linked to food and nutrition as well as to employment and income distribution. In general terms, the determinants of health comprise three factors. The first is people's purchasing power over certain goods and services, including food, housing, fuel, water, and medical services. The second is the health environment—climate, standards of public sanitation, and the prevalence of communicable diseases. The third is people's understanding of nutrition, health, and hygiene.

In the 1970s, there evolved a broad approach to health policy, including attempts to implement universal low-cost basic health care. However, primary and preventive health care is still not a nationwide reality in most African nations. In fact, public health expenditures in Africa are heavily biased in favor of curative care, and the emphasis is on in-hospital rather than outpatient care despite the prevalence of diseases whose incidence could be greatly reduced by preventive measures. It is estimated that Malawi and Sierra Leone, for example, spend more than 90 percent of their health budgets on hospitals, while Tanzania and Togo spend more than 80 percent of their health budgets in a similar manner (UNDP 1991). In the mid-1980s, the major hospitals' share of recurrent health expenditures was 74 percent in Lesotho, 70 percent in Somalia, 66 percent in Burundi, 54 percent in Zimbabwe, and 49 percent in Botswana (Barnum and Kutzin 1993). The diversion of public resources to hospitals that provide high-quality care for relatively few people rather than for safe water, sanitation, and mass immunization, for example, is a costly social waste at the expense of the poor in particular.[6] There is a long list of diseases to which the poor are particularly susceptible and which can be prevented by the better provision of preventive and cost-effective health care.

Health policy in the African nations should therefore reverse existing priorities so as to emphasize comprehensive preventive care with easy access for the poor and slanted toward the needs of such vulnerable groups as pregnant mothers, infants, and children. It must contain elements that address such issues as improved sanitation, maternal and infant care, immunization, family planning, nutrition programs, and, particularly in the context of the AIDS epidemic, the prevention of sexually transmitted diseases.

With respect to transportation policy, it is elementary that both passenger and freight transportation are basically means to other ends. Transportation plays a central role in the development process as the essential link between producers and users of goods and services. In Africa, traffic congestion inevitably occurs as urban areas grow, and mass transport facilities are not being expanded at a sufficiently rapid rate to meet demand. The explosive increase in automobiles in African cities exerts tremendous demand on the existing road space and is a major cause of pollution problems.

The poor are most affected by the transportation dilemma in Africa, in terms of both the cost and their dependence on it for access to employment and services. Thus, disruptions in transportation service create severe hardships for this already hard-pressed group. Considerable scope exists, therefore, for implementing transportation policies that emphasize mass transit facilities; improved access for the poor; appropriate user fees for cost recovery of existing public transportation networks; the enforcement of national regulations that maintain order, accountability, and safety; and an enabling environment for private service provision. In this latter regard, it will be shown, in chapter 4, that the private provision of transportation service is much more efficient and cost-effective than public-sector transportation service, and such private provision must therefore be encouraged to expand.

In terms of housing, there is no doubt that it is a highly visible dimension of poverty. The high concentration and visibility of deficiencies in the urban housing market in Africa make this one of the most urgent problems facing those countries. In Africa, there is an acute shortage of adequate housing, which leads to overcrowding, squatter settlements, and steeply climbing housing prices. For example, in Kumasi, Ghana, three of every four households have only one room to live in. In Lagos, Nigeria, the average density in dwellings is 4.1 persons per room (Gilbert and Gugler 1992).

Squatter settlements may be defined as illegal land occupation. They are largely built by their inhabitants by whatever means may be available and usually lack public utilities and community services. They are referred to as *"bidonville"* in French-speaking Africa and "shantytowns" in English-speaking Africa (Brennan 1993). In recent years, the number and size of squatter settlements have increased. In Dar es Salaam, Tanzania, for example, 51 percent of the total housing stock in 1990 were squatter settlements while in Johannesburg, South Africa, 22 percent of the total housing stock were squatter settlements by 1990 (*The Economist* 1995).

The fundamental housing problem in Africa basically relates to the availability of affordable housing. It is estimated that sub-Saharan Africa, as a whole, needs to build approximately fourteen dwellings per year per thousand population during 1990–99 and another thirteen dwellings per year per thousand population during 2000–9 (Tipple 1994). However, this represents a formidable challenge that would require considerable expenditures. But there are few African governments capable of meeting that challenge. It is considered, for example, that public housing projects account for less than 5 percent of total housing production in most African countries. Moreover, many of these projects yield even less of a share of housing investment by value than their share of housing costs (Tipple 1994). In South Africa, almost 75 percent of new conventional housing is subsidized by the state. However, this is officially considered to be nine times less than what is required to solve the housing problem by the year 2000 (Mainardi 1994).

The ability of African households to afford adequate housing is related to both their earning capacity and the cost of housing. It is estimated that in Dar es Salaam, Tanzania, and Johannesburg, South Africa, the house-price-to-income ratio was approximately two in 1990, while it was approximately twelve in Algiers, Algeria (*The Economist* 1995). That means that the median cost of a house in Dar es Salaam and Johannesburg was twice the median annual household income, while in Algiers it was twelve times. In Zimbabwe, despite government policies encouraging home ownership by the poor, such ownership has proven to be elusive. For example, in the early 1980s one-third of the population could not afford to participate in aided self-help schemes. By the middle of the 1980s only 16 percent of households in high-density areas could have afforded a four-room core house, while in 1991 at least 60 percent of nonowner households could not afford a one-room house in a Phase II project in the capital city of Harare (Rakodi and Withers 1995a). Similar affordability problems were also observed in Gweru, Zimbabwe (Rakodi and Withers 1995b).

Public housing programs such as sites and services schemes have not been very successful in Africa. They have not been able to meet the magnitude required and they were often too costly for the poor. In Zambia and Kenya, for example, where sites and services schemes were widely embraced, they comprised only 5 to 10 percent of total urban low-income housing (Tipple 1994). Generally, there can be no serious housing policy without a bold land policy, and such a land policy faces grave political obstacles. Often, construction of public housing has been combined with slum clearance programs. This is usually regarded as the solution to the social byproduct of the slums by doing away with them easily and quickly. Yet, in most cases, slum clearance has been of little help, and even detrimental to efforts to provide housing (Hope 1996b).

Housing policy in Africa must contain elements that eliminate ob-stacles to private construction and provision efforts; result in the avail-ability of housing finance; encourage the upgrading of slums by private developers; and facilitate self-help and cooperative building projects for the benefit of the poor. One usually overlooked solution to the housing problem in Africa pertains to the provision of rental space rather than home ownership. The availability of rental space increases the access to housing, particularly for the poor in urban Africa. The rental market in Africa, usually of a room or two in some part of a dwelling, has been growing in recent times. This type of housing sup-ply is affordable and also meets the requirements for a large segment of the African population.

Essentially, African governments need to provide an enabling envi-ronment to encourage the private provision of housing, especially for low-income households. It has been shown that incrementally built housing, for example, is a more effective means to increase the volume and improve the quality of shelter than public housing (Brennan 1993). Given the resource constraints in Africa, incremental building emerges as the appropriate framework for solving the continent's housing prob-lem. A considerably larger number of households would therefore be able to acquire basic structures, which can then be extended room by room as their economic and family circumstances permit. In addition, such an approach would certainly encourage the principles of self-help and self-reliance at both the household and wider community levels.

Toward Rural Development

If the rapid growth of the urban areas in Africa is to be controlled, there must also be attempts to develop the rural sector. Trying to confront rapid urbanization by only improving conditions and provid-ing work in the urban centers will simply attract more people from the depressed rural areas. Many urban residents migrated there because they were pushed out of the rural areas by landlessness, joblessness, and hopelessness. Their flight from the rural areas was caused in part by the strong urban bias inherent in the economic and investment policies of almost all African countries. It is therefore in the rural areas that much of the long-term problems of urbanization can most effec-tively be tackled.

Rural development is essential to Africa not only in terms of local improvement but also as a part of overall national economic policy. Rural development is not limited to agricultural development. It also entails the generation of new employment; an increase in rural wages; considerable improvement in basic services such as health, water, education, sanitation, and housing; and the participation of rural residents in the decision-making processes. The essential thrust of rural development is action to raise the standard of living of rural residents, particularly the poor.

Rural development strategies focus particularly, but not exclusively, on the agricultural sector, due to the fact that agricultural activity is the major economic activity in the rural areas of Africa. Rural development promotes agricultural development and should also preserve the integrity of the environment. The primary issues related to rural development in African nations are how to sustain a rate of growth that allows for a balanced expansion of all parts of the economy, and how to ensure that the pattern of agricultural growth is such as to make a strong and direct impact on rural poverty and, indirectly, on the reduction of migration of rural residents to urban areas.

In the process of urbanization it has been relatively easy to overlook the importance of the agricultural sector in the development process in Africa. This has been referred to by Bryceson (1996) as "deagrarianization" which has resulted from "derived urbanization."[7] The political influence of growing, massed, and vocal urban populations has resulted in the disproportionate targeting of public investment and services in the urban areas. As a consequence, there has been an extraordinarily low level of public investment in rural roads, water, health, sanitation, and education in much of sub-Saharan Africa. In those countries where governments have been able to resist some of that pressure for example, Kenya, Togo, and Zimbabwe—there have been positive results in agricultural profitability and growth (Cleaver and Schreiber 1994). However, despite the urban bias in development policy, the rural areas still loom large in Africa since it contains the majority of poor people and it is the birthplace for many of the urban residents.

Realization of the objectives of a broad-based rural development strategy hinges on national commitment and on the translation of that commitment into three areas of action. First, there must be the necessary policy changes, including more equitable distribution of land rights and market pricing for crops produced by subsistence farmers, in particular for cash crops. Second, resources must be allocated on a priority basis to increase the productivity of the rural sector by developing agricultural technology, effective extension, and transportation networks. Third, institutional capability must be developed in the rural agricultural sector to use the existing resources to the maximum and thus ensure effective implementation of the policies directed at rural residents. Rural development must be seen and regarded by African governments as an essential tool to stimulate nonagricultural investment and growth as well as to influence population distribution.

It has been shown in a study of farm–nonfarm linkages in rural sub-Saharan Africa, for example, that each unit of increased agricultural income generated an additional increase of half a unit in nonagricultural rural income. Agricultural growth tended to stimulate growth in services and manufacturing. About 20 percent of the additional rural income generated was attributable to production linkages, while 80 percent was attributable to consumption linkages (Haggblade, Hazell, and Brown 1989). In addition, rising rural incomes are spent largely on labor-intensive products of the rural sector, boosting demand where it does the most good in generating further increases in employment (Mellor 1995).

Back in 1989, the World Bank suggested that the minimum agricultural growth rate required to address poverty, in the average African country, was 4 percent per annum (World Bank 1989b). However, to date, very few countries have been able to reach that target and more than 70 percent of sub-Saharan Africa's agricultural sector has fallen considerably short of the 4 percent growth goal (Cleaver and Donovan 1995). The significance of that goal remains apparent, particularly in the context of rapid urbanization. Consequently, there is still a compelling need to exploit agriculture's growth linkages with the rest of the economy (Cleaver and Schreiber 1994).

Fundamental to any process of organized rural development is the active and willing participation of rural peoples in the development of the area in which they reside. Such participation requires that these people not only share in the distribution of the benefits of development, be they the material benefits of increased output or other benefits considered enhancing to the quality of life, but also that they share in the task of creating these benefits. Participation may be regarded as a substitute for political mobilization. It is therefore, in that sense, the antithesis of politicization. It provides, optimally, political legitimization for institutional programs without significant conflict (Harvey et al. 1979). This then serves to enhance the viability and success of the program or programs.

Former Tanzanian President Julius Nyerere (1979) had argued that "If the people are to be able to develop they must have power. They must be able to control their own activities within the framework of their village communities. The people must participate not just in the physical labor involved in economic development but also in the planning of it and the determination of priorities." Projects of genuine social and economic value are most likely to be identified, planned, and built if rural people are able to play a decisive role in choosing them (Isham, Narayan, and Pritchett 1994). One author argued that optimum participation must be included among development's strategic principles because unless efforts are made to widen participation, development will interfere with people's quest for esteem and freedom from manipulation (Goulet 1971).

That higher levels of participation of the beneficiaries should and do have positive effects on socioeconomic equality in African countries is a foregone conclusion (Narayan 1994). More particularly, widespread participation generally means more widespread access to power, and those who gain access to power will insist that there be actions to broaden their share in the economic benefits of society. In Malawi, for example, there is a very successful community self-help water program, based on strong government and community cooperation. It began in 1969 in two villages with three thousand participants and it now benefits more than one million people. Through district development committees, comprised of local leaders and technical personnel, the requests for piped water are channeled. The district development committees also participate in the design phase. Equipment and training are provided by the government, and the community provides voluntary labor for construction and maintenance (UNDP 1991).

The significance of local participation can also be demonstrated by an examination of the Ghana Water Utilization Project. Between 1973 and 1981 the project installed twenty-seven hundred boreholes and handpumps in a thousand poor villages with a total population of about 600,000–700,000 people. However, it soon became apparent that residents used the wells only when other water was not available and as long as the pumps were working. The pumps were reluctantly repaired by the villagers because they did not regard them as their own. Project improvement began in the early 1980s when the project began to focus on community development rather than on technology. The participation of the villagers, particularly women, was incorporated and project outputs improved tremendously. More than 75 percent of the rural population covered by the project now have access to safe water, about 90 percent of the pumps are working, and health standards have improved. The project did not succeed until the beneficiaries were active partners and participated fully (CIDA 1990; Binswanger and Landell-Mills 1995).

As the Ghana case shows, encouraging participation means responding sensitively to the felt needs of people and communities. Such a response must meet those needs without taking over. There is always the risk of placing too much emphasis on effective delivery and too little on participation (UNDP 1993). The policy advice is clear. People are the best advocates of their own interests, given the opportunity to do so. Moreover, the empowerment that is derived from such participation lends itself to community stability. Experience has also shown that effective participation cannot be commanded but must instead be induced through the advocacy of projects that offer sufficient incentives to attract the personal resources of time, energy, and freedom of action away from other urgent and competing tasks of rural residents (Hope 1996b; Narayan 1995).

Conclusions

Rapid urbanization is indeed a major problem facing African countries, and the consequences of that urbanization suggest that some urgency should be given to implementing policies to manage the situation. Undoubtedly, an urban bias exists in Africa. The urban sector in those countries receives a disproportionately large share of government expenditures and capital investments. Also, urban residents in Africa have much better access to public services than do rural residents.

Urbanization can be regarded as both a contributor to and the result of elusive development in Africa. It contributes to elusive development by placing inordinate demands on the scarce resources of governments. It is the result of elusive development, in turn, because scarce resources are not being used to develop rural areas. Such rural development would contain the rural population, diminish their desire to migrate to the urban areas, and thereby reduce both the rate and negative effects of urbanization. If rural standards of living can be generally improved for the majority of the rural population, rural-urban migration can be checked (Hope 1996b). The growth of the urban centers will not automatically stop. However, with a serious movement away from strategies with an urban bias and a concentrated effort toward rural development, urban growth in Africa could become manageable.

Essentially, African nations need to move further in the direction of encouraging a more intensive commercialization of agriculture; that is, the production of cash crops not only to increase rural incomes and thereby discourage migration, but also as an integral part of the national development strategy. Cash crops, while they can include food crop production surpluses that are sold locally, are generally understood to be crops produced exclusively for sale and, in many instances, crops produced for export. This commercial orientation identifies a cash crop, whether or not the cash crop is a food crop.

Cash crops can play an important part in producing higher incomes in Africa and, thus, in increasing food availability. Food security can only be achieved when people have adequate income (von Braun et al. 1992). Accordingly, a long-term solution to the problem of hunger requires higher levels of rural incomes in the African countries, which can be accomplished through the commercialization of agriculture. Moreover, much needed foreign exchange can also be earned for the African nations where the crops are exported. Such commercialization is not, however, inconsistent with increased food crop production. Countries that have done well in cash crop production have also been among the most successful in expanding food production (Berg et al. 1981). There is a positive relationship between commercialization of agriculture and national development which needs to be seriously taken into account by African governments.

Finally, it should also be observed that urbanization is both a result and a cause of environmental resource degradation. People migrate from rural areas essentially because they can no longer make a living there (Cleaver and Schreiber 1994). Also, some forms of episodic migration, such as flight from ethnic violence, can expose urban centers to massive population increases. As the urban population in Africa becomes further concentrated, they will increasingly overwhelm the natural ability of urban environments to absorb the wastes and emissions of urban populations and their activities. That, in turn, will expose the growing urban populations to health risks (Mink 1993).

Consequently, there will be even further demand upon scarce resources for the environmental protection of urban populations—thus increasing the rural development imperative.

Notes

1. A good discussion on fertility decline in the individual countries can be found in the following publications: For Zimbabwe, see Adamchak and Mbizvo (1993); Thomas and Mercer (1995); and Thomas and Muvandi (1994). For Botswana, see Thomas and Muvandi (1994); and Rutenberg and Diamond (1993). For Kenya, Nigeria, Côte d'Ivoire, Ghana, Mozambique, and Sudan, see Cleaver and Schreiber (1994); Kelley and Nobbe (1990); and Oppong and Wéry (1994).

2. High teenage pregnancy rates lead, in turn, to high female school dropout rates. In Botswana, for example, 65 percent of the female dropouts from secondary school in 1992 were due to pregnancy. Teenage mothers contributed 14 percent of the total number of births in Botswana in 1990–91, for example. See Hope and Edge (1996).

3. The data on Kenya and Zimbabwe are derived from Vandemoortele (1991); for Botswana from Republic of Botswana (1995b); and for Ghana from World Bank (1995c).

4. During the past decade there has been a rapid increase in crime in African urban centers as a direct result of escalating urban unemployment. Car hijackings, drug trafficking, burglaries, bank robberies, and purse snatchings have now become commonplace. The resultant effect has been that security services and the installation of electronic fences and burglar bars, for example, have become growth industries.

5. It is estimated that there are, for example, about 9,000 street children in the cities of South Africa (Kgosana 1992); 2,150 in Namibia (Tacon 1991); about 500–1,000 in Botswana (Campbell and Ntsabane, forthcoming); and about 25,000 in Nairobi, Kenya (UNDP 1993).

6. Many countries that spend a high proportion of their budgets on hospitals also have very high infant mortality rates, for example, Liberia and Tanzania. See UNDP (1991).

7. Bryceson (1996) defines "derived urbanization" in sub-Saharan Africa as the urban growth process that has proceeded without industrial job availability and without a secure domestic food supply.

4

The Subterranean Economy in Developing Societies: The Evidence from Africa

The subterranean economy (sometimes referred to as the informal, hidden, underground, shadow, secondary, black, invisible, or parallel economy) now constitutes an important component in the economic activities and process of development in the developing countries. Although some governments of developing countries made efforts in the past to minimize its relative importance, the subterranean economy continues to thrive in the developing countries where, generally, foreign exchange constraints and inefficiency interfere with the normal functioning of the organized or *formal* economy and therefore disrupt the availability and flow of goods, services, technology, and human resources in and out of those countries. The subterranean economy originally emerged as small-enterprise activities in response to the problems of survival associated with rapid urbanization and unemployment in the developing countries. However, as this chapter makes clear, it is *not now* a set of survival activities performed by destitute people on the margins of society. This chapter examines and analyzes the nature of the subterranean economy and its socioeconomic impact on developing countries with specific reference to Africa.

The Nature of the Subterranean Economy in Developing Societies

The subterranean economy is defined here as consisting of those economic units and workers (both professionals and nonprofessionals) who engage in commercial activities outside of the realm of the *formally* established mechanisms for the conduct of such activities. Included in such activities are barters (exchanging of goods and/or services for other goods and or services); the importation of scarce consumer goods; the importation of production inputs and spare parts; the sale and exchange of hard currency for local currency at black market rates and vice versa; the sale and exchange of certain controlled goods and resources, such as gold, diamonds, and even arms, for hard currency or other goods and services; and unregistered small-scale productive and service activities. It is a process of income generation characterized by the single feature of being unregulated by the institutions of society in an environment in which comparable activities are regulated.

The activities of the subterranean economy do not show up in official statistics. However, such a sector is now widely recognized to have become relatively important, autonomous, and self-propelling in almost all developing countries. Although its exact quantitative magnitude defies any precise estimation, the subterranean economy, by all accounts, operates so "openly" and on such a large scale that any development policy thrust will be senseless unless this economy is recognized and figured into such policy actions.

Originally, the activities of the subterranean economy were conducted primarily by self-employed and urban-based workers, most of whom were rural migrants with little or no formal education and who became known either as the working poor, traders, higglers, hawkers, or hucksters; and who were engaged primarily in marginal production, service activities, and the importation of scarce consumer goods in heavy demand in the urban areas of the developing countries. In their original form, the subterranean economy activities constituted a manner in which those individuals and households at the bottom of the socioeconomic system were able to command and accumulate resources. The subterranean economy provided for people without the requisite educational credentials to participate in the national economy and live an independent life. It also provided the wherewithal for those at the bottom of the economic ladder to exploit those who were in a much more privileged position.

More recently, however, both the activities and the personnel involved have changed considerably. The activities have expanded and the personnel now include the professional and managerial classes, some of whom are even employed in government service or other formal economy activities on a full-time basis and switch between the two economies even during the same workday. As a matter of fact, the activities have now expanded to the point where even the formal economy, in some countries, has to conduct business in the subterranean economy to acquire hard currency, vital medical supplies, basic goods and services, and spare parts, for example. Also, the formal economy now has no alternative but to subcontract, horizontally or vertically, some of its production and other activities to the subterranean economy to take advantage of the latter's efficient production techniques and access to inputs.

The evolution of the subterranean economy has taken place because of the failure of the developing countries to formally make the kind of economic progress that would have allowed for, among other benefits, low urban unemployment rates, a reduction in national poverty rates, wages and salaries that kept pace with inflation, the ready availability of basic goods and services, a functioning infrastructure, and a relatively honest and efficient bureaucracy. Also, in some countries, particularly in Africa, government became such a suffocating force that the private sector went almost completely subterranean to escape it. The subterranean economy represents, therefore, the populace's spontaneous, yet creative and rational, response to the incapacity of their individual nation-state to provide the framework to satisfy their basic needs. In that regard, the citizens of the developing countries have shown more daring, initiative, and dedication to their own individual nation-state than have the politicians and their policy advisers, who seem unwilling and/or incapable of thinking through and implementing policy reform representative of the changing economic environment and the attitudes and desires of their population. A self-reliant and survival network has, consequently, emerged to fill the vacuum, thereby enhancing and entrenching the subterranean economy.

For some time, it was basically accepted that the subterranean economy was somewhat of a transient phenomenon which would gradually disappear as the process of modernization took place and the formal economy thrived and absorbed more labor. However, such a notion was not only inconsistent with the facts and the emerging trends in the developing countries but also was based essentially on the view (a negative one) taken by the International Labor Organization (ILO), in a 1972 mission to Kenya, that deemed such an economy as essentially dysfunctional.

More recent analyses, including those contained in this chapter, provide evidence that the subterranean economy has not disappeared but, in fact, has grown substantially in most parts of the developing world. Viewed from a historical perspective, the subterranean economy today is substantially different from what it was two decades ago. It is no longer the sole domain of the urban poor. As mentioned before, it now includes the professional and managerial classes from the formal economy who, having seen the success of the urban poor, have unleashed their own entrepreneurial spirit to provide a better standard of living for themselves and families and to attempt to rid themselves of the stigma as victims of the failed and discredited bureaucratic model of development found in their countries.

Among the characteristics of the subterranean economy is the increasing rate of participation of women as an entrepreneurial group (Jordan 1994). This, in turn, has further increased the trend toward higher rates of participation of women in the labor force of the developing countries. The currently available evidence indicates that women are overrepresented in the subterranean economy. In Zambia, for example, women account for more than 66 percent of informal production in the services sector,[1] and this has steadily increased their earnings as a share of total household earnings during the 1980s (UNDP 1995). In Ghana, 92 percent of employed women can be found in the subterranean economy compared to 69 percent of employed men; in Tanzania the shares are 95 percent for women and 84 percent for men; and in Egypt the shares are 74 percent and 46 percent for women and men, respectively (World Bank 1995b). In Nigeria, 94 percent of street food vendors are women (UNDP 1995). In Katutura, Namibia, the majority of the hawkers (60 percent) are women (Frohlich and Frayne 1991).

Also significant in terms of the characteristics of the subterranean economy is that the activities have shifted outward from the urban sector and have now become more national in scope encompassing almost all areas of economic activity. For example, the failure of the formal economy to continue to provide, maintain, and monitor a proper transportation network in the developing countries has led to the emergence of ad hoc, but vital, transport systems which link up poor neighborhoods with the capital city and other urban areas, usually in the form of music-filled minibuses. In Kenya, for example, these minibuses are called *matatus,* in Senegal they are referred to as *car rapides,* in Tanzania they are known as *dala dalas,* and in Côte d'Ivoire, they are known as *gbakas*. In Windhoek, Namibia, the transport sector comprises 28 percent of service activities in the subterranean economy (Norval and Namoya 1992). In South Africa, the subterranean taxi industry was estimated to have created 300,000 jobs in just four years in the 1980s, with a fleet value of such taxis on the road equivalent to approximately U.S.$1.2 billion (Norval and Namoya 1992). In Kenya, the subterranean economy commanded a 51 percent market share of the transportation sector in 1989 (Banio 1994).

Undoubtedly, and based on the available evidence, the privately owned and operated transportation networks substantially outperform their state-owned counterparts. For example, in cities such as Harare, Dar es Salaam, Yaoundé, and Douala, private operators perform better than their state-owned counterparts in respect to such key performance indices as vehicle availability, passenger kilometers operated, staff productivity, profitability, and hours of operation (Banio 1994).

Benefits of the Subterranean Economy

The subterranean economy in the developing countries has created a new class of entrepreneurs who have been able to use sheer initiative to function in national economies that have been plagued by very serious economic problems. The emergence of the subterranean economy has allowed for the availability of essential goods and services, which represent, at the same time, the idea that the citizens of the developing countries must be free to choose and to have the opportunity to obtain the basic goods and services they desire. In this respect, a thriving retail sector exists, dominated in part by street vendors.

However, at another level, the success of the retailing business in the subterranean economy serves to further demonstrate the inefficiency and policy vacuum that exists in the formal economy. In particular, it represents a major indictment of the public enterprises that are responsible for the production and/or importation of such goods and services and further makes the case for their privatization. Because of their own mechanisms that allow them to obtain foreign exchange and other inputs, the traders and vendors in the subterranean economy find themselves in the position of having to provide consumers with essential items that the formal economy is no longer capable of providing. Of course, the vendors and traders find these activities to be very lucrative, to say the least.

Another major benefit derived through the subterranean economy is the employment it creates. Jobs are created cheaply and large numbers of individuals, who would otherwise be unemployed and a burden to society, are gainfully employed. Recent studies indicate that the share of the subterranean economy generally exceeded 40 percent of total urban employment in the developing countries (Kannapan 1989). In Africa, the subterranean economy accommodated about 75 percent of the new entrants into the labor force between 1980 and 1985. By the year 2020, it is estimated, 95 percent of African workers will be in the subterranean economy (World Bank 1990; *The Economist* 1990). Available country data indicate that the subterranean economy accounts for more than half of the employment in the urban sectors of Ghana, Nigeria, Kenya, and Tanzania at 53, 69, 58, and 51 percent, respectively, and for about a quarter of total employment in the national economy of those countries (Endale 1995).

The creation of jobs in the subterranean economy is a conclusive demonstration that, given a free-enterprise environment, even amid uncontrolled inflation, large numbers of individuals who are able and willing to work would be in a position to do so. What is taking place here is some of the inevitable results of the experience of a free-market situation that encourages risk-taking and enterprise regardless of class.

Another benefit of the subterranean economy is its contribution to gross domestic and national product. The mere fact that the subterranean economy now permeates so much of economic life in the developing countries means one would expect that the subterranean economy is contributing an increasing share to national income in those countries (Chaudhuri 1989). Overall, the subterranean economy in the developing countries covers economic transactions of anywhere between 30 and 70 percent of national product and there are several studies that have made estimates for individual countries. For example, in Kenya it is estimated at 35 percent of GNP (Main 1989), and for South Africa it is estimated at 40 percent of GDP (Testa 1989). By the year 2020, it is predicted that the subterranean economy in Africa will grow, while the formal economy will stagnate, thereby resulting in a contribution to GDP that will grow from under 50 percent to 66 percent (*The Economist* 1990).

One more benefit of the subterranean economy is that it constitutes an important component in the rural financial markets in many developing countries. It is a dominant source of credit in the rural sector in

Africa where the institutional lenders are absent or ineffective, and the access to formal credit is extremely poor. The numerous types of moneylenders and credit suppliers in the subterranean economy include friends, relatives, landlords, commission agents, storekeepers, agricultural produce dealers, traders, and employers of agricultural labor. Of course, interest rates for such credit tend to vary with the economic interests and the nature of the relationship between the borrower and lender. For example, storekeepers may provide interest-free loans as an integral part of their business in order to retain or expand their share in retail trading in the market. Estimates of the percentage of total loans in the rural areas accounted for by the subterranean economy in Zambia, for example, for 1981–82 were pegged at 43 percent (Mrak 1989); in Niger in 1986 it was 84 percent (World Bank 1989a); and in Gambia for 1987–88 it was 80 percent (Zeller et al. 1994).

At the national level, the subterranean economy accounts for most of the financial services provided to small-scale producers and enterprises (World Bank 1989a). Informal deposit services are provided through group savings associations and temporary loans can be arranged. Perhaps the most popular form of subterranean finance is that of the rotating savings and credit association (ROSCA). ROSCAs have different names in different countries. In Ghana, a ROSCA is called *susu,* in Ethiopia it is referred to as *iqqub* or *iddir,* in Egypt it is known as *gameya,* in Botswana *motshelo,* in Malawi *chiperegani* or *chilimba,* in South Africa *stokvel,* in Mozambique and Burundi *Upato,* in Kenya *Mabati,* in Madagascar *fokontany,* in Senegal *tontine,* in Zimbabwe *chilemba* or *stockfair,* and in Liberia *esusu.*

In ROSCAs, members ranging in number from six to forty pool their money into a fund. The fund is held by a group leader, informally selected from among the members of the group, who is responsible for periodically collecting a fixed share from each member. The money collected is then given in a rotation as a lump-sum payment to each member of the group, thus allowing some members to finance expenditures much sooner than if they had relied on other savings efforts of their own (World Bank 1989a). The basic principle by which resources are shared is balanced reciprocity. Each ROSCA member draws out of the pool or fund as much as he or she puts into it. ROSCAs are said to have existed on the African continent since the mid-nineteenth century with an origin traceable to the Yoruba tribe (Bouman 1995).

ROSCAs represent a very popular form of savings among the low-

and middle-income groups in developing countries. It has been estimated, for example, that approximately 78 percent of market women in Ghana's three principal cities saved in this manner (Aryeetey and Steel 1995). In Addis Ababa, Ethiopia, more than half of the households are members of ROSCAs (Aredo 1993). In a survey of seven regions in Tanzania, 45 percent of the households were found to rely heavily on informal credit to finance their basic needs, small business ventures, and other sources of livelihood (Hyuha, Ndanshau, and Kipokola 1993). In the Cameroon, it was estimated that almost 80 percent of the adults participate in ROSCAs and that these ROSCAs handle about one-quarter of the total volume of money lent in the country as well as manage about one-half of total financial savings nationwide (Schrieder and Cuevas 1992). In Zambia, it was determined that 80 to 90 percent of the urban population participate in ROSCAs (Mrak 1989). In South Africa, it is estimated that *stokvels* currently have more than 3.5 million members who save more than U.S.$25 million per month (Smith 1996).

Although ROSCAs are national in scope in the developing countries, in the rural areas they are widespread among all segments of the rural population, while in the urban areas they are more prevalent among the low- and middle-income classes. Funds collected and saved through ROSCAs in urban areas tend to remain there, while a good portion of the funds collected and saved through rural ROSCAs is transferred to urban areas. The reason for this, of course, is that consumer durables are primarily produced and sold in the urban areas. To acquire them would require expenditure in urban areas.

ROSCAs are widespread and popular in developing countries for two basic reasons. First is the very high responsiveness of ROSCAs to the economic and social requirements of their members; the limited number of participants; the specific duration of the savings/credit cycle; the amount of individual participation; the order of rotation and receipt of funds; the absolute freedom of joining; easily understandable rules and procedures; consistency of rules and procedures with sociocultural norms of the environment; very good accessibility; and so on. The second reason has to do with the very high economic efficiency of ROSCAs. Transaction costs are low or nonexistent since there are no expenses for office space and personnel, or for assessing creditworthiness; and repayment rates are high since there are usually no defaults, due to strong cultural norms and social pressures and cohesion.

Some Disbenefits of the Subterranean Economy

One obvious disbenefit is derived from the fact that the success of the subterranean economy has reduced the pool of skilled labor-force entrants that the formal economy requires for administering and/or implementing programs or delivering essential public or private services. Basically, what the job seekers want is not work as such, but relatively well paid work, as compared to average opportunities. Moreover, the freedom to be self-employed or seek other economic opportunities in the subterranean economy, where the derived income and profits can be relatively higher and be hidden from taxation, is a rational economic decision. With the thriving of the subterranean economy, many employees, or potential employees, assess their wages and salaries not in terms of local purchasing power as dictated by the price index but in terms of the equivalent in United States currency, usually at the black market rate (Ramirez-Rojas 1986; Nowak 1985). In such conditions, the equivalent local income that can be derived in the formal economy seems like a paltry sum. Hence, there are now many jobs that remain available in the formal economy.

What has emerged is a new attitude of no longer wanting to be dependent on paralyzed governments or other players in the formal economy. It embodies the entrepreneurial spirit emanating from individuals striving in admirable ways to become successful even without support, and away from a formal economy that is currently in disarray.

Another disbenefit emanating from the existence of the subterranean economy is that it provides cover for tax evasion, drug trafficking, and smuggling. However, that state of affairs can only exist where tax administration and law enforcement are inept and/or influenced by corrupt actions. It is perhaps understandable that entrepreneurs in the subterranean economy would attempt to evade all the taxes they can, particularly given the consideration that much of the developing world's economy remains in the formal sector where such tax evasion would be more difficult. However, the problem with such tax evasion is that it reduces the national revenues and therefore reduces the government's ability to expend on national programs by a similar amount. This can lead to the possibility of additional tax burdens. Determination of the amount of evasion is very difficult in any country, and particularly in the developing countries. It is often heard in many developing countries that tax evasion is widespread and has reached alarming proportions. However, quantification of such evasion is almost impossible. Although the forms of evasion vary widely among countries, the major methods used for evading taxes in the subterranean economy include failure to report all sales, underinvoicing, overstating nontaxable sales, and the nondeclaration of commissions retained overseas.

Beginning from the days of the first customs duties, smuggling in a great variety of forms has been the primary form of escape. There are a number of factors that may encourage smuggling in developing countries. These include: vast stretches of almost unguarded borders and very lengthy coastlines which make a complete patrol impossible (in this regard, a good example would be the Ghana-Togo border); the general desire to evade taxes; a desire to get contraband goods into countries where there is a heavy demand and rich dividend for such goods; and the nearby availability of cheap supplies, particularly in countries that are just off the coastlines. Smuggling involving the inflow of goods can expose domestic industry to unfair competition.

Bribery is also a problem associated with the subterranean economy and it stems from the now endemic bureaucratic corruption in the developing countries, particularly in Africa, as discussed in chapter 6. Bribery is a major cost of functioning in the subterranean economy. Subterranean economy businesses have to devote a large part of their income to bribing the authorities. Such bribery has the potential of raising the cost of goods and services. However, the payment of bribes also represents purchasing security from prosecution on the one hand, and sanctioning the activities conducted in the subterranean economy on the other.

One disbenefit of the subterranean economy, which can only be corrected through macroeconomic policy, is its contribution to the inflationary spiral in developing countries. Consumer prices have been increasing at an alarming rate in the developing countries, partly in response to the various devaluations of their overvalued currencies and partly as a result of demand for goods and services that exceeds the available supply—a demand, it must be pointed out, that has arisen in the subterranean economy due to the economic deterioration in the developing nations and the diminished capacity of the individual governments to provide and maintain the expected levels of services, goods, and physical infrastructure. However, for sub-Saharan Africa as a whole, the weighted average inflation rate increased only slightly to 16.1 percent for 1980–93 compared to 13.8 percent for 1970–80

(World Bank 1995b). Sierra Leone had the highest rate of inflation among African countries in 1980–93 with an average of 61.6 percent.

Conclusions

Lessons of experience have shown that the subterranean economy in the developing nations is here to stay. Subterranean economy activities are expanding in both scenarios of a contracting formal economy, such as in sub-Saharan Africa, and an expanding formal economy, such as in the newly industrializing countries of Asia and Latin America (Lubell 1991). Where the formal economy contracts, more individuals are forced into the subterranean economy to earn a living, while where the formal economy expands, it generates additional demand for goods and services produced in the subterranean economy, thereby increasing employment in subterranean economy activities.

The subterranean economy in developing countries has therefore emerged to the point where it is directly responsible for the improvement in the standard of living of large numbers of people and, despite some of its shortcomings, contributes significantly to the betterment of life in general in the developing countries. Given this generally positive contribution, the subterranean economy must be regarded and treated as part of the solution to the current economic problems of the developing nations, especially those in Africa.

The subterranean economy has exhibited a vibrancy and a resilience that must be enhanced. The sector is an expression of bottom-up initiative and the culture of entrepreneurship, which development practitioners now agree is a sine qua non for the success of microprojects. It must therefore become a matter of national economic policy to acknowledge the subterranean economy so that its contribution to the national economy can be even further improved. The remaining barriers to the functioning of the subterranean economy must be eliminated. However, this has to be accomplished within a framework that allows for the conduct of business and other activities in a legal manner, thereby minimizing or eliminating the possibility that the subterranean economy will end up with the reputation as a haven for drug traffickers, smugglers, and tax evaders. What is needed, then, is a concerted attempt to accept and legalize the subterranean economy without its being absorbed into the formal economy's bureaucratic and regulatory nightmare, which includes such characteristics as barriers to entry, labor market regulations, controls on marketing and distribution, fiscal regulations, and credit regulations.

Indeed, there is a growing move toward greater flexibility in regulation, brought on primarily by the insistence of some donor agencies on liberalized policy frameworks encompassing, among other things, the encouragement of local entrepreneurship and private-sector activities. Moreover, it is more and more being accepted that the subterranean economy is both competitive with and complementary to the level of activity of the formal economy. Indeed, there is an increasingly widespread belief in some circles that well-targeted programs of support to the subterranean economy can be far more cost-effective in terms of employment promotion, poverty alleviation, and output than certain large-scale programs of investment in and support to the formal economy (ILO 1991).

Among the barriers to the proper functioning of the subterranean economy is inadequate access to credit. This is so despite the success of ROSCAs and other types of subterranean economy finance. This therefore means that access to credit must be equalized. It has been found that loans to small-scale borrowers are not necessarily more risky. In fact, there is no inverse correlation between the size of a loan and the degree of risk, and the proportion of bad and doubtful debts is not higher among small bank customers (Hope 1987a). Moreover, the United States Agency for International Development (USAID) has found that minimalist direct assistance programs that aim to improve the performance of microenterprises by providing short-term credit without attempting to transform the microenterprises into more complex businesses have a better record of success to date than do more ambitious programs (USAID 1989).

The ability to borrow money to legitimately engage in business activity must therefore be facilitated by the banks and other credit-granting agencies. Creating a more flexible set of rules and regulations under which credit can be granted would be a necessary first step in that direction. Providing access to credit further encourages private investment. Given the dismal performance of public enterprises in developing countries and, in particular, the African countries, such private sector initiatives must be soundly supported. Moreover, the formal economy in most developing nations is now in an advanced stage of decrepitude.

Given the failure and negative impact of subsidized formal finance and the success of group lending as practiced, for example, by the People's Bank of Nigeria,[2] there are some important lessons here for the financial institutions in the formal economy. The World Bank's *World Development Report 1990* indicates that only 5 percent of farms in Africa have had access to subsidized formal credit. Subsidized credit has become a transfer program for the nonpoor while the artificially low interest rates and credit regulations have lent themselves to further patronage and corruption. In the subsidized credit programs in the developing countries, loans in arrears range from 30 percent to 95 percent, while the loan programs for the People's Bank of Nigeria, for example, have loan recovery rates exceeding 86 percent (Anyanwu and Uwatt 1993). Clearly, credit programs with low transaction costs, market rates, some linkage between repayment and future lending, and more physical accessibility for borrowers from the subterranean economy should be the desired approach in improving the availability of credit. Additionally, borrowers must face an incentive structure that induces them to repay their loans.

In general, it is good economic reasoning and makes perfect economic sense to recognize the subterranean economy in national economic policy making in the developing countries. As demonstrated here, the subterranean economy has made a major difference between the ability to subsist and abject poverty for large numbers of people in the developing nations. It has encouraged risk-taking and enterprise regardless of class, and perhaps such a sector would not have existed in a well-working market economy without a burdensome public sector. Incentives for the growth of such activities tend to increase with greater state intervention and regulation. Consequently, the subterranean economy needs to be unleashed and the entrepreneurial spirit further nurtured to contribute to the development process. Undoubtedly, the subterranean economy is now a much more efficient system in making goods and services available in the developing countries than is the formal economy.

To promote the subterranean economy, it is desirable for developing country governments to consider removing the obvious disincentives to entrepreneurship by creating a liberalized economic environment that minimizes restrictions. In Africa, for example, it was found that local small-scale entrepreneurship increased as the general economic environment became more open (Elkan 1988). Such an achievement is an example of what can be accomplished if an entire economy is liberalized. The current economic distress in the developing countries dictates that business as usual is no longer a viable option and that alternatives to the current approach to economic organization must be implemented. The subterranean economy is one such alternative (Castells and Portes 1989). The livelihood of millions of developing-country citizens depends on its existence, and the future of many developing societies now depends on its continued evolution and the role now assigned to it in the development process.

Within that scenario, and given the increasing importance of women in the subterranean economy and in the development process generally, the policy framework must also include programs aimed specifically at assisting women. Female entrepreneurship is now an ongoing reality in the developing nations, and consequently all the discriminatory practices against them that are based simply on gender must be terminated. Gender inequality in the developing countries persists, although there have been some improvements in some societies. In many societies, however, women remain invisible in statistics because little value is attached to what they do. For example, although rural women are the majority of agricultural workers in many developing countries, they receive very little credit. In many African countries, they account for more than 60 percent of the agricultural labor force and contribute up to 80 percent of total food production, but they receive less than 10 percent of the credit to small farmers and 1 percent of the total credit to agriculture. Similarly, of the U.S.$5.8 billion allocated by the multilateral banks for rural credit in 1990, only 5 percent reached rural women (UNDP 1995).

Moreover, gender inequality is reinforced in education. For the developing countries as a whole, the female literacy rate is now three-fourths that of the male rate despite the fact that increasing numbers of females have been seeking access to education. In Africa as a whole, the female illiteracy rate was 61 percent in 1990 compared to 38 percent for males (World Bank 1995a). Women in the developing countries must be allowed to participate fully in the development process with all of the rights and abilities now available to men. The lessons learned during the Decade of the Woman would be useful in informing this strategy. Those lessons suggest that female-oriented policies must be implemented within the context of existing organizational structures rather than as special, isolated, sporadic, or politically motivated projects.

Also, a great deal more research needs to be undertaken on the subterranean economy so that much more can be understood of its internal dynamics and a reliable database developed for facilitating optimal decision making. In this regard, the research being undertaken by the African Council of Hawkers and Informal Businesses in South Africa, as well as its advocacy position on behalf of the subterranean economy, deserves both special commendation and a recommendation for continued financial support by the international development agencies. Moreover, the donor agencies need to extend their support for promoting the development role of the subterranean economy to all developing regions, particularly sub-Saharan Africa, where the need for economic reform is great, where the subterranean economy is expanding rapidly, and where the role of aid agencies in the economic reform process looms large. This is especially relevant in those African nations where the failure of government policy is the primary contributor to the rapid growth of the subterranean economy.

In particular, the donor agencies need to continue to tie some of their aid to policy reforms that provide a much more enabling environment, free of bureaucratic red tape and excessive regulation, for microenterprises to flourish. In addition, the donor agencies should follow the lead of USAID and increase their contributions to programs of direct assistance to the subterranean economy in developing countries. Many of the subterranean economy enterprises have benefited immensely from an array of technical assistance projects which have ranged from basic advice on business management to some technology transfer and training. There have also been some small amounts of funding channeled successfully to subterranean economy producers by the ILO/Swiss Cooperation program in Mali, Rwanda, and Togo, for example.

There is also scope for technical cooperation among developing countries in an enabling environment. Through the use of local experts and others who are familiar with the problems of the subterranean economy through hands-on experience, including subterranean economy workers themselves, the cost of technical assistance can be considerably reduced, with an impact much greater than is gained by relying solely on expensive expatriate experts.

Finally, the subterranean economy in developing countries continues to thrive in spite of the hostile environment in which it must operate. Nevertheless, there are encouraging signs of recent movement toward the further development and implementation of policies in support of the subterranean economy. Governments in many developing countries are becoming increasingly interested in the subterranean economy because of the large number of people whom it supports and donor agencies are showing a willingness to do more to support it.

Undoubtedly, the subterranean economy will play a major role in the development process in the developing countries in the immediate future and beyond. However, the magnitude of its contributions will be determined by the extent to which the regulatory framework is diminished.

In any case, however, the evolution of the subterranean economy in the developing nations has provided valuable lessons to those countries that are desperately trying to manage transitions to democratic pluralist and market economic systems. Those involved in subterranean economy activities in the developing countries have shown themselves to be among the most innovative entrepreneurial groups in their societies. This indicates that if they are allowed to function in a nonhostile environment, they would make a much greater contribution not only to their own economic and social progress but to that of their respective countries as well.

Notes

1. Excludes the transport sector.
2. The People's Bank of Nigeria came into existence in 1989. It derives its philosophical focus and operational modalities from the Grameen Bank of Bangladesh. Similar types of institutions providing banking and credit facilities to the poor are the Saving Development Foundation in Zimbabwe, the Malawi Mudzi Fund in Malawi, and the Small Enterprise Foundation in South Africa. See Anyanwu and Uwatt (1993); Christodoulou, Kirsten, and Badenhorst (1993); and Hulme (1993).

5

The Socioeconomic Context
of AIDS in Africa

Acquired Immune Deficiency Syndrome (AIDS) is a fatal disease which strikes an adult, on average, six to ten years after being infected by the human immunodeficiency virus (HIV).[1] Between 1985 and 1996 the cumulative number of persons infected with HIV has risen worldwide from 2.5 million to approximately 30.6 million, and in Africa from 1.5 million to about 19.2 million[2] (World Bank 1991; World Bank 1993a; *The Economist* 1996a). By the year 2000 these figures may more than double (World Bank 1993a). The share for developing countries is expected to grow from 50 percent in 1985 to 75 percent by the year 2000 and to 80 to 90 percent by 2010 (World Bank 1991).

Infection rates among adults in many large African capital cities, and even in some rural areas, already exceed 25 percent and are expected to climb to this level in other cities over the next ten years. Due to the fact that each 10 percent increase in the infection rate increases annual mortality by at least five per thousand, previously high levels of adult mortality are tripling and quadrupling in these areas (World Bank 1991). It was estimated that by 1996 more than 9 million people worldwide had died of AIDS. Of that total 7.6 million of them were in Africa (*The Economist* 1996a).

The AIDS pandemic is imposing and will continue to impose, in the foreseeable future, a significant and potentially crippling burden on the peoples, economies, and already inadequate health care systems of the African countries. It is a human and economic disaster of massive dimensions. Infections tend to strike adults in the prime of life, plus up to one-third of all children born to infected mothers. Babies born to women infected with HIV have a 20 to 40 percent chance of contracting the virus from their mothers. Almost all of these children die before the age of five. By the year 2000, the total number of infants born with HIV infection in Africa alone is expected to exceed one million, of whom more than 600,000 will likely develop AIDS (World Bank 1993a; UNDP 1991).

Millions of children who are not infected with HIV are already suffering emotional and economic deprivation because their parents have died or are chronically ill. It is estimated that during the 1990s more than 10 million children uninfected with HIV will be orphaned by AIDS (Panos Institute 1992). In many parts of sub-Saharan Africa, the extended family system, which has traditionally absorbed orphans, will come under severe strain as parents die of AIDS, leaving aged grandparents to cope with large numbers of young children.

The rapid increase of the rate of mortality due to AIDS in Africa has created a major public health crisis across the continent. In sub-Saharan Africa, unlike in other regions, the principal mode of transmission of the HIV has been heterosexual intercourse.[3] This has been so since the epidemic was first detected and such transmission now accounts for more than 80 percent of infections (Panos Institute 1992). The African AIDS pandemic is, accordingly, very much a family matter and has a major impact on all parts of society. Faced with this calamity, the major concern now for policy makers and socioeconomic development planners is the overall socioeconomic impact that the AIDS pandemic will have on African countries; in other words, determining the long-term effects of AIDS on African population growth and other socioeconomic indicators, and developing strategies to deal effectively with those effects.

Recently, some attempts have been made to help individual countries make some assessments. These attempts have concentrated on three primary issues. The first is the human costs of AIDS; the second is the social costs associated with the disease; and the third is the economic impact of the disease. These are the issues addressed in this chapter. However, first it is necessary to examine those factors that influence the magnitude of the impact of the AIDS pandemic in Africa.

Factors Influencing the Impact of the AIDS Pandemic

The World Health Organization (WHO) and other researchers have identified several major trends within the African AIDS epidemic. It is concentrated primarily in Eastern, Central, and Southern Africa; it is spread largely through heterosexual and perinatal transmission; and it most heavily affects adults of both sexes between the ages of fifteen and forty-four. Giving rise to those characteristics are certain economic, infrastructural, sociocultural, and political factors, which in turn heavily influence the magnitude of the socioeconomic effects of AIDS in Africa.

Economic Factors

Without a doubt, poverty and economic distress in the African countries have contributed greatly to the rapid spread of the HIV and AIDS. Africa remains one of the poorest regions of the world. Low levels of education, crowded and unsanitary living conditions, malnutrition, limited access to basic services, high rates of unemployment, and rapid urbanization are all poverty phenomena that are increasingly associated with HIV/AIDS. Poor people who contract the HIV, moreover, tend to develop AIDS much faster than individuals of a higher socioeconomic status (Storck and Brown 1992).

Limited employment opportunities in the rural areas of Africa have contributed to rural-urban migration, which in turn has increased the urbanization of poverty where cities lack the capacity to absorb the rural poor (Hope 1986). Furthermore, some of the social and economic conditions associated with urban living tend to encourage behavioral patterns, such as drug abuse and prostitution, that increase the risk of being infected with the HIV/AIDS. In addition to rural-urban migration, there is also the problem of cross-border migration. Migrants are a very high risk group. They are primarily single men who suffer loneliness. They also have the potential for spreading the virus when they return home. Single women who migrate may also be forced into sexual activity as a survival mechanism (Whiteside 1993a).

The circulatory nature of most population movements in Africa implies that two points, both the destination and the origin areas, are at risk of an outbreak of the AIDS disease a migrant may transmit. The high sex ratio (male dominance) at migration destinations implies that females are in demand for casual sexual relations; hence the persistence of promiscuity and prostitution in the urban areas, which in turn increases the transmission rate of the AIDS virus (Anarfi 1993). In Ghana, Gambia, Uganda, Zambia, and Tanzania, for example, cross-border migration has been blamed for a very large proportion of the known cases of AIDS (Anarfi 1993).

Generally, the health consequences of poverty are very severe (World Bank 1993a). The poor die younger and suffer more from illness and disability. In Africa, poverty contributes to the heterosexual spread of AIDS most frequently through situations wherein relatively few women (usually commercial sex workers) have sexual contact with large numbers of men (Caldwell, Caldwell, and Quiggin 1989). Thus, work-related, migratory, and other forms of economically based variations in sexual behavior determine to some extent the existing pattern of the AIDS epidemic in different parts of Africa. For example, the HIV might also be spread through temporary residents or transient workers such as soldiers, tradespeople, and truck drivers.

Commercial sex workers, because of the large number of their sexual partners, are the group most at risk for HIV infection in many African countries. Unfortunately, in many African cities this risk has resulted in infection levels approaching 50 percent. In some of these cities, and especially among the poorer prostitutes (who tend to have more clients), infection has become nearly universal (Way and Stanecki 1994). For example, in Abidjan, Côte d'Ivoire, seroprevalence among commercial sex workers rose from 69 percent in 1990 to 86 percent in 1992–93 (Way and Stanecki 1994). In Nairobi, Kenya, and Kigali, Rwanda, commercial sex workers have rates of seropositivity reaching to around 90 percent (Fleming 1993).

Infrastructural Factors

Economic distress in Africa means that countries in the region face increasing pressure for the allocation of scarce resources. Those resources have been declining in their budgetary allocation for infrastructure, including health care. Data for the period 1988–93 indicate that the sub-Saharan Africa population with access to health services stands at 56 percent compared to 79 percent for all developing countries; the population per doctor is 24,180 compared to 5,080 for all developing countries, and public expenditure on health is 2.5 percent of GNP compared to 2.1 percent in all developing countries (UNDP 1995; World Bank 1995b).

The countries of sub-Saharan Africa also have the lowest rate of hospital beds to the population. There are eight to ten times fewer hospital beds than the average for Europe, and beds are much more scarce in rural areas (Cabral 1993). This places considerable strain on the medical staffs in their allocation of hospital beds, given the increasing number of patients with AIDS. As many as 30 percent of inpatient beds in hospitals in Uganda, Malawi, and Zaire are occupied by HIV-infected patients (Cabral 1993). In Addis Ababa, Ethiopia, AIDS patients fill 80 percent of the hospital beds (Kelso 1994).

Given the special care that AIDS patients require and their greater average length of hospital stay compared to most other patients, there is bound to be increased demand on already scarce hospital resources. Moreover, the medical staffs would find themselves with less time to devote to non-HIV patients, who may, in turn, find themselves at greater risk for recovery than would otherwise be the case.

In addition to the health care infrastructure, there are also problems with the infrastructure for education and information communication. In many African countries the education infrastructure is in a state of decrepitude, and access to information is almost nonexistent, especially for rural dwellers. Fortunately, however, some international non-governmental organizations (NGOs) have recognized this problem and have begun to implement education and information programs in many African countries at the grassroots level as a vital intervention measure. Some of these organizations are now being ably assisted and funded by the WHO and other international organizations.

Sociocultural Factors

Some sociocultural traditions and practices that are unique to Africa have a major impact on the transmission of HIV/AIDS in the region. These traditions and practices relate primarily to what is known in the literature as sexual networking (relations with multiple sexual partners).

In many African countries, it is not unusual for women to have transactional sex outside of marriage. This is not frowned upon since the control of female sexuality is often more akin to the control of property. In sub-Saharan Africa, there are also high levels of polygyny. The polygynous system has serious implications for the spread of the AIDS epidemic since entire families may find themselves victims of the disease through polygynous association (Caldwell et al. 1993). Partly because farming and economic strength depend solely on the size of the work force, sub-Saharan Africa is characterized by very high levels of polygyny.

In Africa, 30 to 50 percent of married women are currently in polygynous marriages and nearly all wives must be emotionally and economically adjusted to the possibility of finding themselves in a polygynous marriage at any time. This state of affairs means that African women are aware that the greatest danger presented to them comes from their spouses, and it is most likely that the majority of female AIDS victims have been infected by their husbands (Caldwell et al. 1993).

Another example of sociocultural traditions and practices with implications for the AIDS epidemic is "wife inheritance." Practiced in some parts of Africa, wife inheritance is highly valued by most women for the economic and social security it provides them and their children. The tradition demands that if a woman is widowed she must be inherited either by a younger brother-in-law, or in some cases by an older stepson, in order to safeguard the property of the deceased for his children. This also ensures that future children stay within his clan. However, in this new union either partner may infect the other and thereby increase the spread of the AIDS disease.

In addition to wife inheritance, in some African countries, such as Zambia, there is also the ritual practice of "sexual cleansing." In this practice, the surviving spouse is required to have sexual intercourse with a chosen member of the family of the deceased. In the case of a deceased man, the relative is usually a nephew (on the maternal side), a grandson, a brother, or a grandfather figure. In the case of a deceased woman, they would choose a niece (brother's daughter), a granddaughter, or grandmother by relationship such as the sister of a grandmother. Sexual cleansing is regarded in some areas as an important tradition and an effective way of freeing the surviving spouse of the ghost of the deceased. It is believed that the spirit of the deceased lingers on and the widow or widower would therefore not be set free to get on with their life until this ritual is over. For a widow, the duration of the ritual required for freedom depends on how good or bad, in the eyes of the in-laws, she has been while her husband was alive. Undoubtedly, the practice of sexual cleansing has the potential to significantly increase the spread of the HIV and AIDS.

The final example of sociocultural traditions and practices that have implications for the AIDS pandemic in Africa is male circumcision. Some of the recent research on this issue suggests that there is some direct link between the practice of circumcision and the incidence of disease. More specifically, there exists the view that the lack of circumcision predisposes men to sexually transmitted diseases (STDs) and possibly now directly to AIDS (Caldwell and Caldwell 1994). Moses et al. (1995), for example, have found that in those African locations where male circumcision is practiced, HIV seroprevalence is considerably lower than in areas where it is not practiced. Consequently, the lack of circumcision in males is a risk factor for HIV transmission and some emphasis should now be placed on cautiously searching for acceptable interventions in this area (Mertens and Carael 1995).

Political Factors

In most African countries there is considerable distrust of politicians and governments by the citizenry, and perhaps for good reasons. Two salient features of the politics of sub-Saharan Africa, for most of the period since independence, has been the persistence of highly personalized authoritarian rule and the rampant spread of bureaucratic corruption as discussed in chapter 6. In such circumstances, governmental advice and direction to the people are met with derision and are simply ignored. Lacking credibility, these governments are unable to convince the citizens to comply fully with program implementation, such as AIDS prevention campaigns, that are clearly in both their individual and collective interests.

The Socioeconomic Costs of the AIDS Pandemic

The catastrophic impact of AIDS can be more positively identified by assessing its socioeconomic effects and hence its impact on the already elusive development process in Africa. Agreeably, and as stated by the World Bank (1993a), AIDS deserves special attention because failure to control the epidemic now will result in far more damaging and costly consequences in the future. The AIDS pandemic is much more than a health or medical phenomenon. It also has very significant socioeconomic development ramifications.

Human Costs

The demographic impact of the AIDS pandemic relates primarily to projections about the effects of the disease on population size and growth rates as well as on infant and child mortality. The data project a tragic loss of the primary input needed for development, that of productive human beings.

Although there has been some concern that AIDS could eliminate Africa's future population growth and possibly result in a reduction in overall population levels, current information suggests that AIDS and positive population growth rates are likely to coexist. One study estimates that population growth rates in Eastern and Central Africa will most likely remain positive because of continuing high fertility rates (Bongaarts 1988). The WHO has also released estimates that indicate that AIDS will slow Africa's overall population growth rate of 3 percent by 0.5 percent, resulting in an average annual growth rate of 2.5 percent (WHO 1991). However, another study states that the adult death rates in East and Central Africa are roughly 1.3 percent and that twenty-five years after the start of the epidemic, AIDS deaths may cause it to rise by a further 1.3 percent (Becker 1990).

By the end of this century life expectancy in sub-Saharan Africa could fall to forty-seven years instead of the average of sixty-two years expected in the absence of HIV/AIDS (Panos Institute 1992). However, other studies suggest that the net effect of the AIDS pandemic in Africa would be a reduction of urban life expectancy at birth by seventeen years or approximately a one-year decrease in life expectancy for each percentage-point increase in HIV prevalence levels in the population (Way and Stanecki 1994).

Also of great importance here is the negative impact of AIDS on the progress that has been made to date on child survival in Africa. AIDS has the potential to decrease or completely reverse the gains made in lowering mortality levels for infants and children under the age of five years. One study suggests that, for the typical East African country, AIDS will increase the infant mortality rate by 14 percent and the child mortality rate by 20 percent (Stover 1994). This impact is considered large enough to erase all the gains resulting from investments in child survival programs. Another analysis, using recent seroprevalence data for pregnant women, found that in African urban areas with high HIV seroprevalence levels, between one-tenth and one-third of all deaths under age five already may be attributable to HIV infection (Valleroy, Harris, and Way 1990).

Since both men and women are being infected at an almost equal rate in Africa, large numbers of women of reproductive age are HIV-positive. Over the next ten to twenty-five years, the impact of AIDS on child survival is likely to be much more severe than the impact of the disease on overall population growth rates. AIDS is expected to cause more deaths in children in sub-Saharan Africa than either malaria or measles. Consequently, child and infant mortality rates, which were projected to decrease by 35 to 40 percent in the absence of AIDS, are now expected to increase because of AIDS (WHO 1991). In addition to children dying of AIDS, there is also evidence of higher mortality in the HIV-negative children of HIV-positive mothers. This is so because these children have low birthweight and are generally less healthy than babies born to HIV-negative mothers. Pregnant HIV-positive mothers tend to have malnourished babies who are at greater risk of contracting infections.

In recent years, there has been a consistent and rapid increase in HIV infection levels among pregnant women in the urban areas of most African countries. In Francistown, Botswana, for example, HIV seroprevalence increased from less than 10 percent in 1991 to over 29 percent in 1994. Similar patterns have been observed in the urban centers in Uganda, Zambia, and Malawi (Way and Stanecki 1994).

Social Costs

Because of the human costs of AIDS, and given the traditions of the extended family kinship system as well as the spirit of community living, there are also some significant social costs associated with the AIDS epidemic in Africa. Most predominant here is the issue of the number of children who will be orphaned as a result of losing their parents to AIDS. An estimated ten million uninfected children will lose one or both of their parents to AIDS by the end of the century. These adult deaths will deprive communities of the vitality and skills needed for development while placing new burdens on children and the elderly to care for one another (Storck and Brown 1992).

Already, some evidence has emerged that many families in Eastern and Central Africa are experiencing the breakdown of extended systems as they are already stretched to their limits by the burden of AIDS-related caregiving (Hunter 1990; Kelso 1994). A family's care system is tested not only by the demands of relatives they have long known but also by new infected babies born into the households (Caldwell et al. 1993).

In addition, there is the problem of double orphans. Such children usually have four destinations as reported by Barnett and Blaikie (1992). They can stay on in their parents' house to take care of themselves (often with relatives living a short distance away) with the partial intent of protecting their property rights; they can go to grandparents or aunts and uncles; they can go to more distant relatives or to nonrelatives; or they can go into some kind of institutional care. In terms of the latter, due to cash shortages and little additional room, these orphanages have been unable to meet the challenge of caring for the children left behind due to the AIDS pandemic. In Zimbabwe, for example, the thirty-two public and private orphanages that were in place by 1994 were struggling to meet their daily needs (Kelso 1994). Most of the public institutions are for the older, troubled children and government financial assistance to private homes is not enough.[4]

There is also some evidence that fostered AIDS orphans are likely to be removed from school to force them to help with their own support (Barnett and Blaikie 1992). This, in turn, limits their educational levels and, ultimately, their economic prospects as well as that of their families, communities, and countries (Storck and Brown 1992). Fostered AIDS orphans are also subject to higher mortality than children living with both biological parents, partly because of disputes about who should meet medical costs. Nonrelatives and more distant relatives tend to see fosterage in terms of assistance and a net material return (Caldwell et al. 1993).

The dependency ratios (the number of children and elderly persons dependent on working adults) that are AIDS-related will tend to increase with time as a consequence of the increasing burden of caring for AIDS cases as the pandemic continues to unfold. However, the impact of AIDS on the dependency ratio within a given population will be determined in large part by the demographic and epidemiological patterns present in that particular community, such as the fertility rate, the existing dependency ratio, and the presence of high-risk groups.

Economic Costs

The economic costs of a disease are generally estimated as the direct costs of medical care and the indirect costs of labor, and therefore potential loss of income and decreased productivity and output due to illness, death, and the need to care for loved ones (Panos Institute

1992). The AIDS pandemic, through its effects on savings and productivity, poses a serious threat to the already fragile economies of the African countries. The cumulative direct and indirect costs of AIDS in the developing countries was estimated at U.S.$30 billion for the past decade (UNDP 1993).

First, we look at the direct costs. These costs include both inpatient and outpatient care. One study suggests that the annual worldwide cost of treatment of people with AIDS is U.S.$2.6 billion to $3.5 billion and, of this amount, only 2 percent was spent in Africa, which has the majority of all people with AIDS (Panos Institute 1992). However, estimates done by the World Bank (1993a) show that in the typical developing country the total medical cost per adult AIDS-related death ranges from 8 to 400 percent of annual income per capita, with the average being about 150 percent of annual income per capita. In 1992 the developing countries spent about U.S.$340 million to care for AIDS patients compared to U.S.$4.7 billion spent by the industrial countries for care of their AIDS patients (World Bank 1993a). If spending per patient remains constant, expenditure for the care of AIDS patients in developing countries will exceed U.S.$1 billion by the year 2000.

AIDS patients also require long hospital stays, expensive drugs, and the time of skilled personnel. In some of the Central African capitals, more than 50 percent of hospital admissions are now AIDS cases and the direct costs of treatment have also been estimated to be quite high, ranging from 78 to 932 percent of per capita GNP in Tanzania, for example, depending on the type of treatment recommended (World Bank 1991). Estimates for South Africa suggest that the direct costs of HIV/AIDS will increase seventy-nine-fold during the period 1991–2000, reaching a proportion of between 19 and 40 percent of total health expenditure (Broomberg et al. 1993). In 1995, the estimated direct costs of treatment associated with HIV/AIDS in South Africa was U.S.$252 million.

For many of the African countries, there are no concrete estimates of the overall medical costs of AIDS. Nevertheless, what the available information suggests is that those countries face costs that cannot be met unless there is a substantial increase in per-capita health expenditure. However, given the current and projected economic decline of most of those countries, such an outcome is unlikely. Consequently, some very tough decisions have to be made with respect to the allocation of scarce resources between treatment and prevention of AIDS and other health concerns.

Now to the indirect economic costs. Because those stricken with AIDS are usually from the most productive age group in society, there is considerable concern about how the AIDS pandemic will affect productivity, income, and overall economic development. At the level of the family economy, the death or illness of a main provider may lead to abject poverty for the family even though there may be some extended family or other community support. At the level of the national economy, economic productivity also declines through loss of labor inputs due to illness, early retirement, and death of highly trained and skilled as well as unskilled workers. In addition to the loss of labor and skills and decreased productivity, the AIDS pandemic also has implications for other aspects of employment such as training, sickness and death benefits, pensions, and insurance (Armstrong 1991).

Replacing skilled workers will be very costly. A study of Tanzania projects the cost of replacing teachers lost to AIDS at U.S.$40 million through the year 2010 (World Bank 1993a). Another study on the copper mining industry in Zambia, which earns 75 percent of the country's foreign exchange, demonstrates that workers will die of AIDS faster than replacements can be trained in this labor-intensive sector. The result would be reduced mining output and declining national income (Nkowane 1988). An assessment done on the impact of AIDS on industry in Zimbabwe concludes that if the AIDS epidemic spreads at the rate expected, there is likely to be a shortage of skilled manpower available to industry, which in turn would have very serious implications for the projected economic growth of the country (Whiteside 1993b). Similarly, in Uganda, under the most optimistic scenario, there would be 1.9 million fewer people in the labor force by 2010 or approximately 12 percent less than the labor force would have had without AIDS (Armstrong 1995).

Other assessments have been made of the impact of AIDS on food production. During the past two decades, food security has been under stress in Africa. This situation has now been further threatened by the arrival of AIDS. The labor-intensive nature of food production in Africa means that any prolonged interruption or decline of available labor will considerably jeopardize food production and household income. Declining food production and household incomes, in turn, will make families even more vulnerable to malnourishment and disease in addition to undermining national food security.

The Intervention Imperative

The potential devastating socioeconomic impact of AIDS provides the rationale for serious attempts to be made to contain the pandemic. However, since there is currently no vaccine or cure for AIDS, primary prevention is the only way to fight the disease. Early and effective targeting of HIV interventions is also important because such interventions diminish in cost-effectiveness as the infection moves out of the high-risk, high-transmission core groups (World Bank 1993a).

Since 1987, the WHO's Global Program on AIDS has assisted more than one hundred countries in the developing world to establish National AIDS Control Programs. These programs promote prevention activities such as education, blood screening, and research. Current annual worldwide expenditure on AIDS prevention is about U.S.$1.5 billion a year, of which less than U.S.$200 million is spent in developing countries. Total AIDS spending on prevention in sub-Saharan Africa is approximately U.S.$90 million with only about 10 percent coming from government funds (World Bank 1993a).

Perhaps the primary lesson learned through interventions carried out to date is that the spread of the HIV and AIDS is slowed most effectively by those programs that change sexual behavior and control the spread of other sexually transmitted diseases. Examples of those activities currently targeting behavior change are promotion of condom use, education about the benefits of sexual-partner reduction, and social marketing campaigns promoting AIDS awareness. However, despite these efforts to control the disease, AIDS continues to outpace attempts to contain it and more support now needs to be given to improve the prevention and control of AIDS as well as other STDs. In that regard, the WHO estimates that comprehensive AIDS and STDs prevention programs for all developing countries would cost U.S.$1.5 billion to U.S.$2.9 billion per year. This would be about eight to fifteen times the current level of spending but it would avert new adult HIV infections between 1993 and 2000 by about 9.5 million, of which 4.2 million would be in Africa (World Bank 1993a).

Without a doubt, there are tremendous benefits and savings to be generated by AIDS intervention programs. For example, estimates for Zimbabwe indicate that the cost per primary infection averted is U.S.$11 while the benefits are thirty-six times greater than the costs of intervention. Similar prevention costs of U.S.$8 to $12 per case averted were calculated for Kenya (Panos Institute 1992). The World Bank (1993a) also found that, in nine developing countries, the prevention of a case of AIDS saves, on average, about twice GNP per capita in discounted lifetime costs of medical care, with the savings being as much as five times GNP per capita in some urban areas.

As a solution to a catastrophic socioeconomic problem, AIDS intervention programs have proved to be both necessary and somewhat successful. Such programs now need to be bolstered by political commitment and leadership as well as the additional resources required to properly implement them. However, the great majority of such resources should be channeled to NGOs and other private or community organizations rather than to governments, to avoid the political and bureaucratic culture of maladministration in the developing countries as well as to ensure much greater efficiency and accountability of program implementation.

Conclusions

In contrast to other causes of excess adult mortality in developing countries, AIDS does not spare the elite. In some African cities, relatively well-educated and more productive workers are infected in disproportionately large numbers. The epidemic will therefore have a detectable, and possibly substantial, effect on per-capita income growth and economic welfare for years to come.

Currently, individual avoidance of risky behaviors is the only way tens of millions of people will be able to safeguard themselves and their loved ones from HIV and AIDS (Anderson 1994). In this regard, AIDS education for schoolchildren, married couples, and high-frequency transmitters of STDs has been successful in informing and altering African sexual behavior (Fleming 1993). In Zambia, for example, one line of attack has been through the school system, targeting children before they become sexually active. In Zaire, the promotion of condom use, through a social marketing program, resulted in an increase in condom sales from twenty thousand in 1987 to 18.3 million in 1991 and, as a result, the program averted an estimated twenty-five thousand HIV infections in 1991 (Berkley, Piot, and Schopper 1994). Similar programs have been, and are being, developed in other African countries.

Undoubtedly, the socioeconomic impact of the AIDS pandemic in developing countries is now a matter of great concern to the donor agencies. It is a concern that has transcended the purely health sector and therefore requires greater attention by all development agencies, in a coordinated manner, to attempt to minimize its immense social and economic costs. In fact, controlling the spread of AIDS would release resources for other significant development activities that are currently being neglected.

Notes

1. Some reputable scientists do not agree that HIV is the cause of AIDS. Professor Peter H. Duesberg, for example, who is a world-renowned molecular and cell biologist at the University of California, Berkeley, sets out a compelling theory in his recent book, *Inventing the AIDS Virus,* that HIV is a harmless passenger microbe. Professor Duesberg is supported in his arguments by Professor Kary Mullis, a 1993 Nobel Prize winner for his invention of a gene-identification technique.

2. This is currently 63 percent of the worldwide total.

3. However, there is also substantial vertical (mother to child) transmission.

4. It costs the Harare Children's Home, for example, a monthly average of U.S.$130 to care for each of its ninety children, while the government gives only U.S.$16 per child. See Kelso (1994).

6

Bureaucratic Corruption in Africa: Causes and Consequences

Corruption is an evil, shameful, and despicable phenomenon which impairs administrative capability and impedes social stability and economic development. Consequently, its effective deterrence and prevention have become matters of global concern and particularly so with respect to Africa where acts of corruption and unethical behavior have now become legendary.

The pandemic of corruption in Africa, and its ensuing negative consequences, have given rise to a voluminous literature on the subject. As a matter of fact, one can successfully argue that no other topic, as a case study of Africa, has been so prolifically and sustainably written about. Nonetheless, the modalities through which corruption is perpetrated in Africa always seem to provide something new and interesting with the passing of time, and that in itself leads to further documentation and analyses which, inevitably, contribute to a further multiplication of the literature on the problem of corruption in Africa. Furthermore, the ongoing need to analyze and document the causes and consequences of corruption in Africa remains a legitimate academic and practical exercise.

Drawing on examples from selected countries, this chapter analyzes the phenomenon of bureaucratic corruption in Africa with particular emphasis on its causes and consequences. However, the first task is that of defining the concept of bureaucratic corruption.

What Is Bureaucratic Corruption?

Anyone who is familiar with the literature on corruption would be most aware that no single precise and concise definition of bureaucratic corruption exists. As a matter of fact, there are many and varying perspectives on corruption. In this section, an attempt is made to develop a working definition of bureaucratic corruption to provide the framework for the rest of the discussions to follow.

With independence, most African countries drifted shamelessly into the transformation from a bureaucratic administration that emphasized good governance to one that emphasized the sovereignty of politics. In some countries, such as Tanzania and Zambia, for example, public servants had to be seen to support and subscribe to the ideas and principles of the ruling party if they were to be assured of career advancement. Thus, political neutrality for public servants was thrown overboard (Wamala 1994). This resulted in the creation of a politicized bureaucracy in countries that began to engage in centralized economic decision making and patrimonialism. The new states were not only bureaucratic autocracies but also political and economic monopolies that were now lacking in accountability, transparency, and the rule of law (Dia 1993).

This then was the genesis of rampant bureaucratic corruption in Africa. The politicization of the bureaucracy allowed for the entrenchment of the use of personalism and patronage as the means through which authority and influence were exercised (Adediji 1991). The politicians and the bureaucrats forged a dependent patron (politician)/client (bureaucrat) relationship through which administrative decision making occurred. This relationship involved an exchange between a superior patron or patron group and an inferior client or client group. It is unequal or asymmetrical in nature (Randall and Theobald 1985). This process, inevitably, led to the abuse of public office for private and personal gains.

Bureaucratic corruption can now be defined against that foregoing background. In this work, bureaucratic corruption is, first and foremost, the utilization of bureaucratic official positions or titles for personal or private gain, either on an individual or collective basis, at the expense of the public good, in violation of established rules and ethical considerations, and through the direct or indirect participation of one or more public officials, whether they be politicians or bureaucrats.

In a somewhat more simplistic sense, bureaucratic corruption may be seen as partisanship that challenges statesmanship (Werlin 1994). It is an act or acts undertaken with the deliberate intent of deriving or extracting personal and/or private rewards against the interests of the state (Hope 1985; Hope 1987b; Dwivedi 1978; Dey 1989). Such behavior may entail theft, the embezzlement of funds or other appropriation of state property, nepotism and/or the granting of favors to personal acquaintances, and the abuse of public authority to exact monetary benefits or other privileges (United Nations 1990).

Notwithstanding some recent literature that has criticized definitions such as ours here as placing the emphasis almost entirely on the state sphere and tending to minimize the behavior of those in the private sector who contribute to the corruption of governmental personnel (Harsch 1993), the simple truth is that bureaucratic corruption can only occur with the participation of public officials. Whether or not that participation is direct or indirect is completely irrelevant to the completion of a corrupt act or a set of corrupt acts in which such officials are involved.

Moreover, from the perspective of this author, it is a tautology that "bureaucratic corruption" takes place in transactions between private individuals or firms and public officials. Thus, as has been implied before, the issue is one of the misuse of public office and the abuse of public trust by public officials.

Factors Contributing to Bureaucratic Corruption in Africa

Bureaucratic corruption thrives in Africa for a number of reasons. In this section we seek to discuss and analyze those primary factors that have contributed, and continue to contribute, to the pandemic of bureaucratic corruption in Africa. The point of departure for this section is the fact that public accountability is seriously lacking in the great majority of African states. Public accountability means holding public officials responsible for their actions. It is also central to good governance. Such a lack of real accountability has been regarded elsewhere as a major bane of Africa which has bred irresponsibility among public officials and has further led to resistance and cynicism among the citizenry (Adedeji 1995).

The first factor contributing to bureaucratic corruption in Africa is that of the total exercise, by the ruling elite, of all power attached to national sovereignty. This exercise of state power, as it were, has led to the supremacy of the state over civil society and, in turn, the ascendancy of the patrimonial state with its characteristic stranglehold on the economic and political levers of power. It is through this stranglehold that bureaucratic corruption thrives, for it is through this stranglehold that all decision making occurs and patronage is dispensed. Indeed, the postindependence elites and rulers of Africa quickly reached for those tools that promised the most rapid construction of centralized power, including not only the structures of the modern bureaucratic state, but also the mechanisms of social and economic control. This, in turn, led to the creation of personalist patrimonialism (Le Vine 1980), which in turn provided a mechanism through which bureaucratic corruption would flourish.[1]

Such is the pervasiveness of the patrimonial state in Africa that the citizenry have adapted to it. In Uganda, for example, individuals and other groups of people in positions of authority and/or influence tend to shift their loyalties and political allegiances to the ruling regime of the day for reasons of personal survival and economic gain (Ouma 1991). Likewise, in Sierra Leone a system of patronage thrived during the era of the ruling All People's Congress (APC) 1968–92, primarily because membership of particular groupings was a more acceptable qualification for a given position than an individual's actual capabilities (Kpundeh 1994).

Under such circumstances, bureaucratic corruption tends to run rampant. It becomes truly ubiquitous, reaching into the private sector as well (Elliot 1994). It has now become a way of life in Africa to have transactions at a governmental level that seek to do no more than secure objectives that are not officially sanctioned, thereby corroding popular confidence in public institutions.

The second factor is directly related to the first. Along with the emergence of the patrimonial state came the expanded role of state activity. Economic decision making became centralized and public enterprises proliferated. This resulted in an expanding bureaucracy with increasing discretionary power that was put to use as a conduit for graft. Public enterprises then became a playground for corruption, and state intervention in economic affairs was the precipitating cause of such a situation.

The expanded role of state activity meant that the public bureaucracy was difficult to avoid in Africa. Whatever the transaction, be it getting a driver's license, telephone service, government contracts for goods and/or services, or permits to sell crops, it required the bureaucratic exercise of assumed powers due to the irrational interventions by the state in economic affairs. This, in turn, meant that bribes had to be paid for the transactions to be completed. Thus, bureaucratic corruption in Africa can be seen as an outgrowth of government involvement in the economy. It is that involvement that has allowed for the systematic exploitation of illegal income-earning opportunities by public officials and the enhancement of rent-seeking opportunities (Hope 1987b). In Zimbabwe, for example, virtually all government contracts now require some form of kickback or "commission" to those with political influence or to the bureaucrats who stand guard over regulations. The country's government, led by President Robert Mugabe, is surrounded by influence-peddlers looking for a cut of any contract (*The Economist* 1996b).

It was reported, for example, that Algerian government officials had pocketed U.S.$26 billion in bribes and commissions on foreign contracts in the late 1980s (Ayittey 1992). In Uganda, the various forms of bribes paid to public officials have been principally attributed to a hostile economy and the insensitivity of the state toward the well-being of its servants, among other things (Ouma 1991). In Zimbabwe, twenty-six cases of bureaucratic corruption involving bribes were reported for 1991 alone (Makumbe 1994).

In addition to bribes, the expanded role of state activity also provided additional opportunities for embezzlement and unlawful enrichment. Many African leaders and other government officials have been frequently shown to be in control of wealth and significant assets that are disproportionate to their official earnings. A good litany of the country evidence on this aspect of bureaucratic corruption can be found in Ayittey (1992). Suffice it to say here that Africa represents the classic example of a kleptocracy par excellence. It is not surprising, therefore, that it is this aspect of bureaucratic corruption that is often cited as the justification for the unceremonial removal of African governments from office by the military.

The third factor contributing to bureaucratic corruption in Africa stems from the second. Africa's encounter with centralized economic decision making and increasing state activity has been catastrophic, to say the least. This encounter has resulted in economic retardation and elusive development (Hope 1996b). This in turn has created a situation where the great majority of African countries are now among the poorest in the world. Public officials, being among those experiencing the effects of the hardships associated with these retrogressive economic conditions, have tended to pursue corrupt activities to maintain their living standards and/or to simply make ends meet (Shellukindo and Baguma 1993).

One of the primary fallouts of the deteriorating economic situation in Africa has been the erosion and compression of salaries of public officials. The economic crisis has increasingly worsened the official incomes of almost all public servants in Africa. Shrinking budgets, rising and persistent inflation, and increased taxation, among other things, have all contributed to falling bureaucratic incomes and the erosion of retirement benefits (Mukandala 1992). In Zambia, for example, the salary of an undersecretary in 1986 was worth only 22 percent of its 1976 purchasing power, while in Tanzania in 1969 a top public-sector salary commanded thirty times the minimum wage in government employment compared to a ratio of only six to one in the mid-1980s (Lindauer 1994). Likewise, in countries as diverse as Ethiopia, Kenya, Nigeria, Somalia, and Sudan, it was found that, over the decade 1975–85, the real value of civil service salaries and the real living standards of civil servants recruited in 1975 had fallen even after allowing for the effects of promotion (Robinson 1990).

In such circumstances, quite apart from their declining motivation and efficiency, the bureaucrats in Africa disavow any sense of civic virtue and attempt to supplement their incomes by engaging in corrupt acts. Such acts, although justified in the mindset of the public officials who are engaged in them, are nonetheless corrosive and tend to do economic harm and exacerbate the economic decline of their countries.

The fourth contributing factor to bureaucratic corruption in Africa is the lack of the rule of law and administrative predictability. This factor, important as it is on its own merits, takes on added importance in the context of the patrimonial state, as will be seen shortly. Predictability and the rule of law are characterized by policies and regulations developed and implemented according to a regular process which is institutionalized and which provides opportunities for review (Adamolekun and Bryant 1994).

However, in patrimonial states such as those in Africa, the formal bureaucratic organizations are captured by the ruling regime, which then uses, or interferes with, the powers and functions of government for private gain. This capture includes control over the state instruments for law and order (McCarthy 1994). Such a state of affairs affords considerable discretion in decision making and produces irrational decisions that may be illegal but which cannot be challenged in the courts. Under such circumstances, bureaucratic corruption not only thrives but is more likely to go unpunished.

In Zimbabwe, for example, an exercise to detect and punish those public officials involved in an elaborate scheme to illegally purchase and resell motor vehicles became a farce when the first government minister to be convicted in the affair was pardoned by the president, and the attorney general subsequently dropped all charges against the other government ministers and members of parliament on the grounds that they would be pardoned by the president if convicted (Makumbe 1994). A further example of the lack of the rule of law contributing to corruption can be found in Zaire, whose president's (Mobutu Sese Seko) overseas bank accounts are stuffed with pilfered funds. By 1975, President Mobutu had become one of the world's wealthiest men through large kickbacks on government contracts and outright embezzlement (Young and Turner 1985). Yet, by his own decree, this president has become the embodiment of a homespun philosophy and a national symbol above criticism (Lamb 1982). Bureaucratic corruption, in the case of Zaire, clearly stands out by the magnitude and the impunity with which it is perpetrated (Tshishimbi, Glick, and Thorbecke 1994).

The next factor contributing to bureaucratic corruption in Africa is the lack of exemplary leadership exhibited by politicians and senior public officials. Indeed, the lack of the rule of law automatically suggests that exemplary public leadership would be difficult to find in Africa. This dearth of commendable leadership in most of Africa can be attributed to the fact that personal and private interests take precedence over national interests. The state is often an artificial entity. Consequently, public officials have no fear of being held accountable for their actions. They disobey rules and directives and they display a considerable knack for disregarding their responsibilities. In other words, they tend not to exhibit a public service ethic.

When leadership is not exemplary it provides encouragement for bureaucratic corruption. This, in turn, shapes the attitudes and patterns of behavior of each level of subordinates. However, when leaders are recognized for their integrity and concern for the public welfare, these qualities can be reflected in the ethos and performance of the public service and will also have a profound effect on all sections of society. But if corruption is rife, the public bureaucracy is likely to become demoralized and self-serving (World Bank 1983). In Nigeria, for example, the lack of exemplary leadership has contributed to a fragmentation of political life which continues to channel public service loyalty away from the policy process and the abstract state back to the leaders themselves in a gross display of bureaucratic corruption (Brownsberger 1983).

The final factor has to do with sociocultural norms. In Africa, the widespread existence of personalism results in significant loyalties toward one's family, tribe, and friends (Hope 1987b). Such loyalties are at the expense of loyalty to the state, for they often require the contravention of rules and regulations to maintain them. Bureaucratic corruption is therefore advanced by attitudes and patterns of behavior interwoven throughout the whole sociocultural fabric (Jabbra 1976).

Sociocultural norms may be difficult to grasp in the African context. However, such norms remain as very influential forces in day-to-day African life. They often determine, for example, who gets jobs, who gets promoted, who gets government contracts, and so on. In other words, they have a great deal to do with the organization of life in general, and they are a major source of nepotism and corruption in public life. They breed favoritism and the creation of corrupt social networks within the administrative system. This leads further to the development of a corrupt culture in which terms such as *kalabule* (in Ghana), *dash* (in Kenya), *wako-ni-wako* (in Zambia), and *baksheesh* (in Egypt), reflect the social reference to corruption and demonstrate the corrupt ethos of public officials (Elliot 1994; Prah 1993). Yet, there seems to be no real stigma attached to such corruption.

The Consequences of Bureaucratic Corruption in Africa

There are generally three types of consequences of bureaucratic corruption in developing states, and the African countries are no exception. Bureaucratic corruption produces negative consequences of an economic, political, and administrative nature. These consequences, both individually and collectively, categorically impair the process of development in Africa.

First, we look at the economic consequences. Bureaucratic corruption has done considerable damage to economic growth and prosperity in Africa. Recent studies suggest that no nation can expect to become an advanced high-income economy without attacking its corruption problem. Graft and poverty tend to go hand in hand (Hirsh 1996). Bureaucratic corruption increases the cost to African governments for doing business. Kickbacks and illegal commissions that have to be paid to public officials are simply added to the final costs of contracts, equipment, supplies, and so on. This not only increases government expenditures and siphons off scarce funds, but eventually leads to the need to increase revenues either through more taxes or by borrowing or by reducing development programs of greater importance and ultimately leading to a general welfare loss for the affected country.

Similarly, theft, embezzlement, and fraud by public officials reduces the availability of government funds for development-related activities. In Zimbabwe, for example, the national police disclosed that the government had lost a total of U.S.$3 million in 1991 due to theft and fraud by public officials (Makumbe 1994). Surely, this kind of loss would have a negative impact on development performance, given the country's budgetary constraints. Likewise, the process of economic development has been severely hampered in Mali (one of the poorest African countries with a per capita GNP of U.S.$300) through the looting of the country by the former head of state, Moussa Traoré, who amassed a personal fortune worth over U.S.$2 billion—an amount equal to the size of Mali's foreign debt (Ayittey 1992). Also, the reconstruction and development program (RDP) in South Africa could be severely hampered as a result of bureaucratic corruption. It is estimated that such corruption results in a loss to the South African treasury of approximately as much as U.S.$7 billion per year, an amount that was equivalent to 17 percent of the 1994–95 budget and almost equal to the magnitude of the country's interest payment on its debt (Harverson 1996).

In the trade sector, bureaucratic corruption results in capital flight and price increases at both the wholesale and retail levels. Corruption in the trade sector is perhaps the most systematic of the corrupt activities in Africa. The role of trade in African states, and hence the importance of the import-export sector, looms large and provides many opportunities for corrupt practices to be perpetrated. Bribes have to be paid for the clearance of goods through customs, for obtaining import licenses, for the shipping of contraband, for exclusion from taxes and fees, and so on.

It is estimated that some U.S.$15 billion flees Africa annually

(Ayittey 1992). This is a considerable sum and it is equivalent to about 82 percent of the amount that Africa (excluding North Africa) received in official development assistance in 1992. Undoubtedly, some of this capital flight represents legitimate transfers abroad. However, the great majority is derived from corrupt activities involving public officials. Since capital is scarce in Africa and is much needed to bolster the development effort, its outflow from the region, on a large scale, is a very disturbing matter.

Capital flight can be regarded as a diversion of resources from domestic real investment to foreign financial investments. The country of origin loses the associated benefits of such capital even if the yield from such capital were to be repatriated in the future. The loss of benefits includes income and tax revenues. Also, there is the consequence of the redistribution of wealth from country of origin to country of destination (Polak 1989). Capital flight is bad because of its micro- and macro-impact on development. It destabilizes interest rates and exchange rates, it reflects discrepancies between private and social rates of return, it contributes to erosion of the domestic tax base, it reduces domestic investment, and it necessitates increases in foreign borrowing, which in turn increases the national cost of borrowing (Cuddington 1986).

Bureaucratic corruption also stifles initiative and enterprise in Africa. Rent-seeking activities tend to have the effect of inflating the cost of doing business. In Uganda, for example, it was found that the cost of acquiring a plot in a low-density residential suburb in Kampala was more than ten times the official rate (Ouma 1991). The immediate consequence of such a situation is that entrepreneurs and potential entrepreneurs withdraw from engaging in such investments and the affected economy loses the multiplier benefits that would have been forthcoming with those investments.

Finally, with respect to the economic consequences, bureaucratic corruption also impairs economic efficiency in Africa. As an example, financial gains obtained through bureaucratic corruption are unlikely to be transferred to the investment sector, since ill-gotten money is either used up in conspicuous consumption or is transferred to foreign bank accounts (Gould and Amaro-Reyes 1983). Furthermore, bribes, commissions, or kickbacks result in wasteful expenditure, and usually on suspect projects. The commitment of such expenditure eliminates what would have been viable and cost-efficient alternatives. Kenya, for example, bought fighter jets in 1989 from a French firm rather than a British firm, at twice the cost the latter quoted, because the British firm refused to pay a kickback to the Kenyan official negotiating the sale. However, the French firm offered a free presidential jet to Kenya's president (Ayittey 1992). Kenyan society as a whole was therefore made to bear the corruption opportunity cost.

Another example of the impairment of economic efficiency can be found in Zaire where bureaucratic corruption contributed to the neglect of agriculture in favor of industry. Agriculture was less immediately lucrative to the Zairean kleptocrats than was industrial development. Consequently, the agricultural sector declined throughout the entire postindependence period (Tshishimbi, Glick, and Thorbecke 1994). Similarly, bureaucratic corruption was also an inhibitive factor in the implementation of exchange rate reform. In fact, "Mobutu and his clique have had free access to the state's resources. This group has . . . a preoccupation with foreign exchange—how to obtain it quickly and in large amounts for their own personal needs" (Leslie 1987).

The second type of consequence of bureaucratic corruption in Africa relates to political development and stability. When bureaucratic corruption becomes the status quo, its maintenance tends to involve the use of repressive tactics through the state instruments for law and order. Political leaders, in their own self-interest to maintain the patrimonial state, will suppress political opposition and public criticism of their behavior. In Mobutu's Zaire, for example, where the state bureaucracy has been privatized by the ruling elite, fear and repression have prevented any serious threat from dissenting groups or individuals (Gould 1980). This, in turn, hinders political development (Hope 1987b).

Bureaucratic corruption also affects political stability in Africa because it leads to violence and frequent regime changes. In Uganda under Idi Amin, corruption resulted in violence and social disorganization (Southall 1980). During the past two decades, bureaucratic corruption was the most frequently cited reason for the military takeovers of governments in Africa. In Sierra Leone, for example, Captain Valentine Strasser gave his reasoning for his overthrow of the country's government, on April 29, 1992, as the following:

> The nation as a whole was in a state of virtual collapse. Corruption, indiscipline, mismanagement, tribalism, nepotism, injustice, and thuggery were rampant. Members of government were engaged in the plun-

dering of the state's resources to enrich themselves. . . . (*West Africa* 1992)

Similarly, in Mali, the overthrow of President Moussa Traoré in March 1991 was attributed to the people's outrage at the high-level corruption and embezzlement which had come to characterize his regime (Turrittin 1991). During the twenty-three years Traoré ruled Mali, he, and those close to him, amassed considerable wealth while the standard of living of ordinary Malians fell. Some of the excesses included the squandering of aid funds to build villas for the ruling elite instead of being used to fight droughts, for which they were expressly obtained. As a result, some 300,000 nomads were estimated to have been left destitute (Turrittin 1991).

Going further back, we also have the case of Niger, whose government was overthrown by the military on April 14, 1974. The leader of the coup, Lieutenant Colonel Seyni Kountché, said the army had brought the problem of bureaucratic corruption to the notice of the country's president on several occasions but no action was ever taken (Higgott and Fugelstad 1975). The corruption evidence included the misuse of drought relief aid by the ruling party, and the acquisition by the president's wife of a considerable fortune, including many luxury homes that she rented to foreign embassies and public corporations at exorbitant prices (Higgott and Fugelstad 1975).

More recently, on July 22, 1994, the military also overthrew the government of Gambia. The coup leader, Captain Yahya Jammeh, justified the military takeover on the grounds of widespread corruption, embezzlement of public funds, and mismanagement on the part of the erstwhile government. He said that the rationale of the coup d'état was to respond to the malpractices and misappropriation of funds which were exacerbated by crime, drug trafficking, and rampant corruption (*West Africa* 1995).

When political development and stability are undermined, the process of national development is also undermined. There can be no effective long-term planning under such circumstances and the construction of democracy and the democratic experience become threatened. In other words, things begin to fall apart. That is certainly the experience of Nigeria, whose military government has long since overstayed its welcome and now rules only by brute force.

The final type of consequence stemming from bureaucratic corruption in Africa pertains to administrative development. Bureaucratic corruption hinders administrative development and performance in developing states partly because of its institutional spillover effects. It has been found that corrupt public officials export their corrupt activities to other institutions by extending influence and pressure on other public officials and subordinates as a means of sustaining rent-seeking opportunities (Hope 1987b). It is claimed that in South Africa, for example, as much as 60 percent of corruption is committed by people in management positions (Harverson 1996). Undoubtedly, these managers would have considerable influence on their subordinates as well as on their peers.

Indeed, the damaging effect of bureaucratic corruption on administrative development and efficiency can be very extensive and variegated. Once the corruption syndrome has afflicted a bureaucracy, the resulting negligence, protected through favoritism or other influences, creates innumerable problems and grave consequences for the people. Consequently, bureaucratic corruption may be seen from two perspectives: that inflicted on the people, and that practiced between corrupt public officials (Alatas 1990).

Moreover, such corrupt activities can move from a passive to an active phase where public servants do not wait to be approached and bribed but go out and actively solicit individuals to offer bribes in return for the provision of public services. In countries such as Nigeria, such payments are regarded as necessary and routine but they do not guarantee that transactions will be expedited. However, if such payments are not made, it does guarantee that there will be absolutely no action taken on the transactions. In other words, this type of bureaucratic corruption has become the unofficial but operating administrative order not only in Nigeria but in most African countries.

In Zaire, for example, public servants openly peddle their access to VIPs and their ability to issue official documents. Soldiers hire themselves out as bodyguards to foreign businessmen. As a matter of fact, almost any transaction needs a sweetener. The system has produced the quintessential Zairean kleptocrat, the *protocole,* a professional payer of bribes. The *protocole* will introduce himself whenever any official transaction is to be undertaken. His role is to use his influence to keep the amount of the bribe to be paid to a minimum. In return, of course, he gets a cut for himself (*The Economist* 1994).

Bureaucratic corruption also affects professionalism in the African public services and leads to frustration on the part of the few honest public servants to such an extent that they emigrate. In Uganda, for example, these emigrants have mainly included medical doctors, teachers, engineers, economists, and university lecturers from a wide variety of professional fields (Ouma 1991). This, in turn, contributes to the brain drain dilemma of the African states and thereby further impairs national productivity, output, and the overall development process.

Conclusions

This chapter has analytically shown the causes and consequences of bureaucratic corruption in Africa. Several factors determine the extent to which bureaucratic corruption plays a significant role in the region, including the role of the state in economic activity and the instruments it uses to fulfill that role, sociocultural norms, and the nature of the political system.

Bureaucratic corruption has now reached epidemic proportions in Africa. Most Africans find that there is more to gain than to lose by permitting its existence. Moreover, the African populaces have so little of their own property to protect that they simply accept the systematic pillaging of their respective countries. As a matter of fact, in the African kleptocracies, known also as "vampire states," flagrant dictators like Zaire's Mobutu Sese Seko and their minions suck all of the wealth out of the country while ordinary citizens look on in apathy (Hirsh 1996).

Undoubtedly, bureaucratic corruption retards the process of African socioeconomic development. It siphons off valuable economic resources into unproductive uses and thereby reduces the likelihood of development objectives' being achieved. It also drains off the valuable resource of time into nonproductive use, thus reducing administrative efficiency. In addition, because it is hidden and unaccountable, bureaucratic corruption is essentially undemocratic and hampers the development of democratic processes and institutions (Heeks 1995).

Bureaucratic corruption is now a way of life in Africa. That suggests that its control would be a very difficult task. However, with the emergence of economic and political liberalization in many of those countries, there is considerable optimism that such corruption would be brought under control. The need for such control has also been given additional emphasis in the aid allocation decisions of such donor agencies as the World Bank and the Overseas Development Administration (ODA) of the British government. In chapter 10, we describe and analyze the primary mechanisms that have been implemented in some African states for controlling bureaucratic corruption.

Note

1. Van de Walle (1994a) has demonstrated that public corruption is higher in patrimonial regimes and that public accountability is significantly less well developed in these regimes. He further argues that rent-seeking assumes a particular dynamic in such African regimes because it is inherent in the system of rule.

Part II
Toward Policy Reform and Change

7

Development Policy and the Poor: Toward an Alternative Policy Framework for Africa

During the past two decades the majority of countries in Africa found themselves in a crisis of development that has constrained the access of their citizens to basic goods and services within their respective borders. This is the result of development policy, as discussed in chapter 1, that has failed miserably to move these countries forward on a path toward economic progress and which, in turn, has exacerbated their problem of poverty and elusive development.

Expressed in GNP per capita, in 1992 the average income in the industrial countries was twenty-nine times that of sub-Saharan Africa compared to sixteen times that of the developing countries as a whole (UNDP 1995), and the gap is widening. There were about 1.3 billion poor people in the developing countries by 1990, of which 216 million were in sub-Saharan Africa. This chapter discusses the poverty impact of development policy to date, and suggests an alternative policy framework for improving the well-being of the poor in Africa.

The Poverty Impact of Development Policy in Africa

The debt crisis, balance-of-payments difficulties, environmental disasters, ethnic conflicts, bureaucratic corruption, rapid urbanization, budget deficits, to name a few influences, have all contributed to the development crisis now confronting the African countries. The effect has been, among other things, famine and lack of food security, malnutrition, higher rates of infant mortality, deteriorating infrastructure, capital flight, human flight (brain drain), the return of once eradicated diseases such as polio and tuberculosis, for example, and a general decline in the quality and extent of basic goods and services provided, such as health care, potable water, and sanitation facilities.

With the development crisis there has been the advent of new thinking on development policy (Hope 1992). The new view on development policy is that government intervention is more likely to hurt than help the process of economic growth in developing countries and, by implication, the chances for the poor in those countries to attain a better life (Bird and Horton 1989; Summers 1992). This conclusion is reinforced by evidence that appears to support the now common perception that even those policies and frameworks that were specifically intended to aid the poor have not been very successful and, in some cases, have had quite perverse results. A very good example is "*Ujamaa* socialism" in Tanzania in the 1960s and 1970s.[1]

Expenditure policies, intended to make health, housing, education, and other public services more accessible to the poor, seem to have seldom reached their supposed target groups and often ended up subsidizing and bolstering the more favored and well-off segments of society (Bird and Horton 1989). Primarily for these reasons there has been increased emphasis, in recent times, by the donor agencies on the type of policy reform that emphasizes a serious approach to economic liberalization included in which are public enterprise reform, privatization of government activities, market-determined exchange rates, removal of government subsidies, a dismantling of marketing boards, market-driven interest rates, and export-led growth (Hope 1996b; Summers 1992).

To meet the mandate of the economic liberalization programs, governments throughout the developing world have had to reduce their expenditures on poverty-oriented programs as part of their adjustment to their difficult economic circumstances (Bird and Horton 1989). As a matter of fact, some liberalization programs have, at least in the short term, diminished the capacity of many African countries to provide their citizens with adequate access to basic goods and services. Moreover, this is occurring at a period when their populaces are most vulnerable to economic distress, given the rapidly declining economies of most of those countries (UNICEF 1987; UNICEF 1989; Jolly 1988).

However, and without a doubt, the implementation of liberalization programs has had both positive and negative impacts. On the positive side, some countries such as Ghana and Morocco, for example, have attracted much international attention with their successes in economic growth, improving indicators on balance of payments, declining debt ratios, increasing rates of private investment and the domestic savings ratio, declining rates of inflation and unemployment, and declining overall budget deficits (World Bank 1991).

On the negative side, there have been some adverse distributional consequences (Sadik 1992). This has forced some countries, for example, Zimbabwe and Ghana, to introduce a Social Dimensions of Adjustment Programme (SDA) and a Programme of Action to Mitigate the Social Costs of Adjustment (PAMSCAD), respectively, to cushion the impact of the social consequences of their liberalization programs.[2] Some of the liberalization programs have also contributed to declines in labor's share in the functional distribution of income. This has occurred through some combination of wage freezes, declining formal employment, and rapid inflation, and has resulted in, at least over the short term, many people being worse off than they were before the liberalization programs were put in place and thereby increasing the numbers of the poor (Zuckerman 1991).

The poor in developing countries such as those in Africa are, however, not a homogeneous group. They instead fall into three categories (UNDP 1990). The first category can be designated as the chronic poor. These are individuals at the margin of society and who constantly suffer from extreme deprivation. The second category can be referred to as the borderline poor. These are individuals or households who are occasionally poor, such as the seasonally unemployed. The final category can be termed the newly poor. These are individuals or households who are the direct victims of the structural adjustment and liberalization programs, such as retrenched workers and civil servants.

Recent estimates put the number of people living in absolute poverty in Africa at over 215 million. By the year 2000 the number of poor people living in developing countries is expected to rise to 1.5 billion and, due to the growing concentration of poverty in Africa, it is estimated that Africa's share of the world's poor will rise to more than 40 percent. This would mean that nearly one-half of Africa's population will live below the poverty line at the beginning of the twenty-first century (UNDP 1991; World Bank 1990).

The great majority of the poor in Africa, as discussed in chapter 1, live in the rural areas. However, there has been a trend toward the urbanization of poverty (Hope 1986; World Bank 1994a). Many of the poor are located in urban areas where incomes are generally higher and urban services and facilities more accessible. However, they are usually housed in slums or squatter settlements in overcrowded and contaminated conditions and are under constant threats of forcible eviction, floods, landslides, and inadequate water and sanitation infrastructure (World Bank 1990). The growth of urban poverty in Africa is, to a greater or lesser degree, a reflection of rural poverty in those countries. The cities offer rural migrants a possible escape from joblessness, underemployment, oppressive agrarian structures, or low-wage work. Unfortunately, the number of potential migrants among the rural poor exceeds the capacity of the urban areas to readily absorb them. In many African countries, rural-urban disparities reflect the distribution of income and the locus of power. Moreover, over time, there has been a primary city approach to development that has created and entrenched an urban bias in the implementation of development policy with negative repercussions for the relations between those cities and the rural hinterlands, as discussed in chapter 3.

Poverty in Africa is closely linked with environmental degradation. Approximately 50 percent of the poor in Africa live in ecologically fragile zones (UNDP 1992). They overuse their marginal lands for, among other things, fuel wood and subsistence and cash-crop production, further endangering their physical environment, their health, and the lives of their children. For example, between 1950 and 1983, 24 percent of Africa's forests disappeared, and the pace of this decline accelerated in the early 1980s. Overuse now threatens to turn two-fifths of Africa's nondesert land into desert (Salamon 1994). This, in turn, increases the chances of the poor's becoming environmental refugees. At the same time, the poor are disproportionately threatened by the environmental hazards and health risks posed by pollution, poor sanitation, polluted water, and inadequate housing (UNDP 1992; Mink 1993). The poor are therefore both the victims and the perpetrators of environmental damage (World Bank 1992).

Poverty in Africa is also characterized by a gender bias. Women are often more severely disadvantaged because they are victimized by cultural, social, legal, and economic obstacles that men do not encounter (Buvinić and Lycette 1988). However, women's share in the labor force has been increasing as more and more women have been leaving households to engage especially in gainful self-employment and particularly in the subterranean sector (Hope 1993a). Female entrepreneurship is now an ongoing reality in African countries but general inequality persists, although there have been some improvements in some societies, as discussed in chapter 4. However, in many of those societies women remain invisible in statistics because little value is attached to what they do. They are paid less than men generally and even for similar jobs, and they are discriminated against because of gender-based differences in the distribution of food and other entitlements within the family and society.

Understandably, poverty is by no means a problem confined to the developing countries. Poverty and the poor can also be found in the industrial countries. Therefore, it can be argued that consistent rates of economic growth alone will not guarantee the alleviation of poverty and underdevelopment in African countries. However, it has been demonstrated that the extent to which people can improve their chances to increase their overall human development depends largely on the access they have to basic goods and services (Lewis 1988). Let us now examine the record on access to basic goods and services in sub-Saharan Africa.

Food Security and Nutrition

The concept of food security addresses people's risks of not having access to needed food. At the household level, food security is the ability of the household to secure enough food to ensure adequate dietary intake for all of its members. Consequently, the availability of food and access to food are two essential determinants of food security (von Braun et al. 1992).

The evidence is abundant that hunger and considerable malnutrition continue to be a problem in the developing world. It is estimated that nearly 800 million people are undernourished and this figure continues to increase (UNDP 1995). In 1990 more than 100 million people were affected by famine. Approximately 21 percent of those considered to be hungry in the developing countries live in Africa. Consistent with this distribution is the proportion of low-birth-weight infants in the region, which stood at 16 percent compared to 19 percent for all developing countries (UNDP 1995). At the same time there has been some marginal progress in daily calorie supply per capita, which increased slightly from 2,082 in 1988 to 2,096 in 1992 (UNDP 1992; UNDP 1995).

However, there are differences in calorie consumption and requirements between rural and urban areas. Urbanization is associated with important changes in food consumption patterns (von Braun et al. 1993). Typically, calorie consumption is lower in urban areas and, although the prevalence of food security is higher in the urban areas than in the rural areas, urban poverty with significant food insecurity will increase in the future with the higher rates of urbanization previously alluded to.

Health Care Services

Despite the fact that the developing countries have increased their public expenditure on health as a proportion of GDP by nearly 50 percent in the past thirty years, only about 79 percent of the people in those countries have access to health care services today. For the least developed countries the estimate is 48 percent, and for sub-Saharan Africa the estimate is 56 percent (UNDP 1995). However, during the past three decades average life expectancy increased by over one-third, with more than twenty developing countries achieving a life expectancy of seventy years or more. Unfortunately, due partly to the rampant spread of HIV, which results in the fatal disease of AIDS, life expectancy in Africa is now expected to decline considerably in the near future and beyond until the disease is brought under control, as discussed in chapter 5.

Education

This sector has shown steady progress over the years in every developing region. The number of primary schools, the number of teachers, and the enrollment rates have all increased during the past two decades. In sub-Saharan Africa, adult literacy doubled, increasing from 27 percent to 54 percent. The net enrollment ratio at the primary level doubled, rising from 25 percent to 50 percent, while the secondary enrollment ratio almost tripled, growing from 13 percent to 38 percent, between 1960 and 1991 (UNDP 1995).

On the negative side, more than 80 million African boys and girls are still out of school at the primary and secondary levels and the dropout rate at the primary level is still too high. Only about 50 percent of the entrants to grade one finish grade five. In addition, further progress has been hampered by the low enrollments of females due to reinforced gender inequality in education. However, the enrollment gap is closing. Between 1970 and 1990, the annual rate of growth of female enrollment was more than 1 percent higher than that of men for all levels of education, and the female literacy is now about two-thirds that of the male literacy rate (UNDP 1995).

Water and Sanitation

During the past two decades, the percentage of rural African families with access to safe water has increased from less than 10 percent to almost 35 percent. Overall, the percentage of the population with access to safe water in sub-Saharan Africa for the period 1988–93 was only 43 percent, indicating very slow progress in this area.

With respect to sanitation, about 36 percent of the developing world's population had access to proper facilities for the period 1988–93. In the least developed countries and sub-Saharan Africa, 33 percent and 36 percent of the population, respectively, had access to proper sanitation facilities. The lack of proper sanitation facilities is the primary reason diseases transmitted via feces are so common in Africa.

Toward an Alternative Policy Framework

What does the foregoing exposition of the poverty impact of development policy tell us about the nature of the policy reform needed to improve the situation of the poor in Africa? Well, we first need to accept that the prevailing thinking on development policy implementation is one that limits the role of the state in economic affairs and stresses greater partnerships encompassing the private sector, inclusive of the business community and nongovernmental organizations (NGOs).

We also need to recognize what has been aptly described as the triple challenge of development policy (UNDP 1990). The first of those challenges is that development policy must expand the development opportunities for a growing number of people; the second is that such policy must contribute to the upgrade in living standards; and the third is that such policy must be able to achieve more with less, given stagnating or even declining resources.

Also of significance must be the understanding that such policy reform cannot and should no longer take place in a vacuum. Ideally, and to the extent possible, development policy should have broad national appeal and its implementation must have greater participation by the people whose interests are at stake. This is further predicated on the recognition of the explicit relationship between knowledge and development, and in the acceptance that empowerment through knowledge is a key element in the development of nations, regions, communities, and individuals.

Under this framework, the state intervenes less in the economy. However, it does not disappear. The reduction or the alleviation of poverty provides a straightforward rationale for government intervention (World Bank 1993a). Providing social security services, for example, can only be done by governments. However, governments remain, inevitably, as the principal actors in macroeconomic policy choices, defense, foreign policy, and infrastructure (Klitgaard 1991). Indeed, among other things, macroeconomic policy must be well managed in a way that avoids excessive inflation, an overvalued exchange rate, and much else (Perkins and Roemer 1994).

Given the above premise, the reform framework needs to be accomplished and facilitated through a redefining of the role and responsibilities of governments. African governments must be willing to accept that they can contribute to overall development and growth and the alleviation and reduction of poverty both directly and in close partnership with the private sector, including NGOs, where warranted.

Since access to basic goods and services is an essential part of any long-term strategy for reducing poverty, governments have a major and legitimate role to play in facilitating and enhancing such access. Essentially, all basic goods and services that the private sector is willing and able to deliver, within the economic realities of the individual African countries, should no longer be considered priority areas for governments. Consequently, African governments need to concentrate on investing in human capital and on providing an atmosphere for the private sector to function competitively and efficiently.

Investing in human capital means improved targeting of programs and expenditures in the areas of education and health. Governments need to make a clear commitment to these areas and put them among their highest priorities (World Bank 1991). Inevitably, this requires that both the social allocation and the social priority ratios be increased. The social allocation ratio is the percentage of public expenditure earmarked for social services, while the social priority ratio is the percentage of social expenditure directed at the priority areas.

Increasing the social allocation ratio would require the restructuring of budgets to decrease expenditure on some economic items that are not consistent with current economic and global realities and, therefore, would not negatively impact on the economic sector. For example, African countries can trim, considerably, their military spending, their outlays on inefficient and nonprofitable public enterprises, and their subsidy supports that are not targeted to those most in need. It is not necessary to go into a detailed discussion of each of these here. Suffice it to say, however, that tremendous savings would be realized with these expenditure cuts, some of which can then be used for priority social spending and the reduction of overall budget deficits. For example, in sub-Saharan Africa the losses of public enterprises are estimated at 5 percent of GNP. If African governments did not have to finance such losses, the potential increase in education and health spending in the region would be approximately 77 percent (UNDP 1993). In addition, African governments should attempt to influence donor agencies to increase the social allocation ratio of the development assistance they provide to the region.

The social priority ratio will vary over time and among countries, depending on the degree of success achieved in improving access to basic goods and services. However, for the majority of African countries, the priority remains basic education, with equal access for both males and females, and primary health care, particularly in the rural areas. As mentioned before, some progress has been made in these areas but much more needs to be done in many of the countries because simply increasing spending will not automatically help the poor.

Such spending must tilt the existing pattern of access in favor of the poor. For example, past education policy in some countries has favored spending on tertiary education. However, tertiary education has the lowest social rate of return, 11 percent compared to 24 percent and 18 percent for primary and secondary education, respectively (Psacharopoulos 1994), and usually benefits the higher-income families. "Thus, a large expenditure at the tertiary level is concentrated on a small number of advantaged students, in contrast to the smaller expenditure on primary education, which benefits large numbers of the poor" (Birdsall and James 1993). In Africa, 22 percent of the public education budget is spent on universities, which are attended by only 2 percent of the relevant age group (Birdsall and James 1993). Also, aid donors spend U.S.$1 per head on primary education in the region. That's one-tenth of what they spend per pupil at the secondary level and one-five-hundredth of what they invest in each university student (Watkins 1996).

For many of the African countries, the provision of tertiary education exclusively through government expenditure is not sustainable and now needs to be re-examined. The development success of the East Asian economies, for example, is credited, in part, to their allocation of a bigger share (averaging more than 70 percent) of their public spending on education to basic primary and secondary education rather than to universities (World Bank 1993b). Based on data for ten African countries,[3] it was estimated that eliminating stipends for the living expenses of university students would permit a 20 percent increase in primary school enrollments, even if operating costs of universities continue to be covered out of public funds (Mingat and Tan 1985).

Investment in human capital has a direct positive relationship on productivity, growth, and income distribution. An educated and healthy population is most likely to escape poverty. In this regard, the experience of Malaysia, for example, is most informative. In Malaysia, proper education and health facilities developed a strong base of human capital through which economic progress was enhanced and poverty was considerably reduced from 37 percent of the population in 1960 to less than 5 percent by 1990 (World Bank 1993b). Moreover, programs and expenditures can be targeted at the poor without undermining adjustment programs where needed (Zuckerman 1991). There is no defensible justification for exacerbating poverty as an externality of development policy.

In addition to direct responsibilities, African governments can and should do a great deal more to stimulate private-sector activity generally as well as in the provision of some services. For example, in the provision of tertiary education, some public/private partnership that protects the poor from discrimination, solely on the basis of their lack of ability to pay, can be successfully put in place. Also, with respect to health care, there is no need to put every doctor and nurse on the government payroll. Allowing for protection of the poor, African governments can promote the open functioning of private health clinics which are privately financed and thereby also increase the number of health care professionals willing to relocate to such countries.

African governments must also take a much more active role in decentralizing and deregulating national economic activities to promote greater diversity, competition, and legitimate income-earning opportunities. Of particular significance here to the poor is the need for a sound legal foundation for the subterranean sector to coexist with the formal sector, as discussed in chapter 4. The subterranean sector in sub-Saharan Africa employs some 60 percent of the urban work force and many of these workers are poor (Hope 1993a). Undoubtedly, removing the barriers and disincentives to the functioning of the subterranean sector, such as marketing boards, would encourage, for example, small-holder farming activity, which in turn would improve agricultural production and the food security situation (Ayittey 1989).

In addition to providing a sound legal foundation for the subterranean sector to continue to flourish, African governments must also provide a more enabling environment for the receipt and implementation of development assistance programs for the benefit of the poor. This is particularly of relevance with respect to the role of international NGOs. These NGOs are more and more becoming the conduit through which development assistance is channeled to the developing countries. About two-thirds of their funds come from private contributions and the other one-third from governments. Donor country governments believe that NGOs do a better job of reaching the poor in developing countries and this is certainly borne out by the evidence of development results.

NGOs have been players on the development stage for several decades. They emerged in Africa in response to the region's ongoing development crisis. The activities of NGOs have now expanded into several diverse areas, including the promotion of democratic and human rights, gender justice, and good governance. The emergence and growth of the NGO sector springs essentially from the recognition by citizens, external institutions, and even governments that there is a lack of confidence in the capability of the state to efficiently respond to human needs and catastrophic events. With their small scale, flexibility, and capacity to engage grassroots energies, NGOs are ideally suited to fill the resulting gap (Salamon 1994; Avina 1993).

The emphasis of NGOs is on results at the grassroots level. They tend not to have large bureaucracies, they are more efficient in their use of resources, and they are able to respond rapidly to problems and emergencies in developing countries. They also act as pressure groups lobbying for change and policy reform, as witnessed, for example, by their ability to get the European Community (EC) to increase its food aid to Africa from 1.5 million tons in 1990 to 2.1 million tons in

1991. Moreover, with their concentration on the poor they are most effective in their assistance to rural residents, which is done in a most cost-effective and participatory manner. In Zimbabwe, for example, the Organization of Rural Associations for Progress (ORAP), a local NGO, employed sixty people directly in 1990 and provided funds for technical assistance to rural families to generate income in agriculture. More recently, ORAP has been engaged in education, sanitation, and extension services as well as food security and drought relief (UNDP 1993).

Given such a track record, African governments need to work much more cooperatively with these NGOs and in partnership where justified. One area where such a partnership is most warranted is in improving the access of the rural poor to water and sanitation services based on the use of technology appropriate to individual circumstances and available resources. In some instances, they may even require the imposition of user fees. However, it has been shown that the poor are usually willing to pay for services that are proven to be reliable and better than the status quo (Roth 1987; Briscoe 1992). Consequently, African governments should not be unwilling to accept the imposition of user fees where necessary. As a matter of fact, such services requiring user fees tend to function much better as private sector entities with a role for governments to protect the public through monopoly oversight. Moreover, if properly targeted, such user fees can generate substantial revenue with little or no adverse effect on the poor (Pinstrup-Andersen 1993).

Conclusions

To reduce or alleviate poverty in African countries requires a commitment by their governments to implement a policy framework that recognizes both the role and the limitations of the state in socioeconomic affairs as well as the positive role the private sector can play in stimulating activities that benefit the poor.

The reform framework is clear. To improve the future access of the poor to basic goods and services, African governments must invest directly in human capital and provide an enabling environment for the private sector, including the subterranean economy and NGOs, to function effectively. Apart from investment in human capital, the poor would benefit most from economic activities that allow them to work their way out of poverty. In this regard, the development role of the subterranean sector cannot be overemphasized. It is, after all, absorbing the bulk of labor market entrants, particularly the poor, in Africa.

The policy framework advocated in this chapter builds on current thinking on development policy and calls for African governments to intervene less in certain areas and to take the lead in others. Governments have very important roles to play in national affairs, including empowering the poor. Without government collaboration, the lot of the poor cannot be significantly improved (Friedmann 1992). Consequently, African governments will not become irrelevant to the development process. They must, however, decentralize and privatize some of what they now do consistent with present socioeconomic realities.

Finally, official development assistance needs to be restructured to focus more on the social priority areas. To some extent, this is already being done at the bilateral level, especially with increasing contributions by donor governments to international NGOs. However, the allocation of overall development assistance needs to be guided more by its potential to reach ever larger numbers of the poor rather than the privileged in African countries.

Notes

1. By 1977, ten years after the introduction of *Ujamaa* socialism in Tanzania, the whole country had become poor under what was a policy of repression without growth. See Baregu (1994).

2. Other examples of countries that have introduced such social impact programs include Cameroon (Social Dimensions of Adjustment Project—SDAP), Guinea (Socioeconomic Development Support Project—SEDSP), Madagascar (Economic Management and Social Action Project—EMSAP), and Uganda (Program for the Alleviation of Poverty and the Social Costs of Adjustment—PAPSCA).

3. The ten countries are the Central African Republic, Congo, Côte d'Ivoire, Mali, Niger, Senegal, Togo, Burkina Faso, Malawi, and Tanzania.

8

Structural Adjustment Programmes as Policy Reform: An Assessment of Their Objectives and Impact in the SADC Countries

The deepening of the development crisis in Southern Africa, which began in the 1970s and intensified in the 1980s, as discussed in chapter 1, presented a difficult challenge to the political leadership, policy advisers, and the development community. It required policy measures to reverse the declining trends and place those economies on a path of sustainable growth and development. There was a need to, among other things, arrest the deepening of poverty, reduce the socioeconomic inequalities, lighten the external debt burden, reverse the brain drain, create new employment opportunities, improve the efficiency of the physical infrastructure, narrow down the fiscal deficits, and improve the balance of payments. To avert famine and malnutrition, there was also a critical need to increase productivity. In the early 1980s, the policy response to this crisis emerged in the form of structural adjustment programmes (SAPs). SAPs were formulated by and with the support of the International Monetary Fund (IMF) and the World Bank. However, their efficacy has been the subject of considerable debate. This chapter reviews the nature and objectives of SAPs and analyzes their impact on the economies of the member countries of the Southern African Development Community (SADC).[1]

The Nature and Objectives of Structural Adjustment Programmes

There is no universally accepted definition of SAPs. SAPs are a combination of two types of policy responses—stabilization policies which are the domain of the IMF, and structural adjustment policies which are the province of the World Bank. Stabilization policies aim at returning an economy to an equilibrium path that was followed prior to a shock. They tend to be short-term in perspective and they rely more on demand management (Demery 1994). Structural adjustment policies are designed to address the long-term growth issues through better supply responses to market liberalization and efficient macroeconomic management. In their institutional form, SAPs are comprised of three major components (Demery 1994). These are: (1) the importance of macroeconomic stability; (2) the need for prices to reflect relative scarcities; and (3) a reduction in the role of the state in economic affairs.

Generally, as a precondition for a country to enter into a structural adjustment programme, agreement must be reached on a set of stabilization measures with the IMF. Similarly, bilateral donors and commercial banks insist on the borrowing country reaching an agreement with the IMF and the World Bank as a precondition for rendering economic support. The primary objectives of SAPs are: (1) the restoration of long-term growth; (2) improvement of the balance-of-payments position; (3) a reduction of domestic financial imbalances, including government fiscal deficits; (4) the promotion of trade liberalization; (5) increased domestic savings in the private and public sectors; (6) the elimination of price distortions in various sectors of the economy; and (7) the mobilization of additional external resources (Tarp 1993).

However, in recent years, there has been a shift in emphasis, with higher development objectives assuming equal importance as growth-oriented adjustment. For example, it is now common to conceptualize and formulate adjustment "with a human face" or to evaluate the social dimensions of adjustment. Moreover, the objectives of structural adjustment now include reducing its impact on the poor and other vulnerable groups; avoiding sharp declines in personal consumption; and providing for the delivery of basic social services, which, if neglected, could result in the decay in the fabric of society. More recently, concern has gone beyond the social cost of structural adjustment to consideration of its environmental impact also (World Bank 1994b).

To achieve the objectives of SAPs, the primary policy instruments employed are: (a) exchange rate adjustment, primarily devaluation; (b) control of the money supply and credit ceilings; (c) interest-rate policy, allowing interest rates to respond freely to market forces; (d) debt rescheduling; (e) fiscal policy, including measures to reduce public expenditure and mobilize resources; (f) deregulation of prices of goods, services, and factor inputs; (g) liberalization of trade and payments arrangements; and (h) the reform of institutions with an emphasis on building capacity for policy analysis, implementing public investments, and privatization of public assets (Balassa 1989; Tarp 1993). These instruments are interdependent, and in some cases they are mutually reinforcing.

Usually, these instruments are combined in complex packages, which define the criteria or, in the parlance of the IMF and the World Bank, the conditionalities against which the country's economic performance would be evaluated. It is through these conditionalities that successes or failures of SAPs are judged. For the IMF programmes, conditionalities are a norm for a country intending to borrow more than 25 percent of its IMF quota. However, for the World Bank the imposition of conditionality is a recent phenomenon. Nonetheless, increasingly, there is a tendency toward convergence in approaches between the IMF and the World Bank, and the separate identity of these two institutions seems to be disappearing (Mosley, Subasat, and Weeks 1995). Recently, the IMF stated that "the objective of the IMF policy advice to member countries is to contribute to the promotion and maintenance of high levels of employment and real incomes and to the development of their productive resources" (IMF 1995b). In addition, the IMF now recognizes that its role in alleviating poverty "is to provide support for adjustment programmes that make economic growth sustainable and to mitigate the adverse effects that essential adjustment measures may have on the poor in the short-run" (Bernstein and Boughton 1993). However, in the past, it was primarily the sister organization of the IMF—the World Bank—that was concerned with poverty and development issues.

In the SADC countries, the need for adjustment is no longer a matter of debate. Many policy makers in the SADC countries, as well as in other parts of Africa, have openly recognized the mistakes they made in the past and they are now attempting to address the problems that arose out of those past policies. However, some controversy exists with respect to the distributional aspects of adjustment; that is, the extent of some of the hardships experienced under adjustment and the pace of recovery in economic growth. Initially, it was thought that the period of adjustment would be about five years from the start of implementation of the programmes but it is now widely recognized that adjustment requires a long-term perspective (World Bank 1989b; World Bank 1994b). This is true principally because the supply-side responses have been somewhat weak and have tended to take much longer periods to emerge.

Another controversy relates to the relative balance in the role of market forces and that of the government in the economy. In its advocacy of market-friendly policies, the World Bank states that

> Sustained growth requires more than a high rate of investment. It requires unleashing the market forces so that competition can improve allocation of economic resources. It also requires getting price signals right and creating a climate that allows businesses to respond to those signals in ways that increase returns to investments. . . . But trade, agricultural, and other regulatory reforms . . . are essential complements to reducing the government interventions that distort prices and tie up markets. (World Bank 1994b)

The premise of the World Bank approach is that government allocation of resources is inefficient, while the markets are essentially efficient. However, market failures could have similar adverse impacts on economies as do government failures. Arguably, to create a dynamic set of competitive industries in economies with traditions of weak industrial entrepreneurship and low levels of technological capabilities, selective government interventions may be appropriate (Lall 1995). Moreover, reducing public-sector investment expenditure could have an adverse impact on growth prospects (Mosley, Subasat, and Weeks 1995).

The term "structural adjustment" came into popular use in the early 1980s. It is associated with the policy-based lending of the IMF and the World Bank which were designed to reverse economic decline and stimulate growth. While the IMF and the World Bank sought to demonstrate that countries that had implemented SAPs achieved faster economic growth (Balassa 1989; World Bank 1989b; World Bank 1994b), some critics provided evidence that questioned the effectiveness of SAPs in terms of generating growth (Mosley and Weeks 1993; Mosley, Subasat, and Weeks 1995). The controversy on the impact of SAPs is largely attributable to the fact that results achieved to date seemed to have remained below the expectations of dramatic increases in economic performance. However, it must be borne in mind that it is now recognized that structural adjustment policies seek to stimulate productive capacity and to achieve sustainable economic growth over a longer term than had been originally conceived (Killick 1995).

The Impact of Structural Adjustment Programmes

As a reflection of the diversity and nature of the economies in the SADC group of countries, the experiences with and the impact of SAPs have been somewhat dissimilar. Some countries have experienced stable macroeconomic environments, while others have suffered severe shocks. Some countries have sustained policy reforms for some time, while others have experienced reversals in policy. In this section, the focus of the analysis is on two categories of countries: (1) a country that has implemented SAPs under civil war conditions—Mozambique; and (2) those countries that have implemented comprehensive SAPs in nonwar or relatively peaceful conditions—Lesotho, Malawi, Tanzania, Zambia, and Zimbabwe. Angola, Botswana, Mauritius, Namibia, South Africa, and Swaziland are excluded from the analysis since they have not had SAPs with the IMF/World Bank.

Adjustment Under War Conditions

Mozambique started implementing SAPs under the siege of a devastating civil war. That fact differentiates the Mozambican experience from that of the rest of the SADC countries that had adjustment programmes with the IMF and World Bank. In 1987, Mozambique abandoned its central planning system and began to implement SAPs while the civil war still intensified. That war made much of the countryside an exceedingly risky area for agricultural production and it also resulted in the massive destruction of much of the country's physical and social infrastructure. Moreover, the sudden change from the central planning system to a market-oriented economic system required radical institutional reforms. To rebuild the economy, priority was given to reviving the productive sectors of the economy, primarily agriculture; correcting macroeconomic imbalances, particularly reducing inflation; and strengthening the role of the private sector in the economy. That SAPs could have positive impacts on an economy under such difficult circumstances is remarkable. However, by all measures, the Mozambican economy is in much better shape today than during the era of central planning (de Abreu and Baltazar 1994).

In response to the policy changes, economic performance in Mozambique improved significantly during 1987–89. Over this period, GDP grew at an average annual rate of 10 percent, in sharp contrast to the declining economic activity in all sectors of the economy in the previous five years (Kyle 1994). However, after this initial momentum, the economy contracted during 1990–92. In 1993, there was a robust recovery in the economy with a growth rate recorded at 19 percent and an increase in the share of gross domestic investment in GDP from 26 percent in 1987 to 42 percent in 1993 (World Bank 1995a). In addition, price distortions were corrected and the rate of inflation declined from 91 percent in 1987 to 45 percent in 1992 (IMF 1994a). However, because of the civil war, heavy government military expenditures contributed to large fiscal deficits, averaging around 25 percent of GDP during the adjustment period.

The liberalization of the Mozambican economy has been the most important element in the success of its SAPs. Not only has the volume of exports increased but, in parallel, the composition of exports has diversified as the proportion of new products in total exports increased. Merchandise exports grew at an average annual rate of 9 percent during 1986–1993, compared to a steep decline of 25 percent during 1980–85. Through a series of devaluations, to establish more realistic exchange rates, the ratio of the parallel market rate to the official exchange rate fell sharply from forty-two in 1986 to one in 1992, thus leading to the virtual elimination of the parallel market premium.

Marking an ideological departure from the central planning system, the state also reduced its intervention in the economy. For example, its monopoly on foreign trade was eliminated. The agricultural pricing and marketing systems were liberalized, resulting in a substantial increase in production. Also, to allow for more private-sector participation in the economy, more than two hundred small-scale public enterprises were privatized (de Abreu and Baltazar 1994).

The Mozambican experience with SAPs clearly demonstrates that, even under exceedingly adverse conditions, appropriate policy reforms could have favorable impacts on the macroeconomy (Kyle 1994). Now that the civil war has ended, the challenge currently facing Mozambique is that of maintaining and capitalizing on the gains made to date for sustainable growth and development in the future.

Comprehensive Adjustment Programs

Lesotho, Malawi, Tanzania, and Zambia implemented comprehensive SAPs from the mid-1980s, while Zimbabwe started its SAPs in 1991. As seen in Table 8.1, by 1991 there was some improvement in economic performance, with all of the countries except Zambia recording positive GDP growth rates. In 1992, the Southern African region experienced considerable drought which, combined with the world recession, resulted in marginal or negative growth rates in some of the countries. Malawi and Zimbabwe recorded the steepest declines of around 8 percent, while Zambia's decrease in economic performance was moderate at approximately 3 percent. In 1993, there was a marked improvement in performance, with Lesotho, Malawi, and Zambia all achieving growth rates of more than 6 percent while for Zimbabwe it was 2 percent.

Large fiscal deficits indicate the extent of government failures to achieve fiscal balance. In all five of the countries there have been progressive improvements in their fiscal situation compared to the pre-adjustment period. Between the mid-1980s and 1993, Lesotho, Tanzania, and Zambia showed major improvements in their fiscal performance. Lesotho's fiscal deficit declined from 30 percent of GDP in 1987 to an almost balanced budget by 1993. Equally remarkable, Zambia's fiscal deficits as a percentage of GDP fell from 23 percent in 1986 to 1.2 percent in 1993, while in Malawi and Zimbabwe fiscal performance during the adjustment period has been less spectacular.

The impact of SAPs on fiscal deficits is determined through a set of conditions, including the reduction of government spending. It has also been increasingly recognized that unless the role of government is limited to those activities where market failures predominate, growth of the private sector could be crowded out and stifled. In almost all of the five countries, the share of government expenditure in GDP has continued to decline. Zambia has had the most dramatic decline from 46 percent of GDP in 1986 to 18 percent of GDP in 1993. Similarly, in Malawi, during the adjustment period, government expenditure as a share of GDP declined from 33 percent in 1987 to 25 percent in 1993. Public-sector wage bills account for a large proportion of total government expenditures. Typically, in these adjusting countries, the public-sector wage bill accounts for more than 20 percent of total government spending.

Apart from reductions in government expenditures, maintaining a healthy fiscal balance also necessitates measures to increase revenues. Unfortunately, for some of these countries (Malawi, Zambia, and Zimbabwe) government revenues declined during the adjustment period, and this in turn increased their dependence on external financing.

Table 8.1

Selected Performance Indices, 1980–93

Item	Pre-SAPs period			Sustained SAPs period			
Lesotho	1980	1985	1987	1988	1991	1992	1993
GDP Growth	3.0	3.6	5.7	13.9	2.0	2.8	6.2
Invest/GDP	42.4	49.4	45.4	49.3	69.9	69.6	75.7
Deficit[a]	N/A	−5.8	−29.6	−27.1	−8.8	−3.0	−0.5
Inflation	N/A	N/A	N/A	11.5	31.1	16.9	13.8
Malawi[b]	1980	1984	1986	1987	1991	1992	1993
GDP Growth	0.5	5.6	−0.6	1.7	6.4	−8.0	8.8
Invest/GDP	24.7	12.9	12.3	15.4	20.0	18.8	12.9
Deficit[a]	−20.3	−7.6	−12.3	−11.8	−5.6	−13.0	−8.4
Inflation	N/A	20.0	25.2	33.9	12.6	22.7	N/A
Tanzania	1980	1984	1986	1987	1991	1992	1993
GDP Growth	2.7	4.7	5.5	4.8	1.6	3.7	N/A
Invest/GDP	23.0	15.3	19.5	30.4	38.5	41.9	N/A
Deficit[a]	−11.4	−7.9	−6.9	−7.1	−2.7	−2.6	N/A
Inflation	30.3	36.1	32.4	30.0	22.3	22.1	23.5
Zambia	1980	1984	1986	1989	1991	1992	1993
GDP Growth	3.0	−0.8	0.0	−0.9	−0.6	−2.7	6.8
Invest/GDP	23.3	14.7	23.8	10.8	14.7	14.1	10.7
Deficit[a]	−19.4	−8.9	−23.0	−7.4	−5.6	−2.3	−1.2
Inflation	9.7	20.0	51.8	127.9	92.6	197.4	189.0
Zimbabwe	1980	1985	1990		1991	1992	1993
GDP Growth	10.8	6.5	1.9		4.9	−7.9	2.0
Invest/GDP	18.8	19.8	20.4		25.0	24.3	22.5
Deficit[a]	−10.9	−9.4	−7.7		−7.5	−8.2	−6.4
Inflation	5.4	8.5	17.4		23.3	42.1	27.6

Sources: World Bank, *African Development Indicators 1994–95* (Washington, DC: World Bank, 1995), pp. 25, 33, 46, and 187; IMF, *International Financial Statistics Yearbook 1994* (Washington, DC: IMF, 1994), pp. 106 and 107.
Notes:
[a]Government deficit/surplus (excluding grants) as percentage of GDP.
[b]Malawi had several IMF/World Bank structural adjustment facilities in the early 1980s until September 1986 when the extension of the IMF facility was terminated.

Only Lesotho and Tanzania have experienced modest increases in revenues during the adjustment period. All of the countries have weak and narrow tax bases. In addition, for Zambia, the decline in revenues has also been caused by the erosion in the real value of tax revenues associated with very high rates of inflation (World Bank 1994b).

Under SAPs, there have been serious attempts to reduce the rates of inflation. However, the degree of success has varied. In Zambia, for example, inflation accelerated from approximately 10 percent in 1980 to almost 200 percent by 1992, while in Lesotho and Tanzania there has been some modest success in reducing the rate of inflation during the same period. However, none of the countries have yet achieved single-digit rates of inflation, which are considered desirable for macroeconomic stability. Moreover, inflationary pressures due to seigniorage—average long-term monetary financing which is calculated as the nominal change in the money base divided by the consumer price index—have been a common phenomenon. In Zimbabwe, for example, to collect additional seigniorage of one percentage point of GDP, during 1965–89, required a 10 percent increase in inflation (Easterly and Schmidt-Hebbel 1994).

Increasing investment in the productive capacity of any country is considered central to long-term economic transformation and sustainable growth. During the adjustment period, there has been a sharp contrast among the countries in terms of investment performance. Lesotho had the highest share of gross domestic investment in GDP, which had risen from approximately 49 percent in 1988 to approximately 76 percent by 1993. This has been attributed to massive investments in the Lesotho Highland Water Project (Petersson 1993). Tanzania has also maintained high investment levels, averaging around 37 percent of GDP in the 1988–93 period. In contrast, the data on Malawi and Zambia indicate that there were continuous declines in investment rates. For Malawi, the proportion of gross domestic investment in GDP has declined from approximately 25 percent in 1980 to approximately 13 percent in 1993. Similarly, in Zambia it has fallen from 24 percent in 1987 to approximately 11 percent in 1993. This primarily reflects cuts in public-sector capital expenditure during the adjustment process. However, this declining trend in investment also suggests the need for the pursuit of complementary policies to stimulate private investment. Reversing these declining trends in investment is critical to sustained economic recovery.

The SADC countries have been adjusting under a difficult international economic environment. That environment has been characterized by deteriorating commodity terms of trade; a heavy burden of servicing of debts; and a recession in the industrial countries (Kirkpatrick and Weiss 1995). In Lesotho, Malawi, and Tanzania, for instance, the terms of trade started to deteriorate around the mid-1980s and continued through to the early 1990s. The international prices of the major crops, coffee and cotton, declined by 70 percent and 28 percent, respectively, between 1980 and 1990. One consequence of this state of affairs was that total debt service as percentage of exports rose from 25.3 percent in 1980 to 32.8 percent in 1993 for Zambia, and similarly, over the same period from 3.8 percent to 31.1 percent for Zimbabwe. Malawi and Tanzania have made modest improvements in their debt performance, but still their debt service burden has remained large, at around 20 percent in 1993.

Promoting growth and diversifying exports have been central to SAPs. All five countries experienced rapid growth in the value of their exports. For Malawi and Zambia, for instance, growth in exports almost doubled between 1987 and 1993 (IMF 1994b). Correspondingly, there has been an increase in the export of manufactures, predominantly from the light industries such as textiles and clothing. Furthermore, there has also been export diversification. For instance, in Malawi three major exports—sugar, tea, and tobacco—accounted for 81 percent of the total value of exports in 1987, and that increased to 88 percent in 1991. Since exports have a large impact on growth, all countries should strive to remove policies that impede their export competitiveness (Jones and Kiguel 1994).

There have also been major strides toward the liberalization of imports. In the pre-adjustment period, most of these countries had overvalued exchange rates and they rationed their foreign exchange through administrative measures. However, domestic currency depreciations, combined with appropriate macroeconomic policies, have now eliminated foreign exchange rationing and reduced the import-scarcity premiums which tended to be reflected in the prices in the parallel markets. For instance, Tanzania and Zambia experienced severe distortions in their foreign exchange markets. The ratio of the parallel market rate to that of the official exchange rate decreased from 4.9 in 1986 to 1.4 in 1992 in Tanzania, while in Zambia the ratio increased from 1.3 in 1986 to a peak of 7.8 in 1989 before the black market for foreign exchange was wiped out in 1991 (World Bank 1994b).

Further evidence of import liberalization has been the progressive elimination of nontariff barriers (NTBs). Barriers to imports were pervasive in the 1980s. To have access to foreign exchange, for example, required a valid import license. In some sense, licensing had become a mechanism for rationing foreign exchange. Import licenses were also used to protect inefficient domestic production from foreign competition.

Progress has also been made on reducing the number of goods requiring approval for import. In Malawi, Tanzania, Zambia, and Zimbabwe, before the implementation of SAPs, all imports were subjected to NTBs, including quantitative restrictions and special licensing requirements other than for health and safety reasons. In late 1992, Tanzania still had about one hundred import items subjected to NTBs, while Malawi and Zimbabwe had only a few items. In contrast, Zambia had made greater strides with no items facing NTBs by late 1992 (World Bank 1994b). In addition, the introduction of the open general license (OGL) scheme in all of these countries has contributed to import liberalization. Under the OGL scheme, goods are placed on the list automatically approved for imports and for allocation of foreign exchange. While this falls short of complete import liberalization, the OGL scheme has been an important transitionary mechanism.

Reforming trade policies has been a central feature of the World Bank's structural adjustment loans. All of the adjusting countries in southern Africa have embarked on trade liberalization. This has contributed to improved trade performance, measured in terms of export growth and diversification, particularly shifts toward manufacturing, as noted earlier. Increases in imports have been the immediate impact of trade liberalization. The proportion of imports in GDP has increased considerably during the adjustment period. Zimbabwe's imports as a share of GDP increased from 29 percent in 1990 to 40 percent in 1993. Over the same period, Malawi's import share rose modestly from 24 percent to 27 percent.

For macroeconomic policy reforms to succeed, they should be implemented with corresponding changes in the social and political institutions. Even if the reforms, purely in economic terms, may initially be sustainable, if economic liberalization is politically unacceptable, policy reversals would be inevitable. As Bates and Collier (1995) observe, for example, the government of Zambia in 1985 shifted to a policy of liberalization, and in 1987 it reimposed controls on the markets for commodities, credit, and foreign exchange. Consequently, the donors, following the lead from the IMF and World Bank, suspended their lines of credit. Two years later, the government reversed its position and shifted back to market-based economic policies. These oscillations in economic policy reflected the vacillations in the political arena. The role of politics as a major determinant of sustainability of economic policy reforms has also been demonstrated in Malawi (Killick 1995).

Unless there is political will, implementing public-sector reforms will continue to be intractable. And yet, improving public-sector management has been deemed essential for the success of policy reforms. For example, an effective civil service is central to ensuring that a sound macroeconomic framework can be implemented. However, in recent years considerable progress has been made toward the restructuring of the public sector. For instance, in Zimbabwe, between 1991 and 1993, more than 20,000 public-sector employees were retrenched (Mhone 1995). To a lesser extent, other countries, such as Malawi and Tanzania, have also reduced the size of their civil services.

In addition, reforms have also been directed at improving civil service pay and restructuring grade levels. In many of the countries, the erosion of average salaries was the major issue to be addressed by pay reform. This took the form of attempts to decompress the wage structure so as to be able to recruit and retain higher-level staff whose salaries had sunk to very low multiples of the lowest-ranked employees. In Mozambique, for example, the ratio of the highest-paid echelon to the lowest-paid widened from two to one in 1985 to nine to one by 1991 (World Bank 1994b; Robinson 1990). Likewise, Tanzania adopted a package of pay and employment reforms that decompressed public sector salary scales to a ratio of twelve to one by 1994 (Stevens 1994).

Besides the attempts at public-sector reform in the SADC countries, there has also been some progress in the reduction of state ownership of enterprises. These public enterprises are generally inefficient and are in various stages of dilapidation. Moreover, they absorb large amounts of funds that could be better spent on basic social services. In Tanzania, for example, central government subsidies to public enterprises equal 72 percent of central government spending on education and 150 percent of central government spending on health (World Bank 1995d). The data currently available indicate that Zambia, for instance, has privatized 86 of its 152 public enterprises (Phiri 1995). The government of Zambia has also created a Privatization Trust Fund which will facilitate the acquisition of minority stakes reserved for Zambian citizens (Bell 1995).

Perhaps the most controversial aspect of the debate on SAPs has been their impact on the poor. In the SADC countries, the majority of the poor live in the rural areas. As producers of agricultural commodities, they have benefited from policy reforms in agricultural marketing and also from foreign exchange and trade liberalization. Prices paid to the rural farmers have increased and the delivery of agricultural commodities has improved. However, rising food and other prices as well as declining opportunities for employment in the formal sector have tended to have an adverse impact on both the urban and rural poor (Mlambo 1995; Kayizzi-Mugerwa and Levin 1994). Consequently, some of the countries now have social impact programmes as a part of their SAPs. For example, in 1991, Zimbabwe initiated the Social Dimensions of Adjustment (SDA) programme to mitigate the social costs of adjustment.

Conclusions

This chapter has provided a comparative analytical review of the objectives and impact of structural adjustment programmes as the policy response to the development crisis in the SADC countries. It was determined that the impact of SAPs in the SADC countries has been somewhat mixed and that the full adjustment process was likely to take a good deal longer than had been initially expected.

Nonetheless, there are currently no credible alternatives to SAPs as the policy response to the development crisis in the SADC countries and the rest of Africa as well. As a matter of fact, much of the recent literature on structural adjustment, including that authored by the critics of SAPs, recognizes that adjustment is a necessary condition for an effective long-term attempt at economic recovery and development. Consequently, the issue is not whether adjustment is necessary but rather what the adjustment package should contain (Mosley, Subasat, and Weeks 1995; Mwanza 1992; Killick 1995; Ndegwa and Green 1994).

In that regard, much attention must be given to the problem of the counterfactual, over which there seems to be considerable conceptual confusion. The extreme form of this conceptual confusion is to conflate structural adjustment and the development crisis, which then leads to negative generalizations about the actual impact of SAPs on African economies (van de Walle 1994b). However, the impact assessment approach needs to be one of trying to determine what would have happened in the absence of SAPs. For example, do SAPs result in a worse poverty situation than would have occurred without them? Killick (1995) argues that the critics of SAPs have exaggerated the adverse impact of adjustment on the poor since "adjustment measures are not, for the most part, addressed to variables which are the prime causes of poverty in many developing countries." As a matter of fact, "African governments were never particularly effective in 'reaching the poor' with social services or poverty alleviation policies before the era of structural adjustment" (van de Walle 1994b). Moreover, many SAPs now contain social impact provisions.

Whatever the limitations of SAPs, as implemented in the SADC countries, they contain many of the elements that comprise the list of the necessary conditions for dealing with the development crisis. Consequently, to blame SAPs solely for the continuing development crisis in those countries, or in Africa in general, may be politically appealing in the short run but it would not be credible or helpful in the pursuit of economic recovery in those countries (Ndegwa and Green 1994). Moreover, some of the empirical research now forthcoming on SAPs indicates that intense adjusting countries have a superior growth performance in economic welfare to that of nonadjusting and other-adjusting countries (Kakwani 1995).

Basically, what is required in the SADC countries, and the rest of Africa as well, is not an abandonment of SAPs, since there currently exists nothing better as a replacement to mitigate the development crisis in those countries, but instead a structured approach at indigenous policy making to complement the SAPs. Such a structured approach would require national governments to engage in economic behavior that promotes self-reliance and reduces external dependence, particularly in the post-SAPs era, if the economic crisis is not to be a recurring or permanent one.

A policy of self-reliance remains the only means through which the poor, for example, would be able to improve their circumstances. The poor would benefit most from self-reliant activities that allow them to work their way out of poverty. All African governments must therefore develop and implement policy to empower the poor. Without government collaboration, the lot of the poor cannot be significantly improved (Hope 1996b; Friedmann 1992).

Self-reliance is taken here to mean autonomy of decision making and full mobilization of a society's own resources under its own initiative and direction. It also means rejection of the principle of exploitative appropriation of the resources of others (Hope 1984). A strategy of development emphasizing self-reliance also focuses on increasing cooperative relations in and among African nations and reducing their individual and collective dependence on the industrial countries (Ndegwa and Green 1994).

The operational framework of self-reliance focuses on four elements (Hope 1984). The first element pertains to basic human needs, which means attacking poverty directly and not through the trickle-down process. In other words, it means giving priority to the provision of food, shelter, housing, education, health care, and jobs, at the least. The second element relates to maximization of the use of local resources and values through the educational system as appropriate to the needs, resources, and values of the populace. It entails, therefore, the development of individuals as well as nations. Education should be used to meet the basic needs of individuals to receive a foundation of knowledge, attitudes, values, and skills on which to build a better life for the benefit of themselves and society.

The third element in the framework of self-reliance deals with participation of the poor in the development process (Hope 1983). Participation by intended beneficiaries is a fundamental ingredient for successful development performance. The final element here pertains to the issue of interdependence or collective self-reliance; that is, active economic and political cooperation among African nations for their individual as well as collective development. Such cooperation is aimed at generating or adapting the knowledge and resources needed for endogenous self-sustained development.

Perhaps the most important element of the operational aspect of this self-reliance framework is the need to improve the incomes of the poor through employment. In that regard, one often-overlooked solution is the promotion of growth in the subterranean (informal) sector as discussed in chapters 4 and 7. The subterranean sector currently contributes significantly to GDP and employment in Africa. It is the major source of employment for the urban poor and particularly so for women. All restrictions on this sector should therefore be eliminated so that it can flourish as a means of promoting growth and reducing unemployment and hunger in the region.

Note

1. The current membership of SADC is comprised of Angola, Botswana, Lesotho, Malawi, Mauritius, Mozambique, Namibia, South Africa, Swaziland, Tanzania, Zambia, and Zimbabwe.

9

Managing Development Policy in Botswana: Implementing Reforms for Rapid Change

Botswana has developed an international reputation as a nation that stands out among developing countries, and in Africa in particular, for its generally successful economic management, its adherence to democratic principles, and its development policy emphasis on the need to constantly improve the quality of professional public servants. The country has an apolitical public service which is headed by the permanent secretary to the president. However, there is a close relationship between the government and the public service in the management of development policy that is agreed on through a legitimate political process.

Both the government and public servants play pivotal roles in the management of development policy. This has resulted from the nature of the economy where sustained national development is heavily dependent on the efficient channeling of revenues, primarily from the mineral sector, through the public finance process into public programs and projects designed to support the private sector, to create employment, and to facilitate the expansion and diversification of the economy. Throughout the postindependence period this partnership between the government and the public service worked remarkably well and the country had justifiably acquired an international reputation as a stable democracy with sound and prudent development management and an efficient and accountable public bureaucracy.

However, in the past few years the economy has been in a downturn, with slower growth rates than previous years, as discussed in chapter 1. Moreover, the government has become increasingly concerned with the declining performance of the public service and its apparent drifting away, in some quarters, from the principles of honesty and integrity that had set it apart from the public services in other developing countries and especially those in most of Africa. This concern of the government has been translated into a series of reform measures designed to bring about rapid change and to recapture the postindependence spirit and record of successful and efficient development management.

This chapter discusses and analyzes those reform measures and their potential impact on the development management process in Botswana. However, it may be useful to first give a brief sketch of the current imperatives giving rise to the implementation of reform for rapid change.

The Reform Imperatives

One of the ironic results of Botswana's rapid economic progress is the inability of the public sector to recruit and retain highly skilled personnel. Although the public sector has increased in size, from approximately twenty-eight thousand employees in the 1970s to more than ninety-four thousand in the 1990s, there continues to be a shortage of highly trained and skilled public servants to conduct the development management affairs in the increasing sphere of influence of the public sector (Hope 1995b). Botswana's public sector comprises the central government, local governments, and parastatals. The public sector is the largest economic entity in Botswana in terms of number of employees; assets and expenditures under its management; population served; regional distribution of services provided; and breadth of services delivered (Republic of Botswana 1991a).

The shortage of high-caliber manpower for the management of development policy is the direct result of economic growth and diversification which have created ample alternative opportunities to attract many of the most qualified Botswana nationals away from the usual and traditional career paths in public service (Legwaila 1993). Consequently, economic progress in Botswana has resulted in, among other things, public-sector employment's losing its prestige and attractiveness to the economically active labor force.

This decline in the prestige of public-sector employment is not unique to Botswana. What is unique, however, is the factors that have given rise to it. In other developing countries, such as in Latin America, the Caribbean, and most of Africa, it is economic retardation rather than economic development that has contributed to the decline in the prestige of public-sector employment. That economic retardation created the need to develop alternative forms of employment either on a full-time basis or as supplementary to an individual's existing public-sector employment. Such alternative employment is usually found in the subterranean sector, which has now come to represent a vibrant, self-reliant, resilient, and expanding economic enclave that is directly responsible for the improvement in the standard of living of large numbers of people, as shown in chapter 4.

Combining with the lack of high-level manpower for development management in Botswana is the concern that the efficiency and productivity of some staff are falling below reasonable standards (Republic of Botswana 1991a). However, despite the fact that a presidential commission had used some crude indices of labor productivity in the public sector to declare that they found no evidence that productivity had improved in the public sector during the period 1980–1990, there is still no firm agreement on how productivity is to be measured, and there continues to be a lack of in-depth analyses on the subject (Hope 1995b).

In the private sector, productivity is usually expressed as a ratio of outputs over inputs. Final outputs (goods and/or services) are divided by resources used in production, such as labor, capital, and land. However, applying such productivity measures in the public sector has failed, due primarily to two unique characteristics of public-sector outputs. The first is that most public goods and services are generally nondivisible and therefore no discrimination is possible in their distribution. Consequently, it is difficult to accurately price police outputs as opposed to a bottle of milk, for example.

A second unique characteristic of public-sector outputs is that they are likely to be consumed the moment they are produced. Consumption and production occur almost simultaneously (Kelly 1988). Many public goods are delivered as services to the public and, as such, are created and consumed usually at the same time and, generally, with no tangible evidence that a transaction with economic value had taken place.

These measurement difficulties aside, there are a sufficient number of possible measures and indices for public-sector productivity to provide for effective analyses. In the case of Botswana, one approach would be to look at cost containment through the budgetary process and then relate public expenditure to public-sector employment to derive an index of public expenditure per public-sector employee.

One of the strategies Botswana has used to aid in its postindependence development management effort is that of contracting the services of expatriates. Many of these expatriates hold key positions in the public sector similar to the situation in the countries of the Gulf. Of the established permanent and pensionable positions in the central government, expatriates currently hold 6.2 percent of them while at the local governments and parastatals, expatriates hold 1.2 percent and 4.1 percent, respectively, of the total number of posts at those entities (Republic of Botswana 1991a; Hope 1995b).

After two decades of virtually ignoring the issue, some administrative and political elites have begun to be outspoken about the still too large number of expatriates holding senior positions in the public sector. Expatriates play a much greater role in the management of development policy in Botswana than they do in any other country in Africa. However, the government of Botswana regards the use of expatriates as necessary for implementing development policy and this has been borne out by the postindependence development results. It is the government's stated position that the replacement of expatriates in the Botswana public sector should be done over the long term so as to allow Botswana nationals to acquire the necessary skills and expertise to make meaningful contributions to development management when they assume positions previously held by expatriates. So, while increased participation by Botswana nationals in all aspects of the country's economic development is most desirable, there continues to be a role for expatriates.

The final issue giving rise to the need for reform for rapid change in the management of development policy in Botswana is that of corruption. Corruption takes place in transactions between public officials and private individuals and firms through the utilization of official positions for private gain, as discussed in chapter 6. It is the misuse of public office, funds, and/or trust and, over time, it seriously undermines the effectiveness of government and corrodes popular confidence in public institutions, thus making it harder to raise the standards of public service.

Some recent events have revealed that corruption and economic crime are becoming widespread in Botswana and have the potential to seriously undermine the country's development gains and tarnish its international image. Some of the more popular corruption cases that have been publicized include the loss/disappearance of approximately U.S.$13.5 million with respect to a contract awarded without tender to the International Project Managers (IPM) for the supply of schoolbooks and other teaching materials to the primary schools; alleged illegal land transactions in peri-urban villages; irregularities at the Botswana Housing Corporation which culminated in bribery and fraud involving the misappropriation of at least U.S.$25 million by numerous senior officials and foreign contractors; the near collapse of the National Development Bank and other government financial institutions due to questionable loans made to politicians and senior government officials; and the misuse of funds at construction projects of the Southern District Council.

In all of these publicized cases there were extensive government inquiries and investigations and some of the consequences included the resignations of two government ministers, one of which was the then-Vice President who was also minister of Local Government, Lands, and Housing. However, in August 1994, following three years of battle in the courts, the two former ministers were exonerated by the High Court, which found both the proceedings and the report of the Commission of Inquiry that implicated them to be null and void on the grounds that the commission, in holding hearings in secret, contravened the provisions of the Commissions of Inquiry Act.

More recently, the auditor general announced that he had uncovered several cases of misappropriation, embezzlement, and fraud at various ministries, parastatals, and the Botswana Defence and Police Forces, involving millions of pula (Botswana currency) (Republic of Botswana 1994a). Several of the public servants involved in those cases have since been formally charged, convicted, and/or dismissed from their posts.

The revelations on these corruption cases were, nonetheless, very surprising since Botswana, unlike most of the rest of Africa, was generally regarded to be free of any but the most petty of corrupt activities. Corruption in Botswana was not regarded, and still is not, as part of the bureaucratic routine and administrative culture as found in most other African nations. However, the government of Botswana now regards corruption as a serious reality "especially involving the public service and other public institutions" (Republic of Botswana 1994b). Consequently, it has decided to take it seriously.

Reform Implementation for Rapid Change

The slippage in the performance of development management has influenced the government of Botswana to move toward the implementation of reform measures that are aimed at rapid change for improving the management of development policy. It is a clearly constructed vision of reform linking development management performance to overall economic development and progress. Its primary elements are discussed in this section.

Organization and Methods Review

The organization and methods review (O&M) is a comprehensive undertaking that has been designed to improve the institutional capacity of the development management machinery for successfully implementing development policy. The O&M review has been embarked upon through both internal mechanisms and the use of external consultants provided through donor agencies. The O&M review covers all ministries and departments at all levels of their operations. Similar exercises are also being undertaken at some parastatals and at the local governments.

There are two stages to the O&M review. The first stage covers a review of ministerial organization (objectives, functions, and structures) while the second stage deals with the study and improvement of work systems and methods at all levels of the public service (Hope 1995b). The O&M review is expected to result in, among other things, a stable, adequate, and effective public service that will serve the government of the day; and which will have unequaled ethical standards, high integrity, morale, and competence to effectively discharge all responsibilities at all levels of its operations (Republic of Botswana 1993c).

The O&M review is intended to strengthen the institutional capacity of the public sector to implement development policy and meet national objectives by improving some organizational arrangements, accountability, operational work procedures, and the adequacy of human resources and management.

Training

The training of development managers has become a major undertaking of the government of Botswana in recent years. Considerable emphasis is being placed on improving the skills and competence of public servants in their role as managers of development policy. The basic objective is to improve motivation, performance, and productivity in the interests of the nation.

Botswana, through its political leadership, is one of the few developing countries with a group of truly indigenous institutions capable of dealing with the demands of modern development management training. The country has formally recognized and adopted training policies that integrate public service training with broader human resource development policies such as promotion. The government of Botswana also considers it a reform imperative that more qualified and capable personnel are trained and provided with the necessary skills to move into posts currently held by expatriates (Republic of Botswana 1991a).

Training plans are developed on an annual basis by the Directorate of Public Service Management (DPSM) as well as the Unified Local Government Service (ULGS) and the parastatals. The plans, as well as the practice of training, emphasize both the particular and the general and embrace the development of attitudes as well as the acquisition of knowledge together with skills. For effectiveness, the entire administrative system has been conditioned to regard training as an integral part of the entire process for improving development management. This task has been made easy by Botswana's tradition of excellence in development management.

In concert with the emphasis placed on training, the government of Botswana, with the assistance of some donor agencies, has also been strengthening training institutions to maintain their required capacity to produce appropriately skilled development administrators and to phase out the need for any but the most essential overseas training. In that regard, the four primary training institutions—the Botswana Institute of Administration and Commerce (BIAC), the Institute of Development Management (IDM), the University of Botswana (UB), and the Botswana National Productivity Center (BNPC)—constantly restructure their programs to conform to development objectives and national policies. For example, IDM and UB, respectively, recently introduced a certificate program in local government administration and a Masters in Public Administration (MPA) program.

In addition, the government of Botswana has mandated that there be improved coordination between departments and that the National Industrial Training and Technical Education Council (NITTEC) be used to address appropriate training requirements (Republic of Botswana 1991a). All of these measures are intended to result in a rapid change to enhance the machinery of development management. At the same time, a long-term perspective is being applied to ensure that training needs and the training programs to meet those needs are compatible.

The approach of Botswana to training for effective development management makes a sharp distinction between the mere availability of training programs and their effectiveness in promoting development objectives. Unlike those in some other developing countries, Botswana's formal training programs are not geared directly, or indirectly, to system maintenance but rather are oriented toward change; as such, training programs are developed to meet carefully defined national training requirements. There is no observed tendency to duplicate training programs from abroad. Training is undertaken in an environment of policies, procedures, standards, and national objectives and has an intimate relationship to other strategies for economic development and progress.

Training for rapid change in the management of development policy is a firmly entrenched idea in Botswana that is greatly facilitated by political commitment. Political commitment usually demonstrates an overriding desire to promote rationality, rise of productivity, and improvement of institutions and attitudes, among other things (Hope 1996b). The high priority given to development management training by the government of Botswana is amply demonstrated in its development plans and policies and in its allocation of adequate resources for such purposes. The ultimate aim is to be self-sufficient in human resource development for the country and to eliminate dependence on donor generosity for overseas training.

The Promotion of Productivity

The government of Botswana has identified the improvement of productivity in the public sector as a critical need and is now engaged in a campaign to enhance productivity nationally. To that end, it has, so far, embarked on two related strategies to address the problem more directly.

The first is the establishment of the Botswana National Productivity Center (BNPC) which was created as a parastatal body in 1993. The mission of the BNPC is to work with both the public and private sectors in promoting productivity as a long-term strategy for the creation of employment opportunities, international competitiveness, and improvements in living standards. "This is given effect through the national productivity movement which is an on-going process that fosters productivity consciousness and, thereby, the will of everyone to be productive" (BNPC 1994).

The BNPC has a very impressive and ambitious set of objectives, which include stimulating and generating productivity consciousness in Botswana; promoting increased productivity in all sectors of the economy; improving standards of management; fostering good labor-management relations; promoting the concept of employer responsibility toward the welfare of employees; introducing suitable management practices and techniques; assisting organizations in identifying areas where there is a deficiency in skills, or where performance can be improved, and thereafter advising on how to deal with these; and facilitating equitable sharing of productivity gains among management, employees, and the client public.

The BNPC is attempting to accomplish its objectives through a number of functions which include developing and organizing productivity improvement and management programs, conferences, workshops, and seminars for personnel from all sectors of the economy; providing advisory and consultancy services for all sectors of the economy with the intent of increasing the levels of productivity and efficiency; undertaking productivity measurement exercises for the purpose of establishing and developing national performance standards; conducting studies, inquiries, and research in the fields of management development and productivity; serving as a base for collecting and disseminating information on productivity improvement and related techniques along with the publication of information in relation thereto; taking steps to promote good industrial relations through the formation of joint consultative councils; encouraging and assisting industrial establishments and trade unions to formulate and rationalize wage policies and wage systems; undertaking manpower and wage studies; and the training of employees and their representatives in measures designed to improve labor productivity.

The second direct and related strategy is the creation of Work Improvement Teams (WITS) in the public service. WITS were approved in 1993 by the permanent secretary to the president in his capacity as the head of the civil service and chairman of the Productivity Improvement Committee for the Civil Service (PIC-FORCE). All public officers are required to be members of WITS and their WITS should complete two projects in a year. The primary objective of the overall strategy is to increase productivity in the public service by striving for an emphasis on people who have the power to act and to use their judgment; participative leadership and teamwork rather than authoritarian and coercive leadership; an innovative work style that seeks to solve problems creatively; a strong client orientation rather than an orientation toward serving a bureaucracy; and a mind-set that seeks optimum performance and which drives employees to seek improvement in the performance of their ministries/departments/parastatals (Republic of Botswana 1993d).

WITS are defined as groups of public servants from the same work unit, irrespective of divisional status, who meet regularly to identify, examine, analyze and solve problems pertaining to work in their department or work unit; identify and examine improvement opportunities and propose and implement improvement measures; help to adapt the work unit and, hence, the department to changing circumstances; discuss and conduct studies on how to improve their working environment, efficiency, effectiveness, quality of service, knowledge and skill, teamwork, work performance, use of resources, work goals, objectives and targets, systems, methods and procedures, and so on; develop problem-solving skills; and ensure job satisfaction (Republic of Botswana 1993d).

The objectives of WITS are to enhance team spirit and improve human relations; to develop a much more positive attitude toward work by employees; to create a free flow of communication between management and employees; to facilitate the provision of quality service; to develop problem-solving skills; and to ensure job satisfaction. The WITS concept was adapted from the Japanese framework of Quality Control Circles and its philosophy is based on the belief that employees want to contribute constructively and be part of a team; that employees have self-esteem and desire recognition and do not work for bread alone; that productivity and quality are a consequence of human resource development; that employees can learn and that learning is a continuous process; that management should portray an attitude that brings out positive habits of employees and that builds on intrinsic motivation; and that the needs of employees and the needs of an organization can be integrated.

The WITS program can be seen as an integrated development program. It is aimed at moving from staff inertia into action, from just doing to doing and thinking, and changing and improving. The intent is to instill system, service, group, and quality consciousness into public servants, so that in time all public servants will continually seek improvements in the service they render (Republic of Botswana 1993d).

The WITS hierarchical structure for improving productivity and the management of development policy in Botswana comprises a Productivity Improvement Committee for the Civil Service (PIC-FORCE) which, as already mentioned, is chaired by the permanent secretary to the president; the Ministerial Productivity Improvement Committee for the Civil Service (MINI PIC-FORCE), which is chaired by the permanent secretary of the relevant ministry; Departmental Productivity Improvement Committees (DPCs) comprising top management of departments; facilitators, trained at BIAC or BNPC; leaders who are usually chosen from the supervisory ranks; and members who are public servants of any rank.

The PIC-FORCE is the managing committee for productivity improvement in the overall public service. Its terms of reference include identifying and changing or removing procedures and practices that impede teamwork, productivity, and quality of work in the public service; initiating, examining, and recommending or introducing measures that would promote teamwork, pride in work, morale, and productivity in the public service; discussing ways of measuring or assessing productivity, morale, and teamwork in the public service; formulating strategies for the implementation of WITS; set overall guidelines for WITS operations; and allocate resources for the training, development, and promotion of WITS in the public service (Republic of Botswana 1993d).

A MINI PIC-FORCE is located in each ministry. The mandate of the MINI PIC-FORCE is essentially the same as that of the PIC-FORCE except that it is limited to the level of the ministry. In addition, the MINI PIC-FORCE selects and appoints WITS facilitators and reports on WITS activities to the PIC-FORCE. Similarly, the terms of reference of the DPCs are basically the same as those of the MINI PIC-FORCE except that they are restricted to the departmental level. The DPCs also select and appoint departmental facilitators and they report on departmental WITS activities to the MINI PIC-FORCE.

Facilitators are responsible for facilitating WITS activities and monitoring and reporting on those activities to the MINI PIC-FORCE. Leaders, who are trained and coached by the facilitators, train and coach members in problem solving and group discussion. Leaders also schedule and conduct WITS meetings. Members are required to cooperate with and assist and support the team leader as well as their fellow members. In addition, members are expected to be prepared to accept change, to share and contribute ideas, to reduce any self-centered behavior, and to contribute to teamwork.

Fighting Corruption

In August 1994, the government of Botswana reacted to the potentially negative consequences of corruption by passing into law the Corruption and Economic Crime Bill. The government's attempt to curtail corruption before it becomes endemic, as in other African states, has therefore begun in earnest. The objective is to prevent corruption and economic crime from becoming a way of life in Botswana and to maintain an institutional framework through which corrupt practices can be effectively dealt with. In chapter 10, the government of Botswana's approach to controlling corruption is discussed as a model for other African countries to follow.

The Localization Effort

Localization refers to the replacement of expatriates by Botswana nationals in the public sector. The basic premise of the localization policy is to reduce reliance on expatriate manpower over time to enable Botswana nationals to assume greater responsibility in the management of the economy. Moreover, localization efforts are intended to maximize the employment of citizens as rapidly as possible and to maintain the competitiveness of the country vis-à-vis the marketplace by reducing production costs related to high-cost noncitizen employees.

However, the results of the localization effort have been somewhat uneven. Indeed, the government has been extremely pragmatic in its understanding that the localization effort will only be successful as more and more nationals of Botswana gain appropriate and relevant education and training consistent with current development management needs and future projected staffing requirements.

At independence, in 1966, the government of Botswana was heavily dependent upon European administrators (Picard 1987). At that time, only 3 percent of the senior posts in the public sector were held by nationals of Botswana. Since that time the localization effort has considerably reduced the proportion of expatriates in the public service. Nevertheless, the localization targets that were set in the development plans of the 1980s were not met and the data now suggest that the proportion of expatriate-held positions in the public service in the 1990s exceeds that of the 1980s. In 1987, for example, expatriates held 5 percent of the permanent and pensionable positions compared to 6.2 percent at the present time.

The localization efforts are subject to review by a presidential commission which submits a report containing recommendations for enhancing those efforts. Also, the current development plan has targeted localization for greater scrutiny through adherence to manpower ceilings; by identifying citizens capable of taking over expatriate positions (while retaining competition between candidates); by scrutinizing requests for renewal of expatriate contracts; and by greater use of expatriates for training counterparts (Republic of Botswana 1991a).

Localization is a necessary idea in terms of the need for Botswana nationals to control their own destiny, and for the encouragement of such nationals in opting for careers in the development management machinery without concern that their career paths may be blocked by the presence of expatriates in positions for which they, the nationals, are evaluated as qualified. Moreover, from a strictly national unity standpoint, the effort to localize is a noble one. There are, perhaps, too many expatriates in too many senior positions in the public sector. Consequently, the localization effort should be intensified.

Conclusions

This chapter has shown how the management of development in Botswana has faltered in recent years and the reform measures that have been embarked upon to effect rapid change and recapture the postindependence spirit and record of successful and efficient development management which had garnered international praise.

The government of Botswana has put comprehensive reforms on the national agenda, formulating carefully crafted policies both to reshape the development management machinery and to redraw the boundary between routine policy implementation and policy implementation that enhances economic development and progress rather than retarding it. Bolstered by the national mood for such reforms, their success is virtually guaranteed.

However, from this author's perspective, there is one area that may require some fine-tuning in the immediate future. That area is the promotion of productivity. There is still need for a much clearer focus on the measurement of productivity. Work improvement and productivity are inextricably linked. Hence, there must be an effort to ensure that productivity measurement techniques are incorporated within the WITS structure. Baselines should be established to allow productivity improvements to be monitored. The WITS must be seen to produce some measurable impact beyond an employee's job satisfaction and personal fulfillment, which may or may not affect organizational effectiveness, depending on the nature of the organization and its work environment. It would seem, therefore, that the WITS process should have also provided for a framework for productivity measurement.

The foregoing observation related to productivity notwithstanding, Botswana has again led the way in its approach and policy framework for dealing with deficiencies in its management of development policy. The country's swift reaction and purposeful response to these deficiencies have once again shown it to be a nation with good governance, which is taken here to be synonymous with sound development management; in other words, maintaining the necessary administrative capacity for economic development and progress. Unlike most of Africa, the government of Botswana continues to exhibit a clear capacity and ability to respond to the need for change when shown to be necessary. This augurs well for the future, as the anticipated downturn in economic activity would place considerable demands on the development management machinery to rapidly adapt strategies consistent with current economic realities.

10

Controlling Bureaucratic Corruption in Africa

As shown in chapter 6, bureaucratic corruption has negative consequences on the development process in Africa. It is also of particular concern because it can result in the plunder of public money in countries that are undergoing serious economic and other hardships. The losses caused by corruption significantly exceed the sum of individual profits derived from it, because graft distorts the whole economy (Andreski 1968). Consequently, anticorruption campaigns are necessary and must be sustained if bureaucratic corruption is to be brought under control in Africa.

However, bureaucratic corruption can only be eliminated when both public officials and the public make a concerted effort *not* to tolerate it further. But, due to the softness of African states, public officials are reluctant to uphold laws that would get in the way of their personal or sectional interests. The burden must therefore fall on the political leaders as the only individuals with the power to bring about a stronger allegiance to the nation-state and, hence, a commitment to the national interest rather than to personal or sectional interests. Of course, one recognizes that after several decades of entrenched bureaucratic corruption in the African states, it would be very difficult to totally eradicate it. However, its control is possible and, with that, a significant reduction of its negative effects. This chapter describes and analyzes the primary mechanisms that have been implemented in some African states for controlling bureaucratic corruption.

Mechanisms for Controlling Bureaucratic Corruption

The mechanisms for controlling bureaucratic corruption in African states generally fall into two broad categories. The first category comprises campaigns designed to satisfy a social demand for retribution by punishing wrongdoers to make them public examples for deterrent effect. The second category comprises reform strategies designed to enhance ethical behavior and improve public accountability.

The punishment of corrupt public officials in Africa tends to be much more pronounced and very severe in those countries that have experienced military takeovers of their governments. It is a common practice of the military, in the immediate period following such coups, to publicly demonstrate the excesses of the deposed government by arresting, detaining, jailing, and confiscating property of public officials. Moreover, once an unpopular regime or political leader is replaced, there are usually tremendous demands from the populace for the corrupt officials to be brought to trial or be fired (Harsch 1993).

In Sierra Leone, for example, following the ouster of the Momoh regime in April 1992, the new military government wasted no time in setting up three commissions of inquiry. Although each commission had its own mandate, they were collectively asked to:

1. examine the assets and other related matters of the senior members of the Momoh regime and the Stevens regime that preceded it;
2. inquire into and investigate said regime members to ascertain whether they maintained a standard of living above that which was commensurate with their past official emoluments, whether they were in control of pecuniary resources or property disproportionate to their past official emoluments, whether they engaged in corrupt acts in such a manner as to cause financial damage to the government or a local government or a parastatal, and whether they acquired, directly or indirectly, financial or material gain by fraud or improperly or illegally to the detriment of the central government, a local government, a parastatal, a statutory commission, or the University of Sierra Leone;
3. inquire into and investigate the financial activities of government ministries or departments, local authorities, parastatals, and the Bank of Sierra Leone, or commissions or councils established under the Constitution to ascertain malpractices and irregularities committed and the sums of money and identities of those individuals involved; and
4. inquire into and investigate, under the same terms of reference as for the senior members of the Momoh and Stevens regimes, all

public officers, members of the boards and employees of parastatals, members of the armed forces, and members of the police force (Kpundeh 1994).

Following receipt of the various reports from the commissions, the military governments wasted no time in releasing them as white papers and accepting the recommendations contained therein. This resulted in a number of ex-ministers and senior civil servants being made to pay reparations; the return of illegally acquired state property; and disqualification from public life, for those found guilty of financial impropriety, for periods ranging from fifteen years to life (Zack-Williams and Riley 1993). In addition, some public servants and police officers were fired for embezzlement and accepting bribes.

Moreover, the two former presidents—Momoh and Stevens—had a number of their properties and financial assets confiscated by the state. Those assets and properties formed a considerable list (*West Africa* 1993a; *West Africa* 1993b). They convincingly demonstrated how comprehensively the state coffers had been plundered by these two former presidents and they lent credence to the military regime's reasoning behind their overthrow of the government. Sierra Leone, nonetheless, faces a number of difficult challenges ahead, primary among which is the need to restore democracy following the national elections, and the restructuring of the economy. The military regime had won general praise for its efforts to eliminate corruption, and that campaign needs to continue following the return to civilian rule. Moreover, political instability tends to accompany any prolonged periods of military rule. That, in turn, tends to produce, as in the case of Nigeria, the need to resort to raw force to remain in power.

Although there are other examples, such as Gambia, Niger, Mali, and Ghana, of military-inspired antibureaucratic corruption campaigns designed to punish wrongdoers, the above discussion of the Sierra Leone experience is generally representative of the outcomes in those countries also, despite the differing modalities through which they get there. In Niger, for example, one interesting feature of the military government's anticorruption campaign, in the 1970s and 1980s, was its low-key nature. The military junta had decided to shy away from intensive and sharply focused crusades to concentrate more on delivering exhortations that not only preceded but complemented action (Amuwo 1986).

To that end, the Niger military junta used five instruments of persuasion.[1] These were: (1) the moralization crusade—speeches exhorting public officials to be more publicly accountable; (2) the use of symbols and slogans—speeches, placards, and noticeboards imploring public officers to be "vigilant, upright, honest, and just"; (3) economic, financial, and allied measures—management and other economic and financial reforms designed to stem fraud and embezzlement and protect the public treasury; (4) the use of the presidential security and intelligence network-gathering of intelligence on public officials to keep bureaucratic corruption at bay; and (5) the personality of the president—being secretive and enigmatic, the president was feared by public officials who expected to be severely dealt with if caught engaging in corrupt activities.

The second and final category of mechanisms for controlling bureaucratic corruption in African states comprises reform strategies to enhance ethical behavior and improve public accountability. These are strategies designed to influence behavior modification and resurrect public confidence in public institutions and officials. Obviously, most of these reform strategies have not been successful. Nonetheless, despite their general lack of success, implementing such strategies is much better than simply doing nothing and thereby allowing bureaucratic corruption to become even more entrenched. Frankly, doing nothing to control bureaucratic corruption signals its official acceptance and further suggests that attempts to control such corruption would, a priori, be a failure. However, the lessons from public administration history strongly suggest that reforms in less-than-perfect political and administrative systems are the first milestones in the timely evolution of an ethical and accountable bureaucracy (Rasheed 1995).

One of the most prevalent of the reform strategies to control bureaucratic corruption in Africa is the introduction of codes of conduct for public officials (both politicians and civil servants). These codes can, and do, take many forms. For example, they may be developed as codes of ethics, leadership codes, or codes of public accountability. Whatever form they may take, however, they are all usually designed to achieve the type of public officials who are vigilant, upright, honest, and just; in other words, to instill an atmosphere of moral accountability.

Moral accountability does not mean that public officials respect only their obligations to be honest, obey the laws, and behave within the confines of bureaucratic rules and regulations, but they must also demonstrate the highest standards of personal integrity, honesty, fairness, and justice (Dwivedi 1994). Unfortunately, in most African states, moral accountability is seriously missing. Even in those states with great moral leaders, such as President Nelson Mandela in South Africa, there are still cases of bureaucratic corruption and allegations of "gravy train" administration.

For the most part, codes of conduct for public officials in African states have either been ignored or not enforced. In some instances, they have also been undermined by the political leaders who instituted them. President Robert Mugabe's ruling ZANU party in Zimbabwe, for example, drew up a Leadership Code in 1984 to counteract bureaucratic corruption among the party faithful. However, President Mugabe himself subsequently referred to the Leadership Code as a "despicable piece of paper" (Harsch 1993).

In South Africa, President Nelson Mandela's African National Congress (ANC) party has been forced to react to the public perception that ANC members of parliament (MPs) were riding a gravy train after they assumed power in 1994. In a bold move to clamp down on venality in public office, the ANC had to beef up its code of conduct. The new code, which was released in May 1995, is intended to prevent corruption and money-grabbing by ANC elected officials. It includes prohibition from using government office or parliamentary posts to distribute patronage or obtain personal fortune; the prohibition of ministers, premiers, and provincial executive councillors from playing any active role in profit-making institutions and their surrender of all directorships held prior to taking office; the requirement that ANC members declare their assets and all other posts from which there is financial benefit in other companies, boards, or organizations—in particular consultancies, shareholdings, and directorships or any form of payment received by them or their family from an external source; and the stipulation that MPs should treat their parliamentary posts as full-time and bans them from taking permanent employment in other jobs (*Mail and Guardian* 1995). This is indeed a very tough code of conduct, which also has a high-powered disciplinary committee to implement it.

Other countries, such as the Congo, proposed a code of political ethics in 1991. In Mali, the constitution stipulates that government ministers are to list their assets publicly before taking office (Harsch 1993). However, codes of conduct, despite not being vigorously enforced in most of the African countries where they exist, still represent one formal means at the disposal of future governments, so inclined to enforce them, for controlling bureaucratic corruption.

African states have also attempted to control bureaucratic corruption by creating and/or restructuring, at one time or another, a number of institutional frameworks to coerce discipline and accountability in public officials. Among these institutions, for example, are the Office of the Ombudsman in Zimbabwe, the Public Complaints Commission in Nigeria, the Public Accounts Committee in Uganda, the Anti-Corruption Squad and the Permanent Commission of Inquiry in Tanzania, the Serious Fraud Office in Ghana, and the Directorate on Corruption and Economic Crime in Botswana.

The common purpose of these institutions is to induce fundamental changes in the attitudes and behavior of public officials, in order to promote honesty and integrity in public service, through their watchdog powers to disclose and/or investigate any suspected acts of corruption. However, the activities of these institutions have produced mixed results, which have been due primarily to their lack of sufficient autonomy; their lack of demonstrable support from the political leadership; their lack of good data-gathering and retrieval systems; their vulnerability to changes in political regimes; or their susceptibility to bureaucratization.

In a case study of the Public Complaints Commission (PCC) of Nigeria, for example, Ayeni (1987) found it had assumed a lethargic and conservative posture and had come to see its role as an essentially bureaucratic one. Consequently, the PCC, which had been partly created to check the extent and impact of modern bureaucratization on Nigerians, had itself fallen victim to the same problem with its huge and wasteful bureaucracy. Furthermore, even in some of the regional offices of the PCC, there has been such an increase in the size and complexity of structures and processes that top officers, like the commissioners, are not familiar with the operational details at the lower levels (Ayeni 1987).

On a wider scale, it has also been found that the office of the ombudsman in most African countries lacks both the capacity and the capability to maintain relevant databases to efficiently perform their tasks and uphold their mandates.[2] Most offices of the ombudsman in Africa employ a central filing system, for example, which is both cumbersome and difficult to understand by junior officers. In several instances, files have turned up missing, thus leading to considerable delays in the investigation and decisions on cases (Ayeni 1994).

Another reform strategy that has been attempted to control bureaucratic corruption in African states is what can be termed the "national awareness campaigns." These campaigns seek to publicize the negative effects of corruption, the penalties for engaging in corrupt acts, and the type of behavior that is required of public officials. A good example of this type of campaign can be drawn from Nigeria's War Against Indiscipline and Corruption (WAIC). The WAIC is a rhetoric-filled and symbol-laden campaign. It revolves around a decree that is intended to give legitimacy to efforts "to remove the cancer of indiscipline and corruption" (*The Botswana Gazette* 1995). Through WAIC brigades, activities are designed and implemented with the stated purpose of creating disciplined, patriotic, honest, and dedicated public servants.

The final reform mechanism for controlling bureaucratic corruption in Africa pertains to the civil service. Lest it be misunderstood, it should be pointed out here that civil service reform in Africa goes beyond the narrow focus of bureaucratic corruption. The civil service in most African countries is much larger than those countries require, much more costly than they can absorb, and significantly less effective and productive than they should be. In many of the countries, patrimonialism and expanding state activity have contributed to a civil service that contains many who are superfluous and none who are paid well; and the ministries and agencies in which they work tend to be ill-equipped and poorly structured.

However, this chapter is concerned with bureaucratic corruption and we will now examine those aspects of civil service reform that relate to that concern. Two of the quantifiable factors discussed in chapter 6 as contributing to bureaucratic corruption in African states are the erosion and the compression of salary scales of public servants. Consequently, one of the major components of civil service reform in Africa has been the reform of pay and grading.

As a measure for controlling bureaucratic corruption, pay and grading reform generally has five objectives: (1) an increase in overall real pay levels; (2) the decompression of pay scales to improve the competitiveness of civil service pay at higher levels; (3) a new grading system based on job evaluations; (4) the introduction of performance-based pay; and (5) the improvement of pay policy making and administration (de Merode and Thomas 1994). The experience of pay and grading reform in Africa suggests some success in outcomes which, over the medium term, ought to influence the reduction in bureaucratic corruption.

Aided by tax structure changes, Ghana, for example, was able to improve the net pay compression ratio of its civil service from 5:2 in 1984 to 10:1 in 1991. Similarly, in Mozambique, the ratio of the highest-paid echelon to the lowest-paid widened from 2:1 in 1985 to 9:1 in 1991 (World Bank 1994b). Moreover, the average levels of real remuneration have also substantially increased in some countries. In Guinea, real pay improved spectacularly (118 percent) between the prereform period and the period immediately following reform (de Merode and Thomas 1994).

With respect to the grading system, several African states have made considerable progress in simplifying their grading structures. Notably, the Gambia grading reform resulted in the upgrading of 2,700 posts and the downgrading of 870 others out of a total of some 9,000 posts (de Merode and Thomas 1994). Similar kinds of results have also been recorded in Ghana, Guinea, and Uganda. These accomplishments have, in turn, acted as a magnet to attract and motivate some top professionals (Westcott 1994).

Another aspect of civil service reform in Africa, as a tool for controlling bureaucratic corruption, has been the downsizing of the civil service. Many countries have been taking steps to reduce the number of surplus employees employed in ministries and other government departments. A number of methods have been used, including enforcing mandatory retirement ages, abolishing job guarantees for high school and university graduates, ensuring attrition through hiring freezes, introducing voluntary departure schemes, making outright dismissals, and eliminating "ghost" (fictitious) employees from the payroll. For example, Cameroon and Uganda significantly reduced civil service employment by removing 5,840 and 20,000 ghost employees, respectively, from their payrolls during 1981–90. The Central African Republic reduced its civil service by more than 4,500 through removal of ghost employees, voluntary departures, and retrenchments during the same period. Ghana, Gambia, and Guinea downsized their civil service also, primarily through enforced/early retirement and retrenchment, by a magnitude of 48,610, 3,790, and 38,864, respectively, during the period 1981–90 (World Bank 1994b).

The final aspect of civil service reform to be considered here relates to training. Training is a very important element of the process of behavior modification and instilling values of moral accountability and efficiency. Many African countries now have institutes of public administration or management or administrative staff colleges to train their civil servants. Many of these training activities are supported by donor agencies due to the fact that there is recognition of the importance of training in any attempt to reform any given civil service for improved performance. Training is intended to enhance the knowledge and skills of individuals as well as inculcate proper attitudes toward and about work. In addition, the effectiveness of any civil service is primarily a result of adequate training. Training leads to individual learning, which leads to improved individual job performance, which leads to improved organizational effectiveness and efficiency (Blunt and Jones 1992).

However, the training of civil servants in Africa seems to have had mixed results as a reform measure. For example, Balogun (1989) has argued that the training institutions have made only a limited contribution to civil service reform in Africa due to their perception of the policy framework as "closed," their confused orientation, the narrow background of their staff, and their financial resource constraints. On the other hand, Jacobs (1990) found that the training program for senior managers in the Ugandan civil service was very successful and he even urged its replication in other countries. For Ghana, it was determined that training programs lacked complementarity and needed to have more relevant public policy content (Dotse 1991).

Perhaps the mixed results of training as a reform measure in Africa can be attributed to the management development practices that have been adopted by the region's training institutions. Manamperi (1990) has identified five approaches as comprising those practices. The first is the smorgasbord approach, where training institutions offer a menu of courses served up to their clients without any attempt to find out what training is actually needed. The second is the bandwagon approach, where training institutions offer what seems to be currently in fashion, whether relevant or not. This has been referred to elsewhere as the "copycat syndrome" (Hope and Armstrong 1980). The third is the excursion approach, which assumes that there is a direct relationship between benefits received from training and the distance the trainees have to travel from their place of employment. The fourth is the welfare approach, which exemplifies the view that the purpose of training is to provide demanded certificates. Lastly, there is the justification approach, where training activities are scheduled in order to justify the existence of the training institution.

Controlling Bureaucratic Corruption:
Some Lessons from Botswana for the Rest of Africa

Botswana is an African nation with internationally recognized good governance and it continues to maintain its administrative capacity for economic development and progress. Unlike most of Africa, the government of Botswana continues to exhibit a clear capacity and ability to respond to the need for change when shown to be necessary, as was the case when bureaucratic corruption began to emerge as a problem in the country (Hope 1995b). "Where Botswana departs more radically from other African states is in the uncharacteristically modest lifestyles and moderate personal consumption patterns of Botswana's political and administrative elite" (Charlton 1990).

The key element of Botswana's move to control bureaucratic corruption was the passing into law, in August 1994, of the Corruption and Economic Crime Bill which, among other things, established a Directorate on Corruption and Economic Crime (DCEC) as an independent anticorruption agency. The DCEC is responsible for the investigation of alleged and suspected offenses of corruption and offenses against the fiscal laws of Botswana; it will assist any law enforcement agency of the government in the investigation of offenses involving dishonesty or cheating of the public revenue; and it will assist the attorney general in the prosecution of the offenders, including those instigating and abetting in such offenses (Republic of Botswana 1994b).

In addition, the DCEC will examine the practices and procedures of public bodies in order to facilitate the discovery of corrupt practices and to secure the revision of methods of work or any procedures that are deemed to be conducive to corrupt practices; will instruct, advise, and assist any person requesting ways in which corrupt practices may be eliminated; will educate the public against the evils of corruption; and will enlist and foster public support in combating corruption (Republic of Botswana 1994b).

During the debate on the bill, in both the media and in parliament, those who were opposed felt that too much power was being given to the DCEC. However, on the government side, the minister of Presidential Affairs and Public Administration steadfastly argued that corruption was "a relatively new type of crime which has recently begun to rear its ugly head in our midst at an alarming rate." He further stated that "investors would rather deal with a clean bureaucracy than the one where they have to bribe their way through the various layers of the bureaucracy" (*Contact Botswana* 1994). From its startup of operations in 1994 to the first quarter of 1996, the DCEC had recovered approximately U.S.$2.5 million from fines, forfeitures, seizures, and the recovery of taxes (*Daily News* 1996).

To further promote an honest and efficient bureaucracy, the government of Botswana has also established the Office of the Ombudsman. The Office of the Ombudsman will address administrative shortcomings in the public service and address grievances, as well as uncover breaches of public accountability (*The Midweek Sun* 1994).

Perhaps the most important factor in Botswana's favor for controlling bureaucratic corruption is the country's achievement of good governance. Botswana is a nation where political leaders respect and uphold the rule of law; where patrimonialism, nepotism, and tribalism are virtually nonexistent; and where economic management is sound and eschews state interventionist policies. For example, Botswana has a highly developed, independent, and well-respected legal and judicial system through which laws are enforced fairly and equitably (Westcott 1994). Moreover, the rigorous enforcement of civil service codes requiring honesty have protected the state from being perceived as a source of personal income. In any case, major political and bureaucratic actors do not look upon the state as the area in which they can or should enhance their personal income. Instead, they see economic security as being achieved in the private sector (Holm 1988). Also, the civil service in Botswana has far greater autonomy than its counterparts elsewhere in Africa. Being apolitical in an environment of good governance has therefore allowed the civil service to be virtually free from the influence of corruption (Somolekae 1993).

Another significant factor influencing Botswana's ability to control and minimize corruption is that the pay and standard of living of the country's public servants are relatively high compared with other African countries. Consequently, public servants are not preoccupied with the need to make ends meet and to engage in corrupt activities to do so. Finally, the public service in Botswana is run according to meritocratic principles. Employment and promotion are linked to specific requirements with respect to education and experience, and those requirements are strictly enforced.

Training is also emphasized and has become a major undertaking of the government of Botswana in recent years. Considerable emphasis is being placed on improving the skills and competence of public servants, with the basic objective of improving motivation, performance, productivity, and accountability. Furthermore, the country has formally recognized and adopted training policies that integrate public service training with broader human-resource development policies such as promotion (Hope 1995b). This commitment of the government of Botswana to the training of public officials, at all levels, is amply demonstrated by its allocation of adequate resources for such purposes and the creation of appropriate training institutions, such as the Botswana National Productivity Center and the University of Botswana, to facilitate the process, as discussed in chapter 9.

The control of corruption in Botswana is being accomplished through the fundamentals of good governance, sound economic management, and the implementation of measures designed to make administrative processes more transparent and the actions of officials more visible through the strengthening of systems of political and administrative accountability. This comprehensive approach has proved to be immensely successful and, as such, a highly recommended model for other African nations to follow.

Conclusions

Drawing on the experience of Botswana, as well as on the other evidence presented here, bureaucratic corruption can only be controlled through comprehensive reform measures that have the full support and commitment of the political leadership. Moreover, political leaders must demonstrate their support and commitment by behaving in an ethical and accountable manner. Public servants will not curtail or eliminate their corrupt activities if their political leaders are also engaged in such activities.

In Africa, there has always been an abundance of public pronouncements by government leaders on their intentions to rid their respective countries of corruption. However, these are not usually taken seriously by both the public and public servants because they are not usually followed by serious action. In essence, they are simply regarded as ritualistic. Yet, the most necessary of all conditions to control corruption is a strongly motivated political leadership supported by others of insight and integrity. Given the wave of political liberalization and democratization sweeping across most of the African continent, one can only hope that it will also produce the type of motivated leadership just referred to above.

As a matter of fact, as discussed in chapter 6, it is believed that over the longer term only a profound transformation in social and political relations is likely to significantly weaken corruption's underlying causes, which have their roots very deep in Africa's patrimonial economic and state structures (Harsch 1993). This would necessarily entail a full liberalization of the national political processes, through the development of democratic institutions and practices, including the acceptance of political pluralism, regular and periodic elections, and a free press (Ouma 1991).

In other words, unless and until there is good governance in Africa, bureaucratic corruption will continue to thrive. Good governance has the potential to remove the pervasive stench of corruption because it allows for the functioning of and respect for institutions, laws, conventions, and practices that would effectively discourage corruption and punish those still intent on perpetrating it. Good governance will make corruption a high-risk activity—a high risk that perpetrators will be caught and severely punished since good governance requires the highest standards of integrity, openness, transparency, and respect for the rule of law.

Finally, as the Botswana experience suggests, an independent anti-corruption agency can play a major role in the efforts to control corruption in Africa. This has been found to be true elsewhere also. The establishment of meaningfully focused independent anticorruption agencies can provide a very effective means of promoting integrity in public officials, building up a public service ethic, promoting probity in government, and protection of state income and expenditure, while at the same time offering the means for public redress (Doig 1995). However, as in the Botswana case again, such agencies must necessarily be complemented by good governance, or the potential for such, for them to have a useful impact. Otherwise, they would, inevitably, become bureaucratized and impotent.

Notes

1. For a good discussion and analysis of these instruments of persuasion, see Amuwo (1986).

2. Ayeni (1994) argues that African ombudsmen, being primarily lawyers, civil servants, and politicians, lack the relevant educational orientation toward data gathering and analysis.

11

Decentralization, the New Public Administration, and the Changing Role of the Public Sector in Africa

The role of the public sector in most countries is changing both with respect to public service delivery and the stimulation of economic progress. That change, which was occasioned by the need for policy reform, has resulted in what is now termed the "New Public Administration," reflecting a movement away from the old values and norms of public-sector administration.

The policy reform framework that led to the emergence of the New Public Administration was based on the reality of government failures. Those government failures led to economic stagnation and fiscal crises which reduced the resources available for public service delivery. At the same time, there were increasing demands for quality public service delivery, and this in turn led to the search for realigned structures and institutions capable of meeting those challenges (CAPAM 1995; Kaul and Collins 1995).

The New Public Administration is therefore wedded to the concept of reengineering the public sector or the reinventing of government. Reengineering is a management philosophy that seeks to revamp the process through which public organizations operate in order to increase efficiency, effectiveness, and competitive ability. It calls for changes in the structure of public organizations, their culture, management systems, and other aspects in support of the new initiative. In addition, it encompasses client-oriented, mission-driven, and exercise-participatory management, using resources in new ways to heighten efficiency and effectiveness (Halachmi 1995; Osborne and Gaebler 1992).

The New Public Administration can be seen as a normative reconceptualization of public administration consisting of several interrelated components. It emerged in response to the economic and social realities that governments everywhere have had to face during the past two decades (Borins 1995). Those realities include: (1) too large and expensive public sectors; (2) the need to utilize information technology to increase efficiency; (3) the demand by the public for quality service; (4) the quest for personal growth and job satisfaction by public-sector employees (Borins 1995).

One of the central elements in the changing role of the public sector and the construct of the New Public Administration is the concept of decentralization. Many countries, particularly the African countries after they gained independence, initially emphasized efforts to build a nation-state. That, in turn, had a highly centralizing effect and negative impacts on the efficient delivery of public services. The movement toward decentralization is an attempt to, among other things, improve the delivery of public services and increase the productivity of the public sector. This chapter examines and analyzes the concept of decentralization and its relevance to the changing role of the public sector in Africa, within the context of the New Public Administration.

The Concept of Decentralization

Decentralization can be defined as the transfer of authority or responsibility for decision making, planning, management, or resource allocation from the central government to its field units, district administrative units, local governments, regional or functional authorities, semiautonomous public authorities, parastatal organizations, private entities, and nongovernmental private or voluntary organizations (Rondinelli, Nellis, and Cheema 1983; Rondinelli and Cheema 1983).

Decentralization can also be defined from a public choice perspective. The standard public choice literature provides both ex-ante and ex-post arguments for decentralization. However, the generally basic definition in the public choice literature is that decentralization can be regarded as a situation in which public goods and services are provided primarily through the revealed preferences of individuals by market mechanisms (Rondinelli, McCullough, and Johnson 1989). Decentralized governments are regarded as having better knowledge of local preferences, either in the sense of having access to information denied to central governments, or in the sense of observing preferences with less noise (Cremer, Estache, and Seabright 1994).

The primary objectives of decentralization include, but are not limited to, overcoming the indifference of government bureaucrats to satisfying the needs of the public; improving the responsiveness of governments to public concerns; and increasing the quality of services provided (Rondinelli, Nellis, and Cheema 1983). In addition, within the context of the New Public Administration, decentralization is seen as the means: (1) for governments to provide high-quality services that citizens value; (2) for increasing managerial autonomy, particularly by reducing central administrative controls; (3) for demanding, measuring, and rewarding both organizational and individual performance; (4) for enabling managers to acquire human and technological resources to meet performance targets; (5) for creating a receptiveness to competition and an open-mindedness about which public purposes should be performed by public servants as opposed to the private sector (Borins 1994); (6) for empowering citizens through their enhanced participation in decision making and development planning and management; (7) for improving economic and managerial efficiency or effectiveness; and (8) for enhancing better governance (Silverman 1992).

Decentralization can be either horizontal or vertical. Horizontal decentralization disperses power among institutions at the same level while vertical decentralization, which is more useful, allows some of the powers of a central government to be delegated downward to lower tiers of authority (UNDP 1993). Decentralization can be further differentiated into six types; deconcentration, delegation, devolution, privatization, top-down principal agency, and bottom-up principal agency.

Deconcentration is the passing down of selected administrative functions to lower levels or subnational units within central government ministries. Deconcentration is the least extensive form of decentralization. Although it does result in some dispersal of power, few decisions can be taken without reference to the center (UNDP 1993). However, it is the most common form of decentralization employed in the agriculture services, primary education, preventive health, and population subsectors (Silverman 1992). In Botswana, for example, the central government has created and supervises district councils as well as a national Rural Development Council for the coordination and implementation of, among other things, rural development activities such as drought-relief measures and agricultural development.

Delegation is the transfer of specific authority and decision-making powers to organizations that are outside the regular bureaucratic structure and that are only indirectly controlled by the central government, such as parastatals and semiautonomous agencies. In this type of decentralization the central government retains the right to overturn local decisions and can, at any time, take these powers back (UNDP 1993). Delegation is seen as a way of offering public goods and services through a more businesslike organizational structure that makes use of managerial accounting techniques normally associated with private enterprise (Rondinelli, Nellis, and Cheema 1983). It is increasingly used by donor agencies for implementing or maintaining sector investments primarily in the transport, ports, energy, and communications sectors. Delegation has been used extensively in Africa. In Kenya, for example, public corporations have been used to organize, finance, and manage large-scale agricultural projects such as tea production. Also, in Lesotho, a parastatal was created to finance and manage a huge water development project in the country's highlands area.

One significant feature of delegation, as a mode of decentralization in Africa, is that it is used as a tool for making decisions more relevant to local needs and conditions, especially in rural development programs. In Morocco, for example, the transfer of some implementation powers to the local level is intended to increase the chances that more positive results will be achieved from development projects. Thus, decentralization in this context is designed to reflect unique local circumstances in development plans and their implementation (Smith 1993).

Devolution is the granting of decision-making powers to local authorities and allowing them to take full responsibility without reference back to the central government. This includes financial power as well as the authority to design and execute local development projects and programs (UNDP 1993). The essence of devolution is discretionary authority. To the extent that local governments have discretionary authority, they can do essentially what they decide to do subject only to broad national policy guidelines; their own financial, human, and material capacities; and the physical environment within which they must operate (Silverman 1992).

Devolution is the strongest form of decentralization. It allows for the reduction of the levels of administration through which activities have to pass and it enhances citizenry productivity and participation by increasing their involvement in development activities. Moreover, devolution is an arrangement in which there are reciprocal, mutually benefiting and coordinate relationships between central and local governments (Rondinelli, McCullough, and Johnson 1989). Among the few attempts at devolution is the experience of Nigeria where, in the latter part of the 1970s, it was based on the conventional British local government model. Edicts handed down by each state government established local governments to serve populations of not less than 150,000 and not more than 800,000 constituents; created councils with at least three-fourths elected memberships; and devolved to local governments exclusive responsibility for, and authority to enact, bylaws regarding an extensive list of functions (Koehn 1995).

Similarly, in Ethiopia, in 1992, the transitional government reversed many of the previous regime's centralizing policies and embarked on a more radical devolution to the regional level of "legislative, executive, and judicial powers in respect of all matters within their geographical areas except . . . defence, foreign affairs, economic policy, conferring of citizenship, declaration of a state of emergency, deployment of the army . . . , printing of currency, establishing and administering major development establishments, building and administering major communication networks and the like, which are specifically reserved for the central . . . government because of their nature" (Koehn 1995).

Also, in Senegal, authority is devolved to rural councils, which gives them powers to determine land usage, settlement of land tenure disputes, and the erection of temporary and permanent dwellings within their boundaries (Blunt and Jones 1992). Although budgetary matters are determined at the central government level, many activities are financed from revenues obtained from rural land taxes, the rate of which is also centrally determined (Vengroff and Johnston 1987). In Senegal, rural communities have populations of between five thousand and eight thousand. The rural councils, which govern community affairs, have two-thirds of their council members elected from candidates nominated by political parties, while the remaining members are representatives drawn from cooperatives in the community (Aloki 1989).

Privatization refers here to the transfer of control and responsibilities for government functions and services to the private sector—private voluntary organizations or private enterprises. From a broader perspective, privatization encompasses a wide range of policies to encourage private-sector participation in public service provision and that eliminate or modify the monopoly status of public enterprises (Rondinelli and Kasarda 1993).

This type of decentralization has gained considerable currency during the past decade. Its growing appeal is derived from the economic case for such privatization. That economic case is made by the fact that public-service delivery is much more expensive than can be justified and sustained by central governments; by the poor economic performance of government agencies and ministries when compared to the private sector; and the built-in characteristics of government functioning, such as political interference and bureaucratic failure, that give rise to economic inefficiency (Hope 1996b).

Privatization itself may take several forms. It may be: (1) the commercializing of government services that are contracted out to an outside agency; (2) joint ventures between government agencies/ministries and private entities; (3) the sale of some government services or functions, such as water supply or telecommunications, to the private sector; (4) management contracts for the private sector to manage specific government functions or services such as postal services; (5) the leasing of government assets that are used to provide public services; or (6) the granting of concessions to private entities to operate and finance some public-services delivery.

The sale of government assets or services has a huge advantage over nonownership methods of privatization because it entails the transfer of ownership and the rights to pursue profits. In Guinea, for example, such sales have resulted in a reduction of government-owned assets by more than 50 percent during the period 1980–91. Similarly, during the same period, the government of Togo reduced its ownership of producing assets by 38 percent, while in Tunisia and Nigeria the reductions were 12 percent and 26 percent, respectively (Kikeri, Nellis, and Shirley 1992). In sub-Saharan Africa as a whole, the total revenue collected from the sale of some 200 public enterprises was approximately U.S.$1 billion during the period 1988–93 (Sader 1995).

One method of privatization that is increasing in popularity is the contracting out of services. Increasing emphasis is being placed on efficiency and service delivery, and one of the means identified for improving both is contracting out services. This method leads to cost savings and better value for money by removing the production of such services from inefficient public bureaucracies that are more intent on satisfying the wishes of producer groups than of consumers. Moreover, private contractors can be penalized for poor quality, delays, and lack of reliability (Hoggett 1993). In Botswana, for example, the parastatals have contracted out a number of services, including those related to maintenance and security. Similarly, in Nigeria the National Electric Power Authority contracts out maintenance for power station and transmission facilities. Also, maintenance is contracted out by the Nigerian Telephone Company (Fox 1994).

However, there can also be tremendous benefits from the privatizing of management through management contracts, leases, and concession arrangements. Privatizing management may be a useful alternative method of improving the efficiency of public enterprises where outright sales may not be feasible for economic or political reasons. It can also be used as a tool to improve the performance of such enterprises to ready them for sale in the future.

The most frequently used tool to privatize management is the management contract, an agreement between a government and a private party to operate an enterprise for a fee. Such contracts are most common in the hotel industry. When hotels are excluded, Zambia, for example, was found to have the most management contracts with a total of sixteen, while Tanzania had ten by 1993 (World Bank 1995d).

Excluding hotels, the majority of the worldwide management contracts are concentrated in Africa. The Africa region accounts for approximately two-thirds of these management contracts. Many of the enterprises under management contract in Africa were, ironically, formerly owned by transnational corporations, were nationalized, and then contracted out, sometimes to the former owner. Such management contracts exist in the sugar sector in Kenya and the gold mining sector in Ghana, for example. In the majority of cases, management contracts were found to have improved both enterprise profitability and productivity (World Bank 1995d).

In leases, a private operator pays the government a fee to use its assets and/or facilities and assumes the commercial risks of operation and maintenance of those assets. Fees are usually linked to performance and revenues and some lease arrangements also provide for a percentage of the profits to be paid to the government while the government agrees to guarantee the outstanding debts of the enterprise (Commonwealth Secretariat 1994). Such arrangements are most practicable in those activities where investments are made in an infrequent manner and they allow for responsibility for operations to be separated from responsibility for investment.

Lease arrangements are widely used in Africa, particularly in those sectors to which it is difficult to attract private investors. In Nigeria, for example, a joint foreign-local enterprise has leased ports from the government. Other examples include steel and petroleum refining in Togo, water supply in Guinea and Côte d'Ivoire, electricity in Côte d'Ivoire, road transport in Niger, and mining operations in Guinea (Kikeri, Nellis, and Shirley 1992). These lease arrangements have also brought about considerable improvement in labor productivity and reductions in costs. For example, in Côte d'Ivoire the leased water company reduced the number of highly paid expatriates by about two-thirds, from forty to twelve. In addition, technical efficiency, new connections, billing, and collection of receivables also improved considerably (Kikeri, Nellis, and Shirley 1992).

Concessions incorporate all the features of a lease but give the contractor the added responsibility of investments such as for specified extensions and expansions of capacity or for the replacement of fixed assets. Although concession arrangements exist around the world for railways, telecommunications, urban transport systems, and water supply and treatment, they are not widely used in Africa primarily because private financing tends to be weak in comparison with the size of the investment, and especially so in those countries where the political and economic risks are perceived to be great (Kikeri, Nellis, and Shirley 1992).

In the top-down principal agency model of decentralization, local governments exercise responsibility on behalf of central governments or, in some instances, parastatals under the direction and supervision of central government agencies (Silverman 1992). In this situation, as principal agents, local governments do so under the control and supervision of central government agencies or ministries. The latter is also responsible for the financing of the expenditures associated with the process.

Depending on the degree of autonomy local governments have with respect to their other functions, they can act as principal agents in two ways. They can do so in their entirety and be no more than complete principal agents of central governments or they can serve as principal agents in parallel with their performance of other responsibilities (Silverman 1992). Ghana provides a good example of attempts at decentralization through the principal agency model (Ayee 1994).

The bottom-up type of principal agency is quite the opposite of the top-down model. In this situation, various levels of government or parastatals act as agents of lower levels of government or directly as agents of the consuming public. The source of the discretionary authority is reversed (Silverman 1992). Consequently, a local government department may contract with a central government ministry for the provision of a public good or service, with payment being made by the local government. As is the case with the top-down principal agency model, the fundamental characteristics of the bottom-up principal agency model also do not depend on the extent to which local governments are, or are not, subordinate to higher levels of government with respect to other functions they might perform (Silverman 1992).

Linking Decentralization and the Changing Role of the Public Sector

One central argument or theme of this chapter is that the decentralization framework is a major element in the facilitation of the changing role of the public sector and in the construct of the New Public Administration. Undoubtedly, the changing economic and social conditions in most African countries have led to reduced financial resources within the public sector, a growing concern over cost-consciousness and efficiency, and more pressure for responsiveness and accountability in service delivery (Kaul and Collins 1995). Reducing the size of the public sector while maintaining its effectiveness is therefore a challenging exercise that can best be accomplished through decentralization policies.

Moreover, there is a growing body of evidence indicating that the decentralization of government services can be far more efficient than their supply by bureaus. These methods promise both to reduce the total cost of government and to increase the level and quality of public services. Only the unthinking, uncreative, and inefficient may have any cause to object to such a fundamental fact (Mitchell and Simmons 1994; Hope 1996b). In addition, it has been observed elsewhere that the economic and political crises of the 1970s and 1980s have now discredited service delivery systems based on centralized bureaucracy, forcing theorists of public administration to shift their focus from hierarchy and control to participation and empowerment and, therefore, reflecting the recognition that hierarchical systems do not lead to progress but to inefficiency, autocracy, and corruption (Brett 1996).

Decentralization enables much greater variety of choice while also serving to reduce costs. To the extent, for example, that education is considered a public good, it seems clear that public financing is desirable. However, the consumption of education should be viewed as a private good. Currently, too many African citizens are denied their preferences as to quantity and type of education. Consequently, a case can be made for the full decentralization of schools in Africa.

Highly centralized forms of governance also generate administrative pathologies, including communication overload, long response times, filtering and distortion of information, a failure to grasp spatial connections in sectoral programming, and so on. Moreover, centralized states tend to be unresponsive to local needs as well as to the needs of the disempowered in particular (Friedmann 1992). Restructuring the delivery of public services by decentralizing central functions and resources thus becomes a central claim of the New Public Administration and the changing role of the public sector. Decentralizing governance can also be one of the best means of promoting participation and efficiency in African states.

Some indication of the extent of decentralization in Africa, in the context of the changing role of the public sector, can be gathered through an examination of statistical ratios that indicate the degree of financial decentralization. In Table 11.1, financial decentralization is expressed by the expenditure decentralization ratio, the modified expenditure decentralization ratio, the revenue decentralization ratio, and the financial autonomy ratio.

The expenditure decentralization ratio shows the percentage of total government expenditure spent by local governments. The modified expenditure decentralization ratio takes into account the fact that some government expenditures cannot be decentralized (defense and debt servicing) and they are therefore subtracted to give a modified expenditure ratio that expresses the degree of decentralization of responsibilities that can, in practice, be decentralized. The revenue decentralization ratio indicates the significance of local taxation. It is the percentage of local government revenue in total revenue. The financial autonomy ratio gives an indication of a local government's independence from central government funding. It is the percentage of locally raised revenue in total local expenditure (UNDP 1993).

The ratios indicate that there is greater expenditure decentralization in Zimbabwe, where the ratio exceeds 20 percent, than in the other countries. Likewise, with respect to the revenue decentralization ratios, local governments in Zimbabwe raise considerably more revenue from

Table 11.1

Financial Decentralization in Local Government in Selected Countries

Country	Year	Expenditure decentralization ratio		Revenue decentrali- zation ratio	Financial autonomy ratio
		Total	Modified		
Zimbabwe	1986	22	29	17	58
Nigeria	1988	17	N/A	N/A	N/A
Algeria	1986	14	N/A	16	101
South Africa	1988	10	11	10	79
Kenya	1989	4	5	7	134
Morocco	1987	6	N/A	8	108
Ghana	1988	2	N/A	2	71
Côte d'Ivoire	1985	2	N/A	2	115

Source: UNDP, *Human Development Report 1993* (New York: Oxford University Press, 1993), p. 69.
Note:
N/A: Not available.

taxation than do the other countries. In terms of financial autonomy, in all of the countries the ratio exceeds 50 percent. In four of the countries, Algeria, Kenya, Morocco, and Côte d'Ivoire, the ratio exceeds 100 percent. For all of the countries these statistical ratios indicate considerable financial autonomy irrespective of the absolute magnitude of locally raised revenue.

The financial decentralization ratios, and particularly the financial autonomy ratios, suggest that there is growing recognition that local governments are better placed to make the appropriate decisions with respect to expenditures and revenues for the delivery of public services. Central governments therefore need to find the best combination of feasible policy interventions to facilitate and support the decentralization of public service delivery, financing, and management. The imperative for the changing role of the public sector in Africa demands no less.

Undoubtedly, the poor record of central government performance in Africa has played a major role in the development of policy reforms that have led to the changing role of the public sector and provides ammunition to calls for decentralization. Based on the available evidence on its benefits, decentralization should be implemented at the level that is closest to the people. Such a strategy would also allow for greater economic and political participation among the citizenry and private voluntary groups.

Participation is a dominant aspect of the functioning of private voluntary groups and it is the basic feature that distinguishes them most sharply from the top-down approach of central governments. Many of the successes recorded by private voluntary groups are attributable to their fundamental recognition of the central importance of constituent participation in governance, planning, decision making, distribution of benefits, and project monitoring (Koehn 1995; Hope 1983).

In recent years, both the public policy and development studies literature have moved toward the consensus that participation by the intended beneficiaries improves the delivery of public services. Moreover, the participatory approach is now increasingly advocated by the aid agencies such as the World Bank and the United Nations Development Programme. Increased beneficiary participation is therefore no longer seen as a vague ideology based on the wishful thinking of a few idealists. Indeed, it has become an imperative in the process of decentralization (UNDP 1993).

The changing role of the public sector, within the New Public Administration, is closely linked to private-sector ideas such as efficiency, productivity, scaling down, cost-cutting, client satisfaction, and so on. However, this new awareness in the public sector does not fail to recognize that there are differences between the public and private sectors. Rather, it acknowledges that it is most receptive to learning from and adapting private-sector strategies to the public sector (Borins 1995; Halachmi 1995).

Like the private sector, the public sector in Africa is now forced to cope with a change from ad hoc actions and functional organizational structuring to designing, managing, optimizing, and decentralizing processes. A good example of such change can be found in South Africa where public-sector decision making has evolved from an authoritarian approach with strong sectoral lobbying from the employers to a participative, democratic, and consultative approach where all stakeholders can contribute to the final policies (Boer 1995).

Basically, the current thrust of public-sector reform was pioneered by New Zealand and Australia. That thrust has been an overall policy of decentralization and a switch from centralized input controls to output controls. The impetus for these reforms stemmed from the real-

ity that the traditional model of the civil service was not very successful at adapting to the rapid rates of change in society and that it was no
longer adequate for modern needs. Consequently, reforming the core
public service required the espousing of the philosophies of the New
Public Administration (Byrne et al. 1995; Boston 1991; Scott, Bushnell, and Sallee 1990).

However, one aspect of this change process that warrants further
consideration, with respect to the African countries, is that of capacity
building in the public sector. Capacity building is taken here to mean
specific initiatives undertaken to improve the capacity of the public
sector to plan, implement, and monitor policies designed to improve
socioeconomic performance and public service delivery.

Many African countries still lack sufficient capacity to fully implement fundamental public-sector reforms. Consequently, there are still
large numbers of costly expatriate advisers and consultants in many of
those countries. However, one response to that state of affairs has been
the creation of the African Capacity Building Foundation (ACBF)
based in Harare, Zimbabwe. The ACBF, created in 1991 and funded
by a consortium of donors and African governments, focuses on projects, at least initially, in the key areas of policy analysis and development management that have the clear potential to increase the capacity
of African countries to improve their situation through their own initiatives and abilities. In addition, Botswana, for example, has also created
the Botswana Institute for Development Policy Analysis (BIDPA), an
autonomous research institute which is charged with responsibility in
the areas of development policy analysis and capacity building. Established in 1995 by a deed of trust, BIDPA is funded by the ACBF and
the Botswana government, with additional funding from the Norwe-
gian government. Clearly, building the capacity of governments to plan
and implement public-sector tasks must be given high priority in the
changing role of the public sector and the New Public Administration
(Cohen 1995).

Conclusions

As the changing role of the public sector has become clearer, a managerial approach to the challenges it faces has emerged. That approach
is sufficiently relevant, coherent, and distinct from the old traditional
bureaucratic approaches to have been characterized as the New Public

Administration (Manning 1993). The emphasis is on the quality and effectiveness of governance, efficiency, productivity, competitive ability, client-driven service delivery, results rather than procedural consistency, management autonomy in decision making, and beneficiary participation in program planning and implementation. It also entails the emergence of entrepreneurial government and systems of administration that promote competition between service providers while at the same time seeking to empower citizens.

One crucial element in the facilitation of the changing role of the public sector and the legitimacy of the New Public Administration is the concept of decentralization. Decentralization is seen here as representing the critical means through which the changing role of the public sector, within the context of the New Public Administration, can be most effectively realized, and particularly so in Africa. Decentralization results in better governance, it facilitates the development of more effective and efficient public-sector management, it increases popular participation in government, it allows for better mobilization and use of resources, and it encourages market-like responsiveness to the provision and consumption of public services.

Decentralization is steadily gaining momentum around the world. In the developed countries, it is used as one of the policy instruments to reengineer or reinvent government, while in the developing countries it has mainly been an instrument of policy reform within the framework of political and economic liberalization. As a reform measure, decentralization is much more successful when governments demonstrate a clear vision of the future that is based on leadership and values that are widely shared by society. This requires political commitment, capacity building, and the setting of priorities as well as tangible and realistic objectives (Kaul and Collins 1995).

Finally, from the perspective that better governance will lead to better economic policy making and improved economic performance, decentralization is therefore one instrument that is expected to have very specific effects on the development performance of government institutions at the local level, where government actions usually have the most impact on the lives of ordinary citizens (Crook and Manor 1995). Undoubtedly, there is a direct relationship between decentralization and better governance and it needs to be seriously exploited further, particularly by the African countries.

12

The Challenge of Policy Reform
and Change in Africa

In the preceding chapters a number of factors have been identified as rendering the African continent, as a whole, incapable of sustained growth. Some aspects of policy reform and change have also been discussed and considerable reference has been made to Botswana as a model of prudent economic management and good governance for the rest of Africa to follow.

Essentially, most African nations have not been able or willing to realign their policy frameworks to combat the deepening crisis of development that has plagued them during the past two decades. In particular, sub-Saharan Africa, with its undiversified economic structure and undeveloped policy infrastructure, has been immobilized by its inability to adjust to the external and internal shocks it has experienced. Yet, although the benefits of policy reform and change remain obvious, it is disturbing to think that African leaders and policy makers may have learned nothing from the lost decade of the 1980s. This chapter is a synthesis of the policy reform and change measures that have been discussed in this book. It is intended to blend and further clarify the previous discussions and analyses.

Elements of the Challenge

In March 1996, the United Nations, in association with the World Bank, launched yet another initiative on African development in a desperate attempt to once again contribute in a bold way to solving Africa's development crisis. The aim of this ten-year initiative, which is termed "The UN Systemwide Special Initiative for Africa," is to invest U.S.$25 billion in the region to expand basic education and health care, promote peace and better governance, and improve water and food security. The World Bank will be responsible for mobilizing more than 85 percent of the target sum, the bulk of which will be for education and health services. To date, this is the largest-ever coordinated action plan of the United Nations. It is indeed ambitious and seems to have been proposed in response to charges by African leaders that their continent was being marginalized as exhibited by a lack of response to Africa's problems by the industrialized nations.

But herein lies one of the fundamental problems related to the crisis of development in Africa. African leaders and policy makers still continue to put faith in the notion that Africa's problems are to be solved solely outside of Africa. Yet, internal obstacles to development in Africa are as important as those imposed by the international economic system, and perhaps even more so (Callaghy 1994). Indeed, one recognizes that Africa needs some help to solve its problems. Moreover, continued neglect of these problems can have negative externalities that may have an impact on communities far beyond Africa. However, Africa's destiny lies squarely on the shoulders of its leaders to develop self-reliant initiatives that are sustainable over the long term. Such initiatives will most certainly require not only regional assistance but also some nonregional international assistance. But such external assistance is much more likely to be forthcoming as complementary to indigenous initiatives rather than as sole or stand-alone support.

In any case, the problems faced by Africa are daunting and are, therefore, unlikely to be resolved solely through reliance on UN/World Bank initiatives. It would also be myopic of those two institutions to share the view that their initiatives alone will pull Africa out of its development crisis. However, the UN and World Bank are to be applauded for once again trying to rescue the peoples of Africa from their despair. This work has catalogued the factors contributing to such despair. They include a crippling total external debt which stood at U.S.$313 billion for the region as a whole in 1994;[1] the weakening of the balance of payments; the intensification of the brain drain; the deepening of capital flight; declining agricultural productivity and foreign direct investment;[2] deteriorating physical infrastructure; escalating unemployment and crime; much more pronounced famine and malnutrition; soaring budget deficits; rapid urbanization; expanding environmental degradation; worsening political and civil strife; rampant corruption; and increasing poverty,[3] socioeconomic inequalities, population growth rates, and magnitude of the AIDS epidemic. However, in this sea of despair, there are African countries, such as Botswana, that are models of success for the rest to emulate. Also, several other countries have begun to make the transition from the lost decade of the 1980s to the promise of the twenty-first century. Some countries have even made significant progress toward economic liberalization and democratization. The task, therefore, is one of spreading and sustaining these gains throughout the continent. To accomplish that requires, as discussed before, a much more indigenous vision and long-term-perspective thinking.

In that regard, one laudable attempt has been made under the auspices of the Global Coalition for Africa (GCA)[4] to try to guide African nations to defining and committing themselves to the kind of vision that would lead to the development of strategies that will address the primary economic and political issues facing Africa as the twenty-first century emerges. The GCA suggested, in May 1995, that there are several issues to be addressed.[5] Below, we summarize the content of those issues and analyze them within the context of the policy reform and change measures that have been discussed in this book.

Leadership

The GCA recognizes that leadership has many dimensions. However, the dimension of political leadership is said to be of greatest significance since it determines the development of other forms of leadership. The fundamental principles involved here relate to legitimate leadership, freely chosen or elected by the people, with some regard for honesty, integrity, competence, commitment, accountability, responsibility, and so on. Moreover, mechanisms of sanction and control by neutral and independent institutions should be in place, and leaders should be required to declare their assets before taking office and upon leaving office.

This type of leadership has been missing in most of Africa during the past two decades. When asked about Africa's problems, most African leaders do not discuss the shortcomings of the continent's leadership. Instead, they tend to blame "colonialism, American imperialism, the pernicious effects of slavery, the unjust international economic system, and exploitation by multinational corporations" (Ayittey 1992). In some instances they even blame the international development agencies and donor community from whom they are seeking assistance.

However, much of the blame for the shortcomings of African leadership can be attributed to a tendency toward patrimonialism.[6] "The personalization or patrimonialization of power and authority structures, political and nonpolitical, is pervasive" (Callaghy 1994). For most African leaders, of all ideological and policy persuasions, there is a preoccupation with the need for greater authority over their populaces and territories (Callaghy 1994). Consequently, patrimonial systems have sprung up in which the object of obedience is the personal authority of the leader or ruler, which he enjoys by virtue of the loyalty of his people (Healey and Robinson 1992), and whether or not such loyalty is voluntary or involuntary.

Four essential features of the patrimonial state in Africa have been identified by Callaghy (1986). The first is a highly centralized and personalized executive authority centered around a country's leader, civilian or military. The second is that charismatic and legal-rational doctrines are blended in an attempt to make the exercise of power somewhat routine. The third is that personal rulers are supported by officials and new administrative cadres based on patron-client networks. The final feature is that the state provides the major avenue of upward mobility, status, power, and wealth. These four features of the patrimonial state reveal a system of patronage, clientelism, and personal rule. Moreover, their impacts have further revealed an African leadership that is morally bankrupt and short on vision. This is in sharp contrast to the prevailing situation in the 1960s and early 1970s when the quality of leadership was a major ingredient in Africa's political progress and a key determinant in the improvements in socioeconomic conditions (Sirleaf 1996). The deterioration in the quality of African leadership, which began in the early 1970s, resulted in the replacement of long-term objectives, strategies, and programs with myopic and short-term policies exemplified by large public-sector deficits to support politically determined projects, overvaluation of currencies, inefficient regulation of domestic and foreign trade, and so on. On the political side, partisanship, tribal allegiance, and nepotism replaced inclusion and compromises, ultimately degenerating into a concentration of power and outright dictatorship, many times of a violent and repressive nature (Sirleaf 1996).

Implicit in the GCA's thinking on leadership, although not clearly specified, is the issue of good governance. Good governance exists where there is political accountability; bureaucratic transparency; the exercise of legitimate power; freedom of association and participation; freedom of information and expression; sound fiscal management and public financial accountability; respect for the rule of law; a predictable legal framework encompassing an independent and credible justice system; respect for human rights; an active legislature; enhanced opportunities for the development of pluralistic forces, including civil society; and capacity building.

African leadership, as exhibited through patrimonialism, has undermined good governance on the continent in several ways (Sandbrook 1985). For example, it has diminished or eliminated the independence of the bureaucracy, which in turn led to the misuse of public resources and the entrenchment of corrupt activities; it placed the political requirements of both regime and personal survival over policies that are in the national economic interest; and it promoted a climate in which decision making became based on narrow political considerations or for self-gratification, with total disregard for the negative long-term consequences. In essence, good governance is undermined because African patrimonial leadership is characterized by the inability or unwillingness of rulers or ruling elites to distinguish between personal and public patrimony (property). The power and authority of office are therefore used as a form of "currency," and loyalty of subordinates is exchanged for parcels of power or for privileges from office (Dia 1993).

The good-governance approach in African political economy renews the concern of analysts with political leadership and legitimate politics (Bratton and Rothchild 1992). The conditions that facilitate good governance are said to be (a) citizen influence and oversight; (b) responsive and responsible leadership; and (c) social reciprocities (Hyden 1992). Citizen influence and oversight are related to the degree to which individual citizens can participate in the political process and thereby express preferences about public policy; the means of preference aggregation for effective policy making; and the methods of public accountability. Responsive and responsible leadership refers to the attitudes of political leaders toward their role as public trustees and it entails the degree of respect for the civil public realm; the degree of transparency in public policy making; and the extent of adherence to the rule of law. Social reciprocities are related to the degree of political equality enjoyed by citizens; the degree of intergroup tolerance; and the extent of acceptance in associational organizations bounded by kinship, ethnicity, or race.

Good governance is not a luxury that African countries can barely afford. It is one of the key factors in the process of achieving broad-based socioeconomic growth, which reduces poverty at the fastest rate. Among other things, by checking corruption and incompetence, good governance ensures the most efficient utilization of scarce resources in the promotion of development (Amoako 1996). Africans are acutely aware of the benefits of good governance. It is time for those African leaders who have not already done so to respond to this popular demand.

Institutions

The GCA advocates that democratic institutions be designed to facilitate the peaceful transfer of power and that existing institutions be democratized and their capacities improved. In addition, merit should be the basis for recruitment and promotion in all institutions. In order to ensure checks and balances, separation of power should be a fundamental guiding principle and all players should abide by the constitution.

Given the patrimonial style of leadership that exists in most of Africa, it is expected that there would be very serious institutional weaknesses in those countries. The challenge here is to implement public-sector management and civil service reform to bring all institutions into the realm of democracy and good governance. When institutions are weak, there is limited implementation capacity, and service delivery also remains weak. In such an environment, socioeconomic development also remains elusive.

However, institutional change can be a complicated and lengthy process. Institutions typically change incrementally rather than in discontinuous fashion. Informal cultural constraints embodied in customs and traditions tend to be much more impervious to deliberate policies (North 1990). Consequently, the relative success of institutional change would be a function of the environmental factors that the political leadership have been instrumental in setting in place.

Civil Society

The GCA posits that African civil society is currently weak and fragile, and needs to be strengthened, since democracy can only be consolidated when there exists a vibrant, dynamic, and pluralistic civil society. Furthermore, the GCA is of the view that civil society should not only be conceived in opposition to the state but should also be a locus of continuous exchange of information between society and government.

The recent renewed interest in civil society in Africa stems from the understanding that democratization requires a strong civil society through which people can freely associate, assist in the construction of democratic and participatory institutions, and hold government accountable (Tripp 1994). Civil society can be regarded as a countervailing mechanism to state power while simultaneously engaging the state. It can be defined as "the realm of organized social life that is voluntary, self-generating, (largely) self-supporting, autonomous from the state, and bound by a legal order or set of shared rules" (Diamond 1994). It is an intermediary entity which stands between the private arena and the state. It includes formal and informal associations whose interests may be economic, cultural, informational and educational, professional, developmental, intellectual, or civic (Diamond 1994).

However, civil society should not be confused with a "civic community" since it is not an all-encompassing movement of popular empowerment and economic change (Fatton 1995). In contrast, a civic community is "marked by an active, public-spirited citizenry, by egalitarian political relations, by a social fabric of trust and cooperation. . . . Citizens in a civic community, though not selfless saints, regard the public domain as more than a battleground for pursuing personal interest" (Putnam 1993). Civil society, on the other hand, is influenced by class interests, ethnic identities, individual egotism, and religious and secular fundamentalisms (Fatton 1995).

In Africa, for purely historical and communal reasons, civil society is perceived in a manner different from that in Western societies, or in the rest of the Third World, for that matter. Due particularly to Africa's historically low levels of industrialization, most African countries did not develop extensive economic and social class systems or powerful associational groups whose interests or identities were separate from or opposed to the African state and its leaders. At the same time, however, Africans have always exhibited the capacity to come together to address their local problems wherever and whenever they have been allowed the political latitude to do so (USAID 1994).

On the whole, the vast majority of Africans have been excluded from participation in matters related to national affairs since the patri-

monial state rendered any form of associational activities as impracti-
cal and improbable. Indeed, through coercion, manipulation, and control, the components of civil society have been denied the necessary
autonomy to be effective as a countervailing mechanism to state
power. Due to the weakness of restraining institutions in African patrimonial states, there is little chance of stopping a political leader's use
of coercion, manipulation, and control of the forces of civil society
(Cartwright 1983). Beyond that, there is also the contention that civil
society does not always embrace the peaceful harmony of associational
pluralism (Lemarchand 1992). It is argued by Fatton (1995) that "civil
society in Africa is conflict-ridden and prone to Hobbesian wars of all
against all. It is the prime repository of 'invented' ethnic hierarchies,
conflicting class visions, patriarchal domination and irredentist identities fuelling deadly conflicts in many areas of the continent."

However, assuming that a vibrant civil society will possess the values and the social power to impel a responsive, democratic, and capable state along the road to egalitarian development (Sandbrook 1993),
the challenge therefore is how civil society can be activated and em-
powered in Africa as a key component of the region's democratic
transition. Undoubtedly, such a task will be a lengthy process. It will
take years, for example, just to reorient thinking toward the proven
idea that the state itself benefits in many practical ways from a broad-
based and vibrant civil society. Beyond accomplishing that, both sets
of actors—state and civil associations—would need to engage themselves in efforts aimed at promoting and organizing a vibrant civil
society.

With respect to civil associations, they must themselves be able to
put in place internal democratic procedures and eliminate all forms of
discrimination and inequalities based solely on gender, ethnicity, and
status (Sandbrook 1993). In addition, all civil associations should
strive to develop independent means of support for their activities,
which would further allow them to distance themselves from, and
strengthen their role as a counterweight to, the state. In this latter
regard, civil associations with similar objectives and ideals should
come together and form umbrella groups through which they can pool
their scarce resources to achieve their goals. Moreover, individual
shortcomings would be overcome under the rubric of a group.

It has also been advocated that networking between civil associations enhances their ability to shape government policy. For example,

Clark (1991) has argued that "building up strong networks of similar NGOs and projects can help to overcome any sense of isolation and provide useful forums for learning skills and exchanging techniques." Such networks can be strengthened by external donors who can target their resources toward enhancing how associations interact with each other and their impact on "distributional" issues (Woods 1994). However, there are limits to such assistance, which can also have negative effects. Consequently, the donor community would be well advised not to make a regular practice of bypassing the state to empower civil society as against the state. Such practices may breed suspicions and hamper attempts to reconcile the relationship between the state and civil society in Africa. In effect, it is essential that donors know when to "back off" and refrain from either providing assistance or providing too much of it. This is also important for maintaining the autonomy of African civil associations and for removing the risk of those associations' being perceived as donor creations or donor agents (Barkan and Ottaway 1994).

In terms of the state, there needs to be fundamental acceptance by political leaders and bureaucrats that a vibrant civil society is a vital instrument for complementing a responsive state in the accomplishment of its tasks. A robust associational life supplements the role of political parties in stimulating political participation, increasing the political efficacy and skill of citizens, and promoting an understanding as well as an appreciation of the rights of democratic citizenship (Diamond 1994).

Following on that, the state would need to retreat from coercive behavior and reduce its bureaucracy so as to extend the space for associational activities and create new opportunities for political involvement by previously excluded groups (Healey and Robinson 1992). More particularly, the state would need to offer incentives so that civil associations may become engaged in national affairs in a most vibrant way. Such incentives should include, among other things, clear policy statements that recognize the rights and role of civil society in consolidating and maintaining democracy; the scheduling of regular meetings and consultations between political leaders, the state bureaucracy, and civil associations; and enhanced opportunities for civil associations to make representations and submissions before political leaders, the state bureaucracy, and public institutions at the national, regional, and local levels.

Restructuring the Nation-State

It is the position of the GCA that: (a) existing national boundaries should be respected in accordance with the Organization of African Unity (OAU) charter; (b) balanced growth should be ensured in order to avoid internal conflicts; (c) regional cooperation and integration can reduce interstate conflicts and should therefore be emphasized; (d) the nation-state should pursue cultural equality so that its members, although coming from different ethnic backgrounds, will feel that they are guaranteed equal rights; (e) political power should be shared fairly among all communities, and wealth and resources for development should be equitably redistributed; and (f) a decentralized political, administrative, and fiscal structure is regarded as most essential in creating a sense of fairness and belonging.

The challenge of restructuring the nation-state in Africa is indeed a formidable one although a necessary prerequisite for growth and development in Africa. African states are characterized by, among other things, their centralized nature and their unequal distribution of income. Decentralization of power and financial resources to local governments, and attempts to redistribute income, are therefore important goals. Likewise, regional cooperation and integration are essential to the individual and collective growth and prosperity of African countries. In a world economy marked by the existence of large trading blocks, regional integration would enable Africa to project itself as a large and important destination for trade and investment and also to take advantage of economies of scale offered by a larger market and increased competition (Amoako 1996).

However, progress on regional integration in Africa has been very slow, particularly hampered by counterdemands from potential member states. In May 1994, the treaty on the establishment of the African Economic Community came into force and there is now renewed hope that this attempt at regional integration would be fully implemented in the future as a way of responding to the regionalizing world political economy. Moreover, regional integration has the potential to narrow the various gaps between Africa and the rest of the world's economy as well as among African countries. In the latter case, this also has the potential to reduce or eliminate conflicts between African states. Regional integration promotes industrialization and it is a key element in the quest for reducing Africa's external dependence (Kayira 1993).

Africa's leaders now need to renew their commitment to the achievement of this important goal.

Culture, Values, and Africa's Perception of the World

The GCA has taken the view that there is a need for Africans to overcome a philanthropic vision of the world and develop a better understanding of the mechanisms that govern the world as a necessary condition for the continent's competitiveness; that cultural heritage and values should be harnessed for national development while at the same time creating the right environment to enable Africa to get the best out of her people so as to foster a sense of pride, patriotism, and nationalism; and there should be the promotion of Africa's cultural renaissance through a generalized use of local languages and the development of a continental African language, the teaching of African history, and the recovery of Africa's technological memory.

Undoubtedly, the promotion of cultural values and heritage is a noble idea. To the extent that such values and heritage are consistent with the development process and do not lead to ethnic conflicts or insularity, they should be enthusiastically supported. Essentially, as long as cultural values and attitudes release the creative capacity of Africans, it augurs well for the development process. Cultures are better or worse depending on the degree to which they support innate human capacities as they emerge. At the same time, the creative capacity of human beings is at the heart of the development process. Development happens through the human ability to imagine, theorize, conceptualize, innovate, articulate, organize, manage, solve problems, and do other things with the mind and hands that contribute to the progress of the individual and of humankind (Harrison 1985). Several factors, including climate, natural resources, and government policies, influence the direction and pace of progress. However, the key factor is human creative capacity, as has been demonstrated in the East Asian countries (Naya and McCleery 1994).

With respect to the need for Africans to overcome a philanthropic vision of the world, this is quite consistent with the push for a more self-reliant development. Indeed, one of the fundamental weaknesses of African development policy is that it is too dependent on external forces. The reality of change from external dependence to reliance on local initiatives is also a function of the fact that the rather static quality of African development policy has been superseded by changing global realities, leading to what has now come to be regarded as the marginalization of the continent (Shaw and Inegbedion 1994). Those global realities, including the end of the Cold War, have shifted around the security and economic interests of the industrialized nations, which in turn has led to massive reductions in the foreign assistance made available to Africa.

Africa, therefore, has no other choice but to embark on a path of sustainable local, national, regional, and continental self-reliance that is market-oriented. Past attempts at non-market-oriented self-reliance, such as *Ujaama* socialism in Tanzania, have been grand failures and have long since been discredited (Ayittey 1994a). The challenge here is very clear: African countries must develop and implement market-oriented, self-reliant policies in the interest of their own survival. The new world order suggests that nothing short of that will do. Ironically, such a situation, consonant with marginality, allows for a new creativity and the redefinition of sustainable and democratic development as determined by local peoples rather than foreign entities (Shaw and Inegbedion 1994).

The need to embark on a market-oriented, self-reliant approach cannot be overstressed. Africa's prospects for growth and development lie in such an approach. Moreover, it is necessary to reverse the continent's decline and marginalization.[7] It has been argued by Shaw and Inegbedion (1994), for example, that Africa's decline has reduced it to "Fourth World" status comprising most of the least developed countries and, with the possible exception of South Africa, without any newly industrializing countries (NICs) or even near-NICs. Certainly, such a state of affairs needs to be rectified with some urgency.

Capacity Building

Africa is recognized by the GCA as being behind other regions of the world with respect to skills. Consequently, it is necessary to prioritize needs and develop skills in areas that will catapult the continent into the twenty-first century. In this regard, the retention of skilled individuals is imperative. In addition, the importance of education, at all levels, for national development should be emphasized through the implementation of appropriate national educational policies that are allocated adequate resources.

Capacity is central to African development. It is the combination of human resources and institutions that permits countries to achieve their development goals. "It engenders self-reliance that comes with the ability of people to make choices and take actions to achieve the objectives they set themselves. This entails the ability to identify and analyze problems, formulate solutions and implement them" (World Bank 1996).

Capacity building in Africa is important because, among other things, it generates the capability for those countries to develop indigenous and self-reliant development policies. Moreover, it means the development of the relevant skills without which Africa would be unable to transform its agriculture, effectively link its industrialization with its natural resource base, and become scientifically and technologically advanced. In addition, a skills base would emerge for establishing linkages and complementarities among the production sectors, serving as an effective domestic catalyst for growth and socioeconomic development, and following strategies that are most appropriate to the continent's needs and realities.

Furthermore, the quality of policy analysis, formulation, and implementation depends, in part, on the existence of a substantial and appropriately organized pool of skilled individuals in both the private and public sectors. If that resource does not exist or becomes dissipated, it is very difficult to find people for such tasks who are sufficiently experienced. Furthermore, putting a policy capacity in place is a first order of business, to be inevitably accompanied by more protracted efforts to build even greater capacity. Robust capacity building may also have a long-term payoff for broader institutional development, since it strengthens critical information systems, training, and implementation capacity, and also contributes to the accumulation of staff skills and experience (Lamb 1987).

African governments have a particularly important responsibility for capacity building. Rather than donors, African governments should be providing vision and taking the initiative in implementing means of overcoming gaps in national capacity (World Bank 1996). When capacity is lacking, development policy cannot be adequately implemented.

Science and Technology

It is the view of the GCA that due to the dominance of science and technology in this and the next century, African countries need to bring science and technology to the center of the development endeavor as a part of the political agenda. In that regard, general education of the population, and, in particular, science education during the early stages of the education system, is an important means of inculcating science and technology culture in the general population.

The areas of priority are deemed to be: (a) food and nutrition security—which is not limited to production but includes preservation, and diversification and transformation of staples to different products. It also involves the formulation of appropriate pricing and marketing policies and radical changes in extension services; (b) health security—the rich biological resources that have an enormous potential for the development of pharmaceutical industries and the use of biotechnology as a basis for expanding into new industries, including agroindustries; (c) water—although Africa is rich in natural resources it is water poor and water is going to be a major problem in the future; and (d) population management, the management of the rapid growth of the population.

In all of the above four priority areas, the role of women is viewed as critical. Consequently, the education of women must be given special attention. Science and technology have often been neglected in African development policy. This has led to considerable dependence on external sources for food, medicine, nutrition programs, technology, and so on. African universities and research centers are totally delinked from the productive and marketing sectors and attempts must now be made to forge useful links among them. This is an imperative given the context of self-reliance and the necessity for the use of environmentally sound and appropriate technology suited to local circumstances.

Environmentally sound and appropriate technology refers, in general, to production methods that are less damaging to the environment than previously used methods, consume less energy and fewer resources, and recycle wastes or handle them more acceptably. The idea of appropriate technology must be seen in terms of demand (basic needs goals) and supply (the appropriate production processes). There is an urgent need for the harmonization of these two factors to bring about the management and production techniques that are best suited to the resources and future development potential of the individual African countries. Such technology should contribute to sustainable development (Hope 1996c).

Technological decisions and the pace of technical change affect all development processes and, in turn, are affected by them. The various combinations and proportions in which labor, material resources, and capital are used influence not only the type and quantity of goods and services produced, but also the distribution of their benefits and the prospects for overall growth. The significance of technological choices made in the course of development extends beyond economics to social structure and political processes as well. The growing interest in finding and implementing appropriate technologies reflects an implicit, if not always explicit, recognition of the essential role of technology in sustainable development policy (Hope 1996c).

Because the use of any particular technology is not an end in itself, the criteria of appropriateness for the choice of technology must be found in the goals of sustainable development. These goals are concerned not only with the volumes of output and income generated by a country's economy but also with the way they are produced and distributed among the population. Hence, sustainable development would be unachievable if technology is insufficient in quantity and inappropriate in quality. Consequently, the acquisition of technology in Africa must be limited to appropriate technology.

Economic Performance and Reform

The economies of Africa must perform better and be more competitive. To accomplish that, the GCA advocates that Africa improve and increase its domestic resource mobilization; create productive employment; give priority to developing the agricultural sector while at the same time recognizing the linkage between agriculture and industry and promoting industrial development as the engine for growth in the long term; adequately address the debt problem; create an enabling environment to encourage savings and investment; and use human resources as the basis for improving economic performance. The achievement of these goals would require that governments be efficient, accountable, legitimate, and serviced by an efficient and professional bureaucracy guided by known public policies.

Africa's economic performance can best be improved through the harnessing of market forces. Markets are not perfect. However, when they are free of distortions, they are the most efficient mechanism for mobilizing and allocating scarce resources for poverty-reducing socioeconomic development (Amoako 1996). Moreover, the alternatives—

state planning and intervention in economic affairs—have been disastrous for Africa and are directly linked to the continent's economic crisis.

The harnessing of market forces in Africa has the potential to, among other things, increase private investment, including foreign direct investment, which in turn would create employment opportunities. Prudent fiscal and monetary policies would need to be pursued to reduce or eliminate budget deficits and generally to restore macroeconomic balance and economic confidence. In those African countries that have harnessed market forces and engaged in prudent fiscal and monetary policies, economic performance has been good and, in some instances, even spectacular. Examples are Ghana and Botswana, respectively.

African governments have accumulated huge budget deficits during the past two decades, due in part to parasitic public enterprises, weak fiscal management, questionable expenditures on projects, and misplaced socioeconomic development priorities. Public enterprises, in particular, have been a drain on African treasuries. They operate at a loss; they do not pay taxes; they have yielded a very low rate of return on the large amount of resources invested in them; their cash flows do not even cover running costs; and their operating costs are covered by transfers from government budgets and the banking system.

The consequences of excessive fiscal deficits include inflation, the crowding out of private investment, debt burdens, balance-of-payments difficulties, and low levels of domestic savings, primarily as a result of public dis-saving. Increasing public saving (reducing the deficit) is the only policy measure known to be effective in raising national savings (Easterly and Schmidt-Hebbel 1994), and that, in turn, makes resources available for investment and reduces the need for external borrowing.

The need for African nations to reduce their debt is an obvious conclusion. Debt reduction is necessary for the recovery and resumption of growth in Africa (Amoako 1996). The magnitude of Africa's debt is simply not now sustainable. By 1994, the long-term debt of sub-Saharan Africa as percentage of GNP was approximately 65 percent and as a percentage of exports it exceeded 254 percent.[8] Servicing this debt requires not only an increase in future revenues, but in effect those revenues must be raised in foreign currency since the debt is overwhelmingly denominated in U.S. dollars or other foreign currencies. A few African governments enjoy direct ownership of exportable products, such as minerals. However, most governments are unable to raise revenues directly in foreign currency. Instead, unless they can borrow further abroad, they must buy the foreign currency directly or indirectly from exporters (Little et al. 1993). Since it is unlikely that the majority of African countries would be able to grow their way out of their debt crisis, creditors should consider the possibility of offering them debt relief or extending existing debt relief measures. This ought to be done on a case-by-case basis to benefit only those countries that have made sustained progress in economic and political liberalization.

Natural Resources and Environment

The GCA has enunciated a general principle that Africa must not only exploit its natural resources for export but must also begin to strengthen its processing and production of finished products in the continent. The mining industry is seen as an example in this respect. African countries are also required to balance development with proper protection and conservation of the environment since sustainable development can only be ensured if it is environmentally sound.

Environmental degradation remains a major concern in Africa. Forest cover, estimated at 679 million hectares in 1980, has been diminishing at a rate of 2.9 million hectares per year; the rate of deforestation has been increasing; about 50 percent of the farmland in sub-Saharan Africa is affected by soil degradation and erosion; and as much as 80 percent of Africa's pasture and range areas show signs of degradation (Cleaver and Schreiber 1994). Degraded soils lose their productive capability with significant negative consequences on vegetation. Also, degradation and destruction of forests have a severe impact on wildlife habitat and biodiversity. It is estimated that 64 percent of the original wildlife habitat in sub-Saharan Africa has already been lost (Cleaver and Schreiber 1994).

In the twenty-first century, environmental management will assume even greater importance around the world and Africa will come under increasing pressure to put its environmental house in order. All African countries should therefore prepare environmental action plans (EAPs) which take into consideration not only their own unique circumstances related to pollution, deforestation, agriculture, population growth, conservation, and so on, but also international requirements like the need to phase out the use of ozone-depleting substances such as chlorofluorocarbons (CFCs) as stipulated in the Montreal Protocol on Substances that Deplete the Ozone Layer. By the year 2025, for example, emissions of CFCs in Africa are projected to be 12 percent of the world's total, compared to 2 percent in the Middle East, 8 percent in Latin America, and 16 percent in South East Asia (Hope 1996d).

One factor that African governments must take into consideration in the preparation of their EAPs is the participation of local communities and environmental and/or conservation groups. Without such participation, environmental management and conservation programs would not stir people to action. Instead, such programs are likely to be either ignored or resisted. The Botswana government, for example, has encountered resistance from the Basarwa peoples in the Kalahari desert region over their removal from land that the government has designated as a game reserve. The Basarwa claim that they are being moved from their natural and ancestral habitat without prior and appropriate consultation. However, it is the government's position that the Basarwa peoples are being settled in areas where they would now have access to schools, health facilities, and so on, while at the same time their original habitat would be preserved for the area's wildlife and for ecotourism.

The Role of Government

The GCA regards the role of government as particularly important in defining a new vision for Africa. This is so because governments are needed to change laws and regulations to implement various aspects of the new vision; to provide budgetary allocations to finance the implementation of the new vision; and to take executive action for all phases of adoption and implementation of programs based on the national long-term vision.

Since government represents the legal instrument through which these things are to be accomplished, the role of government is indeed important in the process of implementing this new vision and long-term perspective thinking. African governments would also have to play major roles in negotiations and discussions with regional organizations such as the OAU, the United Nations Economic Commission for Africa (UNECA), and the African Development Bank (AfDB). In addition, African governments would be required to reach out to all stakeholders, including the citizenry and civil associations, to guarantee as much nongovernmental participation as possible to garner popular support for the adoption and implementation of the new development agenda.

Following from the experiences of the East Asian countries, African governments must not only set forth the long-term vision for development, but must also establish a rule of law that is simple and transparent, develop and implement good macroeconomic policies, avoid unnecessary intervention in the marketplace, and develop effective public/private-sector cooperation.

Conclusions

It is undisputed that Africa needs to develop a new shared vision of its future that embraces economic and political liberalization as well as regional cooperation and integration. Improving policies alone can boost growth substantially, but if neighboring countries adopt a policy change together, the effects on growth would be more than double what they would be with one country acting alone (Easterly and Levine 1995).

The postcolonial interventionist state has been a major disaster for Africa, and Africa's ensuing decline and marginalization are nothing short of a major tragedy. Moving from decline and marginalization to progress toward ending absolute poverty and improving the human condition, for example, will come neither on its own nor from outside the region. The challenges on the road to Africa's development have to be overcome in Africa itself (Amoako 1996).

In that respect, the GCA should be commended for putting forward a sober vision and strategy for responding to the continent's crisis. The challenge of policy reform and change is never an easy task to address. However, there now seems to be an emerging consensus on Africa's critical path to revitalization for the twenty-first century. Of course, the most significant variable influencing the outcomes is the extent to which the current and subsequent political leadership would be committed to the goals and vision of this type of initiative.

Policy reform and change are of crucial importance in Africa. But so also are the political processes from which those policy reform and change choices emerge, are implemented, and are sustained. Undoubtedly, politics has been an obstacle to development in postindependence Africa (Killick 1993). This book has amply demonstrated that bad governance has been bad for the development process in Africa. Consequently, if the vision for the twenty-first century is to be realized, Africa's leaders will need to display a new political resolve to disengage from authoritarian or other nondemocratic systems of personal rule, and to dismantle bureaucratic obstacles to policy reform and change. Then, and only then, can such policy reform and change take hold to reverse the continent's tragic decline and its accompanying negative consequences.

Finally, some brief comments on the relevance of the Asian development experience to Africa. It has been pointed out by Naya and McCleery (1994) that the currently dynamic economies of Singapore, South Korea, and Taiwan were also considered hopeless after World War II. The lessons of their development experience suggest that African countries should not be written off as "basket cases." Just as Asians have been able to turn around former basket cases into dynamic centers of growth and prosperity, Africans face the challenge of putting their abundant resources to work in realizing their own visions of development and progress.

Unlocking Africa's potential requires effective policy reform and change as discussed above. Complementary to that, the Asian development experience suggests that there are ten critical policy areas for sustainable development (Naya and McCleery 1994). These are (a) macroeconomic stability; (b) agricultural development; (c) human resource development; (d) mobilization of savings, development of financial intermediation, and incentives for productive investment; (e) outward orientation and attraction of foreign direct investment; (f) effective management of foreign exchange resources and incentives to potential producers of foreign exchange; (g) proper sequencing of structural adjustment policies; (h) institutional capacity building and attention to the problem of governance; (i) development of the information sector; and (j) encouragement of a dynamic private sector working in cooperation with government toward a societywide vision of development.

Notes

1. This was equivalent to approximately 234 percent of their export income.
2. The continent's share of foreign direct investment has declined considerably since 1989 and was at 3 percent for the period 1988–93. See Sader (1995).
3. Africa is the only region in the world whose poverty is projected to rise over the next decade.

4. The Global Coalition for Africa (GCA) is a unique body that provides an informal high-level political forum for organizing a new partnership between Africa and the donor community. Launched in 1991, it provides the framework for a broad consultative process, for a policy dialogue involving, at different stages and at national and international levels, distinguished thinkers and decision makers from among leaders of African governments, the private sector, the nongovernmental organizations active in the region, and the international donor community. The ultimate objective of this body is to be a means of assisting action by African governments to achieve economic growth, poverty alleviation, and social progress, and an effective instrument for mobilizing international support for Africa. The GCA supports the efforts of African countries in designing and implementing their own economic and social policies and programs, improving governance, and fostering popular participation. See GCA (1992) and Pronk (1995).

5. Derived from ACDESS (1996).

6. A formula definition of patrimonialism offered by Dia (1993) is: Patrimonialism = monopoly power + discretion – accountability – transparency.

7. Africa is now the most marginal of the Third World regions in terms of economic, military, technological, and skilled labor resources. See Shaw and Inegbedion (1994) and Sandbrook (1993).

8. Since 1990 the arrears on this debt have doubled and were approximately U.S.$53.2 billion in 1994.

References

Abugre, Charles. 1993. "When Credit is Not Due—Financial Services by NGOs in Africa." *Small Enterprise Development* 4 (4): 24–33.

Adamchak, Donald J., and Michael T. Mbizvo. 1993. "Structural and Attitudinal Change: Fertility Decline in Zimbabwe." *Genus* 49 (3–4): 101–13.

Adamolekun, Ladipo. 1991. "Promoting African Decentralization." *Public Administration and Development* 11 (3): 285–91.

Adamolekun, Ladipo, and Coralie Bryant. 1994. *Governance Progress Report: The Africa Region Experience.* Washington, DC: World Bank.

Adams, Dale W., and Delbert A. Fotchett, eds. 1992. *Informal Finance in Low-Income Countries.* Boulder, CO: Westview Press.

Adedeji, Adebayo. 1991. *Preparing Africa for the Twenty-First Century: Agenda for the 1990s.* Addis Ababa, Ethiopia: United Nations Economic Commisssion for Africa.

———. 1995. "The Challenge of Pluralism, Democracy, Governance and Development." *The Courier,* no. 150 (March–April): 93–95.

Adediji, Oyeniran. 1991. "Role of Government in Bureaucratic Corruption: The Case of the Politicization of the Civil Service." *Quarterly Journal of Administration* 25 (2): 208–19.

African Center for Development and Strategic Studies (ACDESS). 1996. *Bulletin* (January): 3–6.

African Development Bank (AfDB). 1993. *Economic Integration in Southern Africa: Volumes 1–3.* Abidjan, Côte d'Ivoire: African Development Bank.

Alatas, Syed Hussein. 1990. *Corruption: Its Nature, Causes and Functions.* Aldershot: Avebury.

Alderman, Harold. 1994. "Ghana: Adjustment's Star Pupil?" in *Adjusting to Policy Failure in African Economies,* ed. David E. Sahn. Ithaca, NY: Cornell University Press.

Aloki, A. Otshomampita. 1989. "Rural Development in Sub-Saharan Africa: A Different View of Political and Administrative Decentralization." *International Review of Administrative Sciences* 55 (3): 401–32.

Alpers, Edward A. 1995. "Africa Reconfigured: Presidential Address to the 1994 African Studies Association Annual Meeting." *African Studies Review* 38 (2): 1–10.

Amoako, Kingsley Y. 1996. "Africa: Development Challenges of the Twenty-

First Century." Paper presented to the Conference of African Ministers of Planning and UNDP Resident Representatives in the Africa Region, Ouagadougou, Burkina Faso, January 30–31.

Amuwo, Kunle. 1986. "Military-Inspired Anti-Bureaucratic Corruption Campaigns: An Appraisal of Niger's Experience." *The Journal of Modern African Studies* 24 (2): 285–301.

Anarfi, John K. 1993. "Sexuality, Migration and AIDS in Ghana: A Socio-Behavioral Study." *Health Transition Review* 3 (Supplement): 45–67.

Anderson, David. 1994. *Toward a More Effective Policy Response to AIDS.* Liège, Belgium: International Union for the Scientific Study of Population.

Andreski, Stanislav. 1968. *The African Predicament: A Study in the Pathology of Modernization.* London: Michael Joeseph.

Anyanwu, J. C., and U. B. Uwatt. 1993. "Banking for the Poor: The Case of the People's Bank of Nigeria." *African Review of Money, Finance and Banking* 1: 87–103.

Aredo, Dejene. 1993. "The Iddir: A Study of an Indigenous Informal Financial Institution in Ethiopia." *Savings and Development* 17 (1): 77–90.

Armstrong, Jill. 1991. "Socio-economic Implications of AIDS in Developing Countries." *Finance and Development* 28 (4): 14–17.

———. 1995. *Uganda's AIDS Crisis: Its Implications for Development.* Discussion Paper 298. Washington, DC: World Bank.

Aryeetey, Ernest, and William F. Steel. 1995. "Savings Collectors and Financial Intermediation in Ghana." *Savings and Development* 19 (2): 191–212.

Avina, Jeffrey, 1993. "The Evolutionary Life Cycles of Non-Governmental Development Organizations." *Public Administration and Development* 13 (5): 453–74.

Ayee, Joseph R. A. 1994. *An Anatomy of Public Policy Implementation: The Case of Decentralization Policies in Ghana.* Aldershot: Avebury.

Ayeni, Victor. 1987. "Nigeria's Bureaucratized Ombudsman System: An Insight into the Problem of Bureaucratization in a Developing Country." *Public Administration and Development* 7 (3): 309–24.

———. 1994. "The Ombudsman's Statistics: On Data-Gathering and Management in the Enforcement of Public Accountability in Africa." *International Review of Administrative Sciences* 60 (1): 55–70.

Ayittey, George B. N. 1989. "Why Can't Africa Feed Itself?" *International Health and Development* 1 (2): 18–21.

———. 1992. *Africa Betrayed.* New York: St. Martin's Press.

———. 1994a. "The Failure of Development Planning in Africa" in Boettke 1994.

———. 1994b. "Aid for Black Elephants: How Foreign Assistance Has Failed Africa" in *Perpetuating Poverty: The World Bank, the IMF, and the Developing World,* ed. Doug Bandow and Ian Vásquez. Washington, DC: Cato Institute.

Baker, Jonathan, and Paul Ove Pedersen, eds. 1992. *The Rural-Urban Interface in Africa: Expansion and Adaptation.* Uppsala: Scandinavian Institute of African Studies.

Balassa, Bela. 1989. *A Conceptual Framework for Adjustment Policies,* Working Paper no. 139. Washington, DC: World Bank.

Balogun, M. Jide. 1989. "The Role of Management Training Institutions in Developing the Capacity for Economic Recovery and Long-Term Growth in Africa" in *Economic Restructuring and African Public Administration,* ed. M. Jide Balogun and Gelase Mutahaba. West Hartford, CT: Kumarian Press.

Banio, G. Adegboyega. 1994. "Deregulation of Urban Public Transport Services." *Third World Planning Review* 16 (4): 411–28.

Bank of Botswana. 1994. *Annual Report 1993.* Gaborone, Botswana: Bank of Botswana.

Baregu, Mwesiga. 1994. "The Rise and Fall of the One-Party State in Tanzania" in Widner 1994.

Barkan, Joel D., and Marina Ottaway. 1994. "Democratization and Civil Society." Paper prepared for the Democracy Roundtable Series, Overseas Development Council, Washington, DC, May 24.

Barnett, Tony, and Piers Blaikie. 1992. *AIDS in Africa: Its Present and Future Impact.* London: Bellhaven Press.

Barnum, Howard, and Joseph Kutzin. 1993. *Public Hospitals in Developing Countries: Resource Use, Cost, Financing.* Baltimore: Johns Hopkins University Press.

Bates, Robert H. 1981. *Markets and States in Tropical Africa.* Berkeley: University of California Press.

———. 1994. "The Impulse to Reform in Africa" in Widner 1994.

Bates, Robert H., and Paul Collier. 1995. "The Politics and Economics of Policy Reform in Zambia." *Journal of African Economies* 4 (1): 115–43.

Bayart, Jean-Francois. 1986. "Civil Society in Africa" in Chabal 1986.

———. 1993. *The State in Africa: The Politics of the Belly.* London: Longman.

Becker, C. 1990. "The Demo-Economic Impact of the AIDS Pandemic in Sub-Saharan Africa." *World Development* 18 (4): 1599–1619.

Bell, Stuart W. 1995. *Sharing the Wealth: Privatization through Broad-Based Ownership Strategies.* Discussion Paper no. 285. Washington, DC: World Bank.

Berg, Elliot, et al. 1981. *Accelerated Development in Sub-Saharan Africa.* Washington, DC: World Bank.

Berkley, Seth, Peter Piot, and Doris Schopper. 1994. "AIDS: Invest Now or Pay More Later." *Finance and Development* 31 (2): 40–43.

Bernstein, Boris, and James M. Boughton. 1993. *Adjusting to Development: The IMF and the Poor.* Washington, DC: IMF.

Binswanger, Hans P., and Pierre Landell-Mills. 1995. *The World Bank's Strategy for Reducing Poverty and Hunger: A Report to the Development Community.* Washington, DC: World Bank.

Bird, Richard M., and Susan Horton. 1989. Introduction in *Government Policy and the Poor in Developing Countries,* ed. Richard M. Bird and Susan Horton. Toronto: University of Toronto Press.

Birdsall, Nancy. 1980. *Population and Poverty in the Developing World.* Staff Working Paper no. 404, Washington, DC: World Bank.

Birdsall, Nancy, and Estelle James. 1993. "Efficiency and Equity in Social Spending: How and Why Governments Misbehave" in *Including the Poor,* ed. Michael Lipton and Jacques Van Der Gaag. Washington, DC: World Bank.

Blomstrom, Magnus, and Mats Lundahl, eds. 1993. *Economic Crisis in Africa: Perspectives on Policy Responses.* London: Routledge.

Blunt, Peter, and Merrick L. Jones. 1992. *Managing Organizations in Africa.* New York: Walter de Gruyter.

Boeninger, Edgardo. 1991. "Governance and Development: Issues and Constraints" in Summers and Shah 1991.

Boer, J. H. 1995. "Re-engineering the Consultative Process Between Industry, Labor and Government Trade Authorities in South Africa." *International Review of Administrative Sciences* 61 (3): 343–54.

Boettke, Peter J., ed. 1994. *The Collapse of Development Planning.* New York: New York University Press.

Bongaarts, John. 1988. *Modelling the Spread of HIV and the Demographic Impact of AIDS in Africa.* New York: The Population Council.

———. 1995. "Global and Regional Population Projections to 2025" in *Population and Food in the Early Twenty-First Century: Meeting Future Food Demand of an Increasing Population,* ed. Nurul Islam. Washington, DC: International Food Policy Research Institute.

Borins, Sandford. 1994. *Government in Transition: A New Paradigm in Public Administration.* A Report on the Inaugural Conference of CAPAM. Toronto: Commonwealth Association of Public Administration and Management.

———. 1995. "The New Public Management Is Here to Stay." *Canadian Public Administration* 38 (1): 122–32.

Boston, J. 1991. "The Theoretical Underpinnings of Public Sector Restructuring in New Zealand" in *Reshaping the State: New Zealand's Bureaucratic Revolution,* ed. J. Boston et al. Auckland: Oxford University Press.

Botswana National Productivity Center (BNPC). 1994. *Productivity Improvement in the Workplace: Management Training Programs 1994.* Gaborone, Botswana: BNPC.

Bouman, F. J. A. 1995. "ROSCA: On the Origin of the Species." *Savings and Development* 19 (2): 117–48.

Boutros-Ghali, Boutros. 1995. "Democracy: A Newly Recognized Imperative." *Global Governance* 1 (1): 3–11.

Bratton, Michael, and Donald Rothchild. 1992. "The Institutional Bases of Governance in Africa" in Hyden and Bratton 1992.

Bratton, Michael, and Nicolas van de Walle. 1992. "Toward Governance in Africa: Popular Demands and State Responses" in Hyden and Bratton 1992.

Brennan, Ellen M. 1993. "Urban Land and Housing Issues Facing the Third World" in Kasarda and Parnell 1993.

Brett, E. A. 1996. "The Participatory Principle in Development Projects: The Costs and Benefits of Cooperation." *Public Administration and Development* 16 (1): 5–19.

Briscoe, John. 1992. "Poverty and Water Supply: How to Move Forward." *Finance and Development* 29 (4): 16–19.

Bromley, Ray. 1993. "Small Enterprise Promotion as an Urban Development Strategy" in Kasarda and Parnell 1993.

Broomberg, Jonathan, et al. 1993. "The Economic Impact of the AIDS Epidemic in South Africa" in Cross and Whiteside 1993.

Brownsberger, William N. 1983. "Development and Governmental Corruption: Materialism and Political Fragmentation in Nigeria." *The Journal of Modern African Studies,* 21 (2): 215–33.

Bryceson, Deborah Fahy. 1996. "Deagrarianization and Rural Employment in Sub-Saharan Africa: A Sectoral Perspective." *World Development* 24 (1): 97–111.

Business Focus (1995), no. 2 (July): 24.

Buvinić, Mayra, and Margaret A. Lycette. 1988. "Women, Poverty, and Development in the Third World" in Lewis and Contributors 1988.

Byrne, Denis, et al. 1995. "Strategic Management in the Irish Civil Service: A Review Drawing on Experience in New Zealand and Australia." *Administration* 43 (2): 5–150.

Cabral, A. Jorge R. 1993. "AIDS in Africa: Can the Hospitals Cope?" *Health Policy and Planning* 8 (2): 157–60.

Caldwell, John C., Pat Caldwell, and Pat Quiggin. 1989. "The Social Context of AIDS in Sub-Sarahan Africa." *Population and Development Review* 15 (2): 185–234.

Caldwell, John C., et al. 1993. "African Families and AIDS: Context, Reactions and Potential Interventions." *Health Transition Review* 3 (Supplement): 1–16.

Caldwell, John C., and Pat Caldwell. 1994. "The Neglect of an Epidemiological Explanation for the Distribution of HIV/AIDS in Sub-Sahran Africa: Exploring the Male Circumcision Hypothesis." *Health Transition Review* 4 (Supplement): 23–46.

Callaghy, Thomas M. 1986. "Politics and Vision in Africa: The Interplay of Domination, Equality and Liberty" in Chabal 1986.

————. 1994. "State, Choice, and Context: Comparative Reflections on Reform and Intractability" in *Political Development and the New Realism in Sub-Saharan Africa,* ed. David Apter and Carl G. Rosberg. Charlottesville, VA: University Press of Virginia.

Callaghy, Thomas M., and John Ravenhill, eds. 1993. *Hemmed In: Responses to Africa's Economic Decline.* New York: Columbia University Press.

Campbell, Eugene K., and Tidimane Ntsabane. Forthcoming. *Street Children in Gaborone, Botswana: Causes and Policy Implications.* Dakar, Senegal: Union for African Population Studies.

Canadian International Development Agency (CIDA). 1990. *The Water Utilization Project: A Case Study on a Water and Health Education Project.* Ottawa: CIDA.

Cartwright, J. 1983. *Political Leadership in Africa.* London: Croom Helm.

Castells, Manuel, and Alejandro Portes. 1989. "World Underneath: The Origins, Dynamics, and Effects of the Informal Economy" in *The Informal Economy: Studies in Advanced and Less Developed Countries,* ed. Alejandro Portes, Manuel Castells, and Lauren A. Benton. Baltimore: Johns Hopkins University Press.

Chabal, Patrick, ed. 1986. *Political Domination in Africa.* Cambridge: Cambridge University Press.

Charlton, Roger. 1990. "Exploring the Byways of African Political Corruption: Botswana and Deviant Case Analysis." *Corruption and Reform* 5 (1): 1–27.

Chaudhuri, Tamal Datta. 1989. "A Theoretical Analysis of the Informal Sector." *World Development* 17 (3): 351–55.

Chazan, Naomi. 1988. "State and Society in Africa: Images and Challenges" in Rothchild and Chazan 1988.

Chileshe, Jonathan H. 1992. *Nothing Wrong With Africa Except. . . .* New Delhi: Vikas Publishing House.

Christodoulou, N. T., Marie Kirsten, and Johan Badenhorst. 1993. "Financing South African Micro-entrepreneurs." Paper delivered at the International Council for Small Business Conference, Las Vegas, NV, June.

Clapham, Christopher. 1993. "Democratization in Africa: Obstacles and Prospects." *Third World Quarterly* 14 (3): 423–38.

Clark, John. 1991. *Democratizing Development: The Role of Voluntary Organizations.* West Hartford, CT: Kumarian Press.

Clarke, Laurence C. 1995. *The Financial Emergence of Southern Africa.* Gaborone, Botswana: Bank of Botswana.

Cleaver, Kevin M., and W. Graeme Donovan. 1995. *Agriculture, Poverty, and Policy Reform in Sub-Saharan Africa.* Washington, DC: World Bank.

Cleaver, Kevin M., and Gotz A. Schreiber. 1994. *Reversing the Spiral: The Population, Agriculture, and Environment Nexus in Sub-Sarahan Africa.* Washington, DC: World Bank.

Cochrane, Susan H. 1979. *Fertility and Education: What Do We Really Know?* Baltimore: Johns Hopkins University Press.

Cohen, John M. 1995. "Capacity Building in the Public Sector: A Focused Framework for Analysis and Action." *International Review of Administrative Sciences* 61 (3): 407–22.

Commonwealth Association for Public Administration and Management (CAPAM). 1995. "The New Public Administration: Global Challenges–Local Solutions." Malta Conference Theme Paper, *Commonwealth Innovations* 1 (2): 8–11.

Commonwealth Secretariat, ed. 1993. *Administrative and Managerial Reform in Government: A Commonwealth Portfolio of Current Good Practice.* London: Commonwealth Secretariat.

———. 1994. *Management of the Privatization Process: A Guide to Policy Making and Implementation.* London: Commonwealth Secretariat.

Contact Botswana. 1994. July 30: 1.

Conyers, Diana. 1986. "Future Directions in Development Studies: The Case of Decentralization." *World Development* 14 (5): 593–603.

Cornia, Giovanni Andrea, and Gerald K. Helleiner, eds. 1994. *From Adjustment to Development in Africa: Conflict, Controversy, Convergence, Consensus.* London: Macmillan.

Cremer, Jacques, Antonio Estache, and Paul Seabright. 1994. *The Decentralization of Public Services: Lessons from the Theory of the Firm,* Policy Research Working Paper 1345. Washington, DC: World Bank.

Crook, Richard C., and James Manor. 1995. "Democratic Decentralization and Institutional Performance: Four Asian and African Experiences Compared." *Journal of Commonwealth and Comparative Politics* 33 (3): 309–34.

Cross, Sholto, and Alan Whiteside, eds., 1993. *Facing Up to AIDS: The Socio-Economic Impact in Southern Africa.* New York: St. Martin's Press.

Cuddington, John T. 1986. *Capital Flight: Estimates, Issues, and Explanations.* Princeton: Princeton University Studies in International Finance no. 58.

Curry, Robert L. 1987. "Poverty and Mass Unemployment in Mineral-Rich Botswana." *American Journal of Economics and Sociology* 46 (1): 71–87.

Daily News. 1996. no. 45 (March 6):1.

Davidson, Basil. 1992. *The Black Man's Burden: Africa and the Curse of the Nation-State*. New York: Times Books.

de Abreu, António Pinto, and Ruy A. Baltazar. 1994. *The Role of the State and its Fiscal and Monetary Policies in the Successful Implementation of Reform Programmes*. Harare: Konrad Adenauer Foundation.

Decalo, Samuel. 1990. *Coups and Military Rule in Africa*. New Haven, CT: Yale University Press.

de Merode, Louis, and C. S. Thomas. 1994. "Implementing Civil Service Pay and Employment Reform in Africa: The Experiences of Ghana, the Gambia, and Guinea" in Lindauer and Nunberg 1994.

Demery, Lionel. 1994. "Structural Adjustment: Its Origins, Rationale and Achievements" in Cornia and Helleiner 1994.

de Soto, Hernando. 1989. *The Other Path: The Invisible Revolution in the Third World*. New York: Harper and Row.

Dey, Harendra Kanti. 1989. "The Genesis and Spread of Economic Corruption: A Microtheoretic Interpretation." *World Development* 17 (4): 503–11.

Dia, Mamadou. 1993. *A Governance Approach to Civil Service Reform in Sub-Saharan Africa*. Washington, DC: World Bank.

———. 1996. *Africa's Management in the 1990s and Beyond: Reconciling Indigenous and Transplanted Institutions*. Washington, DC: World Bank.

Diamond, Larry. 1994. "Rethinking Civil Society: Toward Democratic Consolidation." *Journal of Democracy* 5 (3): 4–17.

Doig, Alan. 1995. "Good Government and Sustainable Anti-Corruption Strategies: A Role for Independent Anti-Corruption Agencies." *Public Administration and Development* 15 (2): 151–65.

Dollar, David. 1992. "Outward-Oriented Developing Economies Really Do Grow More Rapidly: Evidence from 95 LDCs, 1976–1985." *Economic Development and Cultural Change* 40 (3): 523–44.

Dornbusch, Rudiger. 1992. "The Case for Trade Liberalization in Developing Countries." *Journal of Economic Perspectives* 6 (1): 69–85.

Dotse, F. Mawuena. 1991. "The State of Training in Public Policy Management in Ghana." *Public Administration and Development* 11 (6): 525–39.

Drakakis-Smith, David. 1993. *The Nature of the Third World Cities*. Copenhagen: Center for Development Research.

Dwivedi, O. P. 1978. *Public Service Ethics*. Brussels: International Institute of Administrative Sciences.

———. 1994. *Development Administration: From Underdevelopment to Sustainable Development*. New York: St. Martin's Press.

Easterly, William, Carlos Alfredo Rodríguez, and Klaus Schmidt-Hebbel, eds. 1994. *Public Sector Deficits and Macroeconomic Performance*. New York: Oxford University Press.

Easterly, William, and Klaus Schmidt-Hebbel. 1994. "Fiscal Adjustment and Macroeconomic Performance: A Synthesis" in Easterly, Rodríguez, and Schmidt-Hebbel 1994.

Easterly, William, and Ross Levine. 1995. *Africa's Growth Tragedy: A Retrospective, 1960–89*. Policy Research Working Paper 1503. Washington, DC: World Bank.

Edwards, Michael, and David Hulme, eds. 1993. *Making a Difference: NGOs and Development in a Changing World*. London: Earthscan Publications.

Elkan, Walter. 1988. "Entrepreneurs and Entrepreneurship in Africa." *Finance and Development* 25 (4): 20, 41–42.

Elliot, Michael. 1994. "Money Talks." *Newsweek* (November 14): 10–15.

Endale, Derseh. 1995. *Changing Patterns of Employment and Unemployment in Africa*. World Development Studies 7. Helsinki: World Institute for Development Economics Research, United Nations University.

Escobar, Arturo. 1995. *Encountering Development: The Making and Unmaking of the Third World*. Princeton: Princeton University Press.

Fardi, Mohsen A. 1991. "Zambia: Reform and Reversal" in Thomas et al. 1991.

Fatton, Robert, Jr. 1992. *Predatory Rule: State and Civil Society in Africa*. Boulder, CO: Lynne Rienner.

———. 1995. "Africa in the Age of Democratization: The Civic Limitations of Civil Society." *African Studies Review* 38 (2): 67–99.

Findlay, Allan, and Anne Findlay. 1987. *Population and Development in the Third World*. London: Methuen.

Findley, Sally E. 1993. "The Third World City: Development Policy and Issues" in Kasarda and Parnell 1993.

Fleming, Alan. 1993. "Lessons from Tropical Africa for Addressing the HIV/AIDS Epidemic in South Africa" in Cross and Whiteside 1993.

Fox, William F. 1994. *Strategic Options for Urban Infrastructure Management*. Washington, DC: World Bank.

Friedmann, John. 1992. *Empowerment: The Politics of Alternative Development*. Cambridge: Blackwell.

Frohlich, Christine, and Bruce Frayne. 1991. *Hawking: An "Informal" Sector Activity in Katutura, Windhoek*. Windhoek, Namibia: Namibian Institute for Social and Economic Research.

Gilbert, Alan, and Joseph Gugler. 1992. *Cities, Poverty and Development: Urbanization in the Third World*. New York: Oxford University Press.

Glickman, Harvey. 1988. *The Crisis and Challenge of African Development*. New York: Greenwood Press.

Global Coalition for Africa (GCA). 1992. *Global Coalition for Africa: Documents on: Development, Democracy and Debt*. The Hague: Netherlands Ministry of Foreign Affairs.

Good, Kenneth. 1992. "Interpreting the Exceptionality of Botswana." *The Journal of Modern African Studies* 30 (1): 69–95.

———. 1993. "At the Ends of the Ladder: Radical Inequalities in Botswana." *The Journal of Modern African Studies* 31 (2): 203–30.

Goody, Jack. 1990. "Futures of the Family in Rural Africa" in McNicoll and Cain 1990.

Gordon, April A., and Donald L. Gordon, eds. 1996. *Understanding Contemporary Africa*. Boulder, CO: Lynne Rienner.

Gould, David J. 1980. *Bureaucratic Corruption and Underdevelopment in the Third World: The Case of Zaire*. New York: Pergamon.

Gould, David J., and Jose A. Amaro-Reyes. 1983. *The Effects of Corruption on Administrative Reform: Illustrations from Developing Countries*. Washington, DC: World Bank.

Goulet, Denis. 1971. *The Cruel Choice.* New York: Atheneum.

Green, Cynthia P., ed. 1994. *Sustainable Development: Population and the Environment: Proceedings of a Workshop on Sustainable Development in Sub-Saharan Africa.* Washington, DC: United States Agency for International Development and the Academy for Educational Development.

Greenway, David. 1990. "Export Promotion in Sub-Saharan Africa" in *Export Promotion Strategies, Theory and Evidence from Developing Countries,* ed. Chris Milner. New York: New York University Press.

Grosh, Barbara, and Rwekaza S. Mukandala, eds. 1994. *State-Owned Enterprises in Africa.* Boulder, CO: Lynne Rienner.

Gugler, Josef. 1991. "Life in a Dual System Revisited: Urban-Rural Ties in Enugu, Nigeria, 1961–1987." *World Development* 19 (5): 399–409.

Gulhati, Ravi. 1990. *Zambia: The Economics and Politics of Reform.* Washington, DC: World Bank.

Hadjimichael, Michael T., et al. 1995. *Sub-Saharan Africa: Growth, Savings, and Investment, 1986–93.* Washington, DC: IMF.

Haggard, Stephan, and Steven B. Webb, eds. 1994. *Voting for Reform: Democracy, Political Liberalization, and Economic Adjustment.* New York: Oxford University Press.

Haggblade, Steven, Peter B. Hazell, and James Brown. 1989. "Farm-Nonfarm Linkages in Rural Sub-Saharan Africa." *World Development* 17 (8): 1173–1201.

Halachmi, Arie. 1995. "Re-engineering and Public Management: Some Issues and Considerations." *International Review of Administrative Sciences* 61 (3): 329–41.

Harbeson, John, Donald Rothchild, and Naomi Chazan, eds. 1994. *Civil Society and the State in Africa.* Boulder, CO: Lynne Rienner.

Harden, Blaine. 1990. *Africa: Dispatches from a Fragile Continent.* New York: W. W. Norton.

Harrison, Lawrence E. 1985. *Underdevelopment Is a State of Mind.* Lanham, MD: Madison Books.

Harsch, Ernest. 1993. "Accumulators and Democrats: Challenging State Corruption in Africa." *The Journal of Modern African Studies* 31 (1): 31–48.

Harverson, Karen. 1996. "Corruption Could Cripple SA, but . . ." *Mail and Guardian* (March 1–7): B2.

Harvey, Charles. 1992. "Botswana: Is the Economic Miracle Over?" *Journal of African Economies* 1 (3): 335–68.

———, ed. 1996. *Constraints on the Success of Structural Adjustment Programmes in Africa.* London: Macmillan.

Harvey, Charles, and Stephen R. Lewis. 1990. *Policy Choice and Development Performance in Botswana.* New York: St. Martin's Press.

Harvey, Charles, et al. 1979. *Rural Employment and Administration in the Third World: Development Methods and Alternative Strategies.* Geneva: ILO.

Healey, John, and Mark Robinson. 1992. *Democracy, Governance and Economic Policy: Sub-Saharan Africa in Comparative Perspective.* London: Overseas Development Institute.

Healey, John, Richard Ketley, and Mark Robinson. 1992. *Political Regimes and Economic Policy Patterns in Developing Countries, 1978–88.* Working Paper 67. London: Overseas Development Institute.

Heeks, Richard. 1995. "Computerizing Corruption in Developing Countries." *Information Technology in Developing Countries* 5 (2): 2–5.

Herbst, Jeffrey. 1989. "Political Impediment to Economic Rationality: Explaining Zimbabwe's Failure to Reform its Public Sector." *The Journal of Modern African Studies* 27 (1): 67–84.

Hettne, Bjorn. 1995. *Development Theory and the Three Worlds: Towards an International Political Economy of Development.* Harlow, Essex: Longman.

Higgott, Richard, and Finn Fugelstad. 1975. "The 1974 Coup d'État in Niger: Towards an Explanation." *The Journal of Modern African Studies,* 13 (3): 383–98.

Hill, Catharine B. 1991. "Managing Commodity Booms in Botswana." *World Development* 19 (9): 1185–96.

———. 1994. "Trade Policies and the Promotion of Manufactured Exports" in Lindauer and Roemer 1994.

Hirsh, Michael. 1996. "Graft Busters." *Newsweek* (January 1): 56–59.

Hoggett, Paul. 1993. "Administrative Reform of Central Government: Choosing Appropriate Organizational Structures" in Commonwealth Secretariat 1993.

Holm, John D. 1988. "Botswana: A Paternalistic Democracy" in *Democracy in Developing Countries, Vol. 2: Africa,* ed. Larry Diamond, Juan Linz, and Seymour Martin Lipset Boulder, CO: Lynne Rienner.

Hope, Kempe Ronald, Sr. 1983. "Self-Reliance and Participation of the Poor in the Development Process in the Third World." *Futures* 15 (December): 455–62.

———. 1984. "Self-Reliance as a Development Strategy: A Conceptual Policy Analysis." *Scandinavian Journal of Development Alternatives* 3 (4): 17–27.

———. 1985. "Politics, Bureaucratic Corruption, and Maladministration in the Third World." *International Review of Administrative Sciences* 51 (1): 1–6.

———. 1986. "Urbanization and Economic Development in the Third World." *Cities* 3 (2): 41–57.

———. 1987a. *Development Finance and the Development Process.* Westport, CT: Greenwood Press.

———. 1987b. "Administrative Corruption and Administrative Reform in Developing States." *Corruption and Reform* 2 (2): 127–47.

———. 1989. "Managing Rapid Urbanization in the Third World: Some Aspects of Policy." *Genus: An International Journal of Demography* 45 (3–4): 21–35.

———. 1992. "Development Theory and Policy in the Third World." *South African Journal of Economics* 60 (4): 333–53.

———. 1993a. "The Growth and Impact of the Subterranean Economy in the Third World." *Futures* 25 (8): 864–76.

———. 1993b. "The Subterranean Economy and the Role of Private Investment in Developing Countries." *Journal of Social, Political and Economic Studies* 18 (2): 181–95.

———. 1995a. "Urbanization and Urban Management in the Third World." Mimeo., University of Botswana.

———. 1995b. "Managing the Public Sector in Botswana: Some Emerging Constraints and the Administrative Reform Responses." *International Journal of Public Sector Management* 8 (6): 51–62.

———. 1996a. "Growth, Unemployment, and Poverty in Botswana." *Journal of Contemporary African Studies* 14 (1): 53–67.

————. 1996b. *Development in the Third World: From Policy Failure to Policy Reform.* Armonk, NY: M.E. Sharpe.

————. 1996c. "Promoting Sustainable Community Development in Developing Countries: The Role of Technology Transfer." *Community Development Journal* 31 (3): 193–200.

————. 1996d. "International Trade and International Technology Transfer to Eliminate Ozone-Depleting Substances." *International Environmental Affairs* 8 (1): 32–40.

Hope, Kempe Ronald, Sr., and Aubrey Armstrong. 1980. "Toward the Development of Administrative and Management Capability in Developing Countries." *International Review of Administrative Sciences* 46 (4): 315–20.

Hope, Kempe Ronald, Sr., and Wayne Edge. 1996. "Growth with Uneven Development: Urban-Rural Socio-Economic Disparities in Botswana." *Geoforum* 27 (1): 53–62.

Huffman, Sandra L., and Adwoa Steel. 1995. "Do Child Survival Interventions Reduce Malnutrition? The Dark Side of Child Survival" in *Child Growth and Nutrition in Developing Countries: Priorities for Action,* ed. Per Pinstrup-Andersen, David Pelletier, and Harold Alderman. Ithaca, NY: Cornell University Press.

Hulme, David. 1993. "Replicating Finance Programmes in Malawi and Malaysia." *Small Enterprise Development* 4 (4): 4–15.

Hunter, S. S. 1990. "Orphans as a Window on the AIDS Epidemic in Sub-Saharan Africa: Initial Results and Implications of a Study in Uganda." *Social Science and Medicine* 31 (6): 681–90.

Husain, Ishrat, and Rashid Faruqee, eds. 1994. *Adjustment in Africa: Lessons from Country Case Studies.* Washington, DC: World Bank.

Hyde, Karin A. L. 1993. "Sub-Saharan Africa" in *Women's Education in Developing Countries: Barriers, Benefits, and Policies,* ed. Elizabeth M. King and M. Anne Hill. Baltimore: Johns Hopkins University Press.

Hyden, Goran. 1990. "Local Governance and Economic-Demographic Transition in Rural Africa" in McNicoll and Cain 1990.

————. 1992. "Governance and the Study of Politics" in Hyden and Bratton 1992.

Hyden, Goran, and Bo Karlstrom. 1993. "Structural Adjustment as a Policy Process: The Case of Tanzania." *World Development* 21 (9): 1395–1404.

Hyden, Goran, and Michael Bratton, eds. 1992. *Governance and Politics in Africa.* Boulder, CO: Lynne Rienner.

Hyuha, M., M. O. Ndanshau, and J. P. Kipokola. 1993. *Scope, Structure and Policy Implications of Informal Financial Markets in Tanzania.* Nairobi, Kenya: African Economic Research Consortium.

International Labor Organization (ILO). 1991. *The Dilemma of the Informal Sector: Report of the Director General.* Geneva: ILO.

International Monetary Fund (IMF). 1994a. *Financial Statistics Yearbook 1994.* Washington, DC: IMF.

————. 1994b. *Direction of Trade Statistics Yearbook 1994.* Washington, DC: IMF.

————. 1995a. *Botswana—Background Papers and Statistical Appendix.* Washington, DC: IMF.

————. 1995b. *Social Dimensions of the IMF Policy Dialogue.* Pamphlet Series no. 47. Washington, DC: IMF.

Isham, Jonathan, Deepa Narayan, and Lant Pritichett. 1994. *Does Participation Improve Performance?" Empirical Evidence from Project Data.* Policy Research Working Paper 1357. Washington, DC: World Bank.

Jabbra, J.G. 1976. "Bureaucratic Corruption in the Third World." *Indian Journal of Public Administration* 22 (4): 673–91.

Jacobs, Colin. 1990. "Training for Change in the Ugandan Civil Service." *Public Administration and Development* 10 (3): 315–30.

Jefferis, Keith. 1991. "The Economy in 1990." *Barclays Botswana Economic Review* 2 (1): 1–24.

————. 1993. "The Economy in 1992." *Barclays Botswana Economic Review* 4 (1): 1–22.

————. 1994. "The 1994 Budget." *Barclays Botswana Economic Review* 5 (1): 17–22.

Jolly, Richard. 1988. "Poverty and Adjustment in the 1990s" in John P. Lewis and Contributors 1988.

Jones, Christine, and Miguel Kiguel. 1994. "Africa's Quest for Prosperity: Has Adjustment Helped?" *Finance and Development* 31 (2): 2–9.

Jordan, Nhlanhla. 1994. "The Informal Sector: Its Historical Context for African Women." *Women's Studies* 6: 26–39.

Kakwani, N. 1995. "Structural Adjustment and Performance in Living Standards in Developing Countries." *Development and Change* 26 (3): 469–502.

Kakwani, N., Elene Makonnen, and Jacques van der Gaag. 1993. "Living Conditions in Developing Countries" in *Including the Poor,* ed. Michael Lipton and Jacques van der Gaag. Washington, DC: World Bank.

Kannapan, Subbiah. 1989. "Urban Labor Markets in Developing Countries." *Finance and Development* 26 (2): 46–48.

Kasarda, John D., and Allan M. Parnell, eds. 1993. *Third World Cities: Problems, Policies, and Prospects.* London: Sage.

Kashambuzi, Eric. 1995. "Poverty Still Deepening in Zambia." *Africa Recovery* 9 (1): 13.

Kaul, Mohan, and Paul Collins. 1995. "Governments in Transition: Towards a New Public Administration." *Public Administration and Development* 15 (3): 199–206.

Kaunda, Mayuyuka, and Katabaro Miti. 1995. "Promotion of Private Enterprise and Citizen Entrepreneurship in Botswana." *Development Southern Africa* 12 (3): 367–77.

Kayira, Gladson K. 1993. "A Comparative Analysis of Approaches to Regional Economic Cooperation and Integration—The African Experience" in *Integrating SADC Economies: From Resolutions to Action,* ed. Gladson K. Kayira, Amy G. Luhanga, and Ponny N. L. Walakira. Gabrorone, Botswana: IDM Publications.

Kayizzi-Mugerwa, Steve, and Jorgen Levin. 1994. "Adjustment and Poverty: A Review of the African Experience." *African Development Review* 6 (2): 1–39.

Keller, Edmond J. 1995. "Liberalization, Democratization and Democracy in Africa: Comparative Perspectives." *Africa Insight* 25 (4): 224–30.

Kelley, Allen C., and Charles E. Nobbe. 1990. *Kenya at the Demographic Turn-*

ing Point? Hypotheses and a Proposed Research Agenda. Discussion Paper 107. Washington, DC: World Bank.

Kelly, Rita Mae. 1988. "Introduction: Success, Productivity and the Public Sector" in *Promoting Productivity in the Public Sector*, ed. Rita Mae Kelly. London: Macmillan.

Kelso, B. J. 1994. "AIDS: Orphans of the Storm." *Africa Report* 39 (1): 50–55.

Kgosana, P. 1992. "Children in Especially Difficult Circumstances: The South African Case" in *Children in Especially Difficult Circumstances*, ed. UNICEF. Gaborone, Botswana: UNICEF.

Khan, Azizur Rahman. 1994. *Overcoming Unemployment*. Geneva: International Labor Organization.

Kikeri, Sunita, John Nellis, and Mary Shirley. 1992. *Privatization: The Lessons of Experience*. Washington, DC: World Bank.

Killick, Tony. 1993. *The Adaptive Economy: Adjustment Policies in Small, Low-Income Countries*. Washington, DC: World Bank.

———. 1995. "Structural Adjustment and Poverty Alleviation: An Interpretative Essay." *Development and Change* 26 (2): 305–31.

Kirkpatrick, Colin, and John Weiss. 1995. "Trade Policy Reforms and Performance in Africa in the 1980s." *The Journal of Modern African Studies* 33 (2): 285–98.

Klitgaard, Robert. 1991. *Adjusting to Reality: Beyond "State Versus Market" in Economic Development*. San Francisco: ICS Press.

Koehn, Peter H. 1995. "Decentralization for Sustainable Development" in Rasheed and Luke 1995.

Kossoudji, Sherrie, and Eva Mueller. 1983. "The Economic and Demographic Status of Female-Headed Households in Rural Botswana." *Economic Development and Cultural Change* 31 (4): 831–59.

Kpundeh, Sahr John. 1994. "Limiting Administrative Corruption in Sierra Leone." *Journal of Modern African Studies* 32 (1): 139–57.

Kraus, Jon. 1991. "The Political Economy of Stabilization and Structural Adjustment in Ghana" in *Ghana: The Political Economy of Recovery*, ed. Donald Rothchild. Boulder, CO: Lynne Rienner.

Kyle, Steven. 1994. "Structural Adjustment in a Country at War: The Case of Mozambique" in *Adjusting to Policy Failure in African Economies*, ed. David E. Sahn. Ithaca, NY: Cornell University Press.

Lall, Sanjaya. 1992. "Structural Problems of African Industry" in *Alternative Development Strategies in Sub-Saharan Africa*, ed. Frances Stewart, Sanjaya Lall, and Samuel Wangwe. New York: St. Martin's Press.

———. 1995. "Structural Adjustment and African Industry." *World Development* 23 (12): 2019–31.

Lamb, David. 1982. *The Africans*. New York: Random House.

Lamb, Geoffrey. 1987. *Managing Economic Policy Change: Institutional Dimensions*. Discussion Paper 14. Washington, DC: World Bank.

Landell-Mills, Pierre. 1992. "Governance, Cultural Change, and Empowerment." *Journal of Modern African Studies* 30 (4): 543–67.

Landell-Mills, Pierre, and Ismail Serageldin. 1991. "Governance and the External Factor" in Summers and Shah 1991.

Legwaila, E. W. M. J. 1993. "Botswana: Coherence With a Strong Central Government." *International Review of Administrative Sciences* 59 (4): 617–28.

Lemarchand, René. 1992. "Uncivil States and Civil Societies: How Illusion Became Reality." *Journal of Modern African Studies* 30 (2): 177–91.

Leslie, Winsome J. 1987. *The World Bank and Structural Transformation in Developing Countries: The Case of Zaire.* Boulder, CO: Lynne Rienner.

LeVine, Victor T. 1980. "African Patrimonial Regimes in Comparative Perspective." *Journal of Modern African Studies* 18 (4): 657–73.

Lewis, John P., ed. 1988. *Strengthening the Poor: What Have We Learned?* NJ: Transaction Books.

Lewis, Jeffrey D., and Malcolm F. McPherson. 1994. "Macroeconomic Management: To Finance or Adjust?" in Lindauer and Roemer 1994.

Lindauer, David L. 1994. "Government Pay and Employment Policies and Economic Performance" in Lindauer and Nunberg 1994.

Lindauer, David L., and Barbara Nunberg, eds. 1994. *Rehabilitating Government: Pay and Employment Reform in Africa.* Washington, DC: World Bank.

Lindauer, David L., and Michael Roemer, eds. 1994. *Asia and Africa: Legacies and Opportunities in Development.* San Francisco: ICS Press.

Little, I. M. D., et al. 1993. *Boom, Crisis, and Adjustment: The Macroeconomic Experience of Developing Countries.* New York: Oxford University Press.

Livi-Bacci, Massimo. 1994. *Poverty and Population.* Liège, Belgium: International Union for the Scientific Study of Population.

Love, Roy. 1994. "Drought, Dutch Disease and Controlled Transition in Botswana Agriculture." *Journal of Southern African Studies* 20 (1): 71–83.

Lubell, Harold. 1991. *The Informal Sector in the 1980s and 1990s.* Paris: OECD Development Center.

Luckham, Robin. 1994. "The Military, Militarization and Democratization in Africa: A Survey of Literature and Issues." *African Studies Review* 37 (2): 13–75.

Lundahl, Mats, and Lena Moritz. 1993. "Macroeconomic Stagnation and Structural Weaknesses in the South African Economy" in Blomstrom and Lundahl 1993.

MacGaffey, Janet. 1991. *The Real Economy of Zaire: The Contribution of Smuggling and Other Unofficial Activities to National Wealth.* Philadelphia: University of Pennsylvania Press.

———. 1987. *Entrepreneurs and Parasites: The Struggle for Indigenous Capitalism in Zaire.* Cambridge: Cambridge University Press.

MacKenzie, Fiona. 1992. "Development from Within? The Struggle to Survive" in Taylor and MacKenzie 1992.

Mail and Guardian. 1995. (May 26–June 1): 9–10.

Main, Jeremy. 1989. "How to Make Poor Countries Rich." *Fortune* 119 (January 16): 101–6.

Mainardi, Stefano. 1994. "Poor Housing Conditions: An Analysis Across South African Development Regions." *Savings and Development* 18 (4): 427–55.

Makumbe, John. 1994. "Bureaucratic Corruption in Zimbabwe: Causes and Magnitude of the Problem." *Africa Development* 19 (3): 45–60.

Manamperi, S.A. 1990. "Training Provision and the Trainer's Role in the 1990s." *Sri Lanka Journal of Development Administration* 7 (1): 40–64.

Manning, Nick. 1993. "Administrative and Managerial Reform in Government: Identifying and Sharing Commonwealth Good Practice" in Commonwealth Secretariat 1993.

Marc, Alexandre, et al. 1995. *Social Action Programs and Social Funds: A Re-*

view of Design and Implementation in Sub-Saharan Africa. Washington, DC: World Bank.

Martin, Denis-Constant. 1991. "The Cultural Dimensions of Governance" in Summers and Shah 1991.

Mason, Karen Oppenheim, 1995. *Gender and Demographic Change: What Do We Know?* Liège, Belgium: International Union for the Scientific Study of Population.

Mayer, Marina, and Harry Zarenda. 1994. *The Southern African Customs Union: A Review of Costs and Benefits.* Halfway House, South Africa: Development Bank of Southern Africa.

McCarthy, Stephen. 1994. *Africa: The Challenge of Transformation.* London: I. B. Tauris.

McNicoll, Geoffrey, and Mead Cain, eds. 1990. *Rural Development and Population: Institutions and Policy.* New York: Oxford University Press.

Mellor, John W. 1995. "Agriculture on the Road to Industrialization." *Food Policy Statement,* no. 22 (December). Washington, DC: International Food Policy Research Institute.

Mertens, Thierry E., and Michel Carael. 1995. "Sexually Transmitted Diseases, Genital Hygiene and Male Circumcision May Be Associated: A Working Hypothesis for HIV Prevention." *Health Transition Review* 5 (1): 104–8.

Mhloyi, Marvellous. 1994. *Status of Women Population and Development.* Liège, Belgium: International Union for the Scientific Study of Population.

Mhone, Guy C. Z. 1995. "The Social Dimensions of Adjustment (SDA) Program in Zimbabwe: A Critical Review and Assessment." *European Journal of Development Research* 7 (1): 101–123.

Mingat, Alain, and Jee-Peng Tan. 1985. "Subsidization of Higher Education Versus Expansion of Primary Enrollments: What Can a Shift of Resources Achieve in Sub-Saharan Africa?" *International Journal of Educational Development* 5 (4): 259–68.

Mink, Stephen D. 1993. *Poverty, Population, and the Environment.* Washington, DC: World Bank.

Mitchell, William C., and Randy T. Simmons. 1994. *Beyond Politics: Markets, Welfare, and the Failure of Bureaucracy.* Boulder, CO: Westview Press.

Mlambo, A.S. 1995. "Towards an Analysis of IMF Structural Adjustment Programmes in Sub-Saharan Africa (SSA): The Case of Zimbabwe 1990–94." *Africa Development* 20 (2): 77–98.

Morandé, Felipe, and Klaus Schmidt-Hebbel. 1994. "Zimbabwe: Fiscal Disequilibria and Low Growth" in Easterly, Rodríguez, and Schmidt-Hebbel 1994.

Morgan, S. Philip. 1993. "Third World Urbanization, Migration, and Family Adaptation" in Kasarda and Parnell 1993.

Morton, James. 1994. *The Poverty of Nations: The Aid Dilemma at the Heart of Africa.* London: British Academic Press.

Moses, Stephen, et al. 1995. "Male Circumcision and the AIDS Epidemic in Africa." *Health Transition Review* 5 (1): 100–3.

Mosley, Paul, and John Weeks. 1993. "Has Recovery Begun? 'Africa's Adjustment in the 1980s' Revisited." *World Development* 21 (10): 1583–1606.

Mosley, Paul, Turan Subasat, and John Weeks. 1995. "Assessing Adjustment in Africa." *World Development* 23 (9): 1459–73.

Mrak, Mojmir. 1989. "Role of the Informal Financial Sector in the Mobilization and Allocation of Household Savings: The Case of Zambia." *Savings and Development* 13 (1): 65–85.

Mukandala, Rwekaza S. 1992. "To Be or Not to Be: The Paradoxes of African Bureaucracies in the 1990s." *International Review of Administrative Sciences* 58 (4): 555–76.

Murdoch, William W. 1980. *The Poverty of Nations: The Political Economy of Hunger and Population*. Baltimore: Johns Hopkins University Press.

Mwanza, Allast M. 1992. "Structural Adjustment Programmes in SADC: What Have We Learned?" in *Structural Adjustment Programmes in SADC*, ed. Allast M. Mwanza. Harare: SAPES Books.

Narayan, Deepa. 1994. *Contribution of People's Participation: Evidence from 121 Rural Water Supply Projects*. ESD Occasional Paper Series, no. 1. Washington, DC: World Bank.

———. 1995. *Designing Community Based Development*. Environment Department Papers, Participation Series, no. 007. Washington, DC: World Bank.

Naya, Seiji, and Robert McCleery. 1994. *Relevance of Asian Development Experiences to African Problems*. San Francisco: ICS Press.

Ndegwa, Philip, and Reginald Herbold Green. 1994. *Africa to 2000 and Beyond: Imperative Political and Economic Agenda*. Nairobi: East African Educational Publishers.

Nellis, John R. 1994. "Public Enterprises in Sub-Saharan Africa" in Grosh and Mukandala 1994.

Nkhoma-Wamunza, Alice. 1992. "The Informal Sector: A Strategy for Survival in Tanzania" in Taylor and MacKenzie 1992.

Nkowane, B. M. 1988. "The Impact of Human Immunodeficiency Virus Infection and AIDS on a Primary Industry: Mining (A Case Study of Zambia)" in *The Global Impact of AIDS*, ed. Alan Fleming et al. New York: Alan Liss.

Norberg, Helene, and Magnus Blomstrom. 1993. "Dutch Disease and Management of Windfall Gains in Botswana" in Blomstrom and Lundahl 1993.

Norgaard, Richard B. 1994. *Development Betrayed*. London: Routledge.

North, Douglas C. 1990. *Institutions, Institutional Change and Economic Performance*. Cambridge: Cambridge University Press.

Norval, Dixon, and Rosy Namoya. 1992. *The Informal Sector Within Greater Windhoek*. Windhoek, Namibia: Namibia Development Corporation.

Nowak, Michael. 1985. "Black Markets in Foreign Exchange." *Finance and Development* 22 (1): 20–23.

Nyati-Ramahobo, Lydia. 1992. *The Girl-Child in Botswana: Educational Constraints and Prospects*. Gaborone, Botswana: UNICEF.

Nyerere, Julius K. 1979. *On Rural Development*. Address to the FAO World Conference on Agrarian Reform and Rural Development, Rome, Italy, July 13.

Oberai, A. S. 1993. "Urbanization, Development, and Economic Efficiency" in Kasarda and Parnell 1993.

Olukoshi, Adebayo O., and Lennart Wohlgemuth, eds. 1995. *A Road to Development: Africa in the 21st Century*. Uppsala: The Nordic Africa Institute.

Oppong, Christine, and René Wéry. 1994. *Women's Roles and Demographic Change in Sub-Saharan Africa*. Liège, Belgium: International Union for the Scientific Study of Population.

Osborne, David, and Ted Gaebler. 1992. *Reinventing Government: How the En-*

trepreneurial Spirit Is Transforming the Public Sector from Schoolhouse to State House, City Hall to Pentagon. Reading, MA: Addison-Wesley.

Osterfeld, David. 1992. *Prosperity Versus Planning: How Government Stifles Economic Growth*. New York: Oxford University Press.

Ouma, Stephen O. A. 1991. "Corruption in Public Policy and its Impact on Development: The Case of Uganda Since 1979." *Public Administration and Development* 11 (5): 472–90.

Pack, Howard. 1993. "Productivity and Industrial Development in Sub-Saharan Africa." *World Development* 21 (1): 1–16.

Page, Sheila. 1994. *How Developing Countries Trade: The Institutional Constraints*. London: Routledge.

Panos Institute. 1992. *The Hidden Cost of AIDS: The Challenge to Development*. London: Panos Institute.

Parker, Ronald L., Randall Riopelle, and William F. Steel. 1995. *Small Enterprises Adjusting to Liberalization in Five African Countries*. Washington, DC: World Bank.

Peke, Dan. 1994. "Inequality Prevalent in Botswana." *The Botswana Guardian* (September 22): 2.

Perkins, Dwight H., and Michael Roemer, eds. 1991. *Reforming Economic Systems in Developing Countries*. Cambridge, MA: Harvard Institute for International Development.

———. 1994. "Differing Endowments and Historical Legacies" in Lindauer and Roemer 1994.

Petersson, Lennart. 1993. "Structural Adjustment and Economic Management in a Dependent Economy: The Case of Lesotho" in Blomstrom and Lundahl 1993.

Phiri, M. J. (Zambian High Commissioner to Botswana). 1995. Speech on the Occasion of Zambia's 31st Independence Anniversary, Gaborone, Botswana.

Picard, Louis A. 1987. *The Politics of Development in Botswana: A Model for Success?* Boulder, CO: Lynne Rienner.

Picard, Louis A., and Michele Garrity, eds. 1994. *Policy Reform for Sustainable Development in Africa: The Institutional Imperative*. Boulder, CO: Lynne Rienner.

Pickett, James, and Hans Singer, eds. 1990. *Towards Economic Recovery in Sub-Saharan Africa*. London: Routledge.

Pinstrup-Andersen, Per. 1993. "Economic Crises and Policy Reforms During the 1980s and Their Impact on the Poor" in *Macroeconomic Environment and Health: With Case Studies for Countries in Greatest Need,* ed. WHO. Geneva: WHO.

Pleskovic, Boris, and Petros Sivitanides. 1993. "Priorities for the Poor: A Conceptual Framework for Policy Analysis." *Journal of Developing Areas* 27 (2): 399–416.

Polak, Jacques J. 1989. *Financial Policies and Development*. Paris: OECD.

Popiel, Paul A. 1994. *Financial Systems in Sub-Saharan Africa: A Comparative Study*. Washington, DC: World Bank.

Prager, Jonas. 1994. "Contracting Out Government Services: Lessons from the Private Sector." *Public Administration Review* 54 (2): 176–84.

Prah, K. K. 1993. "Socio-Cultural Dimensions of Ethics and Accountability in African Public Services." In Rasheed and Olowu 1993.

Pronk, Jan. 1995. "Global Coalition Looks to the Year 2000." *Africa Recovery* 9 (1): 18.

Psacharopoulos, George. 1994. "Returns to Education: A Global Update." *World Development* 22 (9): 1325–43.

Putnam, Robert D. 1993. *Making Democracy Work.* Princeton: Princeton University Press.

Rakodi, Carole, and Penny Withers. 1995a. "Sites and Services: Home Ownership for the Poor? Issues for Evaluation and Zimbabwean Experience." *Habitat International* 19 (3): 371–89.

———. 1995b. "Housing Aspirations and Affordability in Harare and Gweru: A Contribution to Housing Policy Formulation in Zimbabwe." *Cities* 12 (3): 185–201.

Ramachandran, K. 1993. "Promoting Small Enterprises—An Interventionist Mechanism." *Small Enterprise Development* 4 (4): 34–41.

Ramirez-Rojas, C. L. 1986. "Monetary Substitution in Developing Countries." *Finance and Development* 23 (2): 35–38.

Randall, Vicky, and Robin Theobald. 1985. *Political Change and Underdevelopment.* London: Macmillan.

Rasheed, Sadig. 1995. "Promoting Ethics and Accountability in African Civil Services" in Rasheed and Luke 1995.

Rasheed, Sadig, and David Fasholé Luke, eds. 1995. *Development Management in Africa: Toward Dynamism, Empowerment, and Entrepreneurship.* Boulder, CO: Westview Press.

Rasheed, Sadig, and Dele Olowu, eds. 1993. *Ethics and Accountability in African Public Services.* Nairobi: African Association for Public Administration and Management/ICIPE Press.

Republic of Botswana. 1988. *Household Income and Expenditure Survey: 1985/86.* Gaborone, Botswana: Government Printer.

———. 1991a. *National Development Plan 7: 1991–1997.* Gaborone, Botswana: Government Printer.

———. 1991b. *A Poverty Datum Line for Botswana: November 1989.* Gaborone, Botswana: Government Printer.

———. 1993a. *Labor Statistics 1991/92.* Gaborone, Botswana: Government Printer.

———. 1993b. *Planning for People: A Strategy for Accelerated Human Development in Botswana.* Gaborone, Botswana: Ministry of Finance and Development Planning/UNDP/UNICEF.

———. 1993c. *O&M Review: Report on Organization Review.* Gaborone, Botswana: Directorate of Public Sector Management.

———. 1993d. *Strategy for Productivity Improvement in the Botswana Public Service.* Gaborone, Botswana: Office of the President.

———. 1994a. *Report of the Auditor-General on the Accounts of the Botswana Government for the Financial Year Ended 31st March, 1993.* Gaborone, Botswana: Government Printer.

———. 1994b. *Government Gazette: Extraordinary* 32 (25). Gaborone, Botswana: Government Printer.

———. 1995a. *Budget Speech 1995.* Gaborone, Botswana: Government Printer.

———. 1995b. *Household Income and Expenditure Survey: 1993/94.* Gaborone, Botswana: Government Printer.

————. 1996a. *Annual Economic Report 1996.* Gaborone, Botswana: Government Printer.

————. 1996b. *Budget Speech 1996.* Gaborone, Botswana: Government Printer.

Rimmer, Douglas. 1995. "Development and Africa: Changing Perceptions." *Africa Insight* 25 (2): 122–28.

Robinson, Derek. 1990. *Civil Service Pay in Africa.* Geneva: ILO.

Robinson, Mark. 1993. "Aid, Democracy and Political Conditionality in Sub-Saharan Africa." *European Journal of Development Research* 5 (1): 85–99.

Rodwin, Lloyd, and Donald A. Schon, eds. 1994. *Rethinking the Development Experience: Essays Provoked by the Work of Albert O. Hirschman.* Washington, DC/Cambridge, MA: Brookings Institution/Lincoln Institute of Land Policy.

Roemer, Michael, and Steven C. Radelet. 1991. "Macroeconomic Reform in Developing Countries" in Perkins and Roemer 1991.

Rondinelli, Dennis A. 1983. *Secondary Cities in Developing Countries: Policies for Diffusing Urbanization.* London: Sage.

Rondinelli, Dennis A., and G. Shabbir Cheema. 1983. "Implementing Decentralization Policies: An Introduction" in *Decentralization and Development: Policy Implementation in Developing Countries,* ed. G. Shabbir Cheema and Dennis A. Rondinelli. London: Sage.

————. 1988. "Urban Services for the Poor: An Introduction" in *Urban Services in Developing Countries: Public and Private Roles in Urban Development,* ed. Dennis A. Rondinelli and G. Shabbir Cheema. London: Macmillan.

Rondinelli, Dennis A., James S. McCullough, and Ronald W. Johnson. 1989. "Analyzing Decentralization Policies in Developing Countries: A Political-Economy Approach." *Development and Change* 20 (1): 57–87.

Rondinelli, Dennis A., and John D. Kasarda. 1993. "Privatization of Urban Services and Infrastructure in Developing Countries" in Kasarda and Parnell 1993.

Rondinelli, Dennis A., John R. Nellis, and G. Shabbir Cheema. 1983. *Decentralization in Developing Countries: A Review of Recent Experience,* Staff Working Paper, no. 581. Washington, DC: World Bank.

Rosenau, James N. 1995. "Governance in the Twenty-First Century." *Global Governance* 1 (1): 13–43.

Roth, Gabriel J. 1987. *The Private Provision of Public Services in Developing Countries.* New York: Oxford University Press.

Rothchild, Donald, ed. 1991. *Ghana: The Political Economy of Recovery.* Boulder, CO: Lynne Rienner.

————. 1994. "Structuring State-Society Relations in Africa: Toward an Enabling Political Environment" in Widner 1994.

Rothchild, Donald, and Naomi Chazan, eds. 1988. *The Precarious Balance: State and Society in Africa.* Boulder, CO: Westview Press.

Rutenberg, Naomi, and Ian Diamond. 1993. "Fertility in Botswana: The Recent Decline and Future Prospects." *Demography* 30 (2): 143–57.

Sader, Frank. 1995. *Privatizing Public Enterprises and Foreign Investment in Developing Countries, 1988–93.* Washington, DC: World Bank.

Sadik, Nafis. 1992. "Global Development Challenges: The Population Dimension" in *Change: Threat or Opportunity for Human Progress: Volume IV—Social Change,* ed. Uner Kirdar. New York: United Nations.

Sahn, David E., ed. 1994. *Adjusting to Policy Failure in African Economies.* Ithaca, NY: Cornell University Press.

Salamon, Lester M. 1994. "The Rise of the Nonprofit Sector." *Foreign Affairs* 73 (4): 109–22.

Salih, Siddig A. 1994. *Impacts of Africa's Growing Debt on Its Growth.* Helsinki: United Nations University, World Institute for Development Economics Research.

Salkin, J. S. 1994. "The Economy in 1993." *Barclays Botswana Economic Review* 5 (1): 1–16.

Sandbrook, Richard. 1985. *The Politics of Africa's Economic Stagnation.* Cambridge: Cambridge University Press.

———. 1986. "The State and Economic Stagnation in Tropical Africa." *World Development* 14 (3): 319–32.

———. 1988. "Liberal Democracy in Africa: A Socialist-Revisionist Perspective." *Canadian Journal of African Studies* 22 (2): 240–68.

———. 1993. *The Politics of Africa's Economic Recovery.* Cambridge: Cambridge University Press.

Sarris, Alexander H., and Rogier van den Brink. 1994. "From Forced Modernization to Perestroika: Crisis and Adjustment in Tanzania" in Sahn 1994.

Schatz, Sayre P. 1994. "Structural Adjustment in Africa: A Failing Grade So Far." *Journal of Modern African Studies* 32 (4): 679–92.

Schrieder, Gertrud R., and Carlos E. Cuevas. 1992. "Informal Financial Groups in Cameroon" in Adams and Fitchett 1992.

Scott, Graham, P. Bushnell, and N. Sallee. 1990. "Reform of the Core Public Sector: The New Zealand Experience." *Governance* 3 (2): 138–67.

Seligman, Adam. 1992. *The Idea of Civil Society.* New York: The Free Press.

Seshamani, Venkatesh. 1992. "The Economic Policies of Zambia in the 1980s: Towards Structural Transformation With a Human Face?" in *Africa's Recovery in the 1980s: From Stagnation and Adjustment to Human Development,* ed. Giovanni Andrea Cornia, Rolph van der Hoeven, and Thandika Mkandawire. New York: St. Martin's Press.

Sharer, Robert L., Hema R. DeZoysa, and Calvin A. McDonald. 1995. *Uganda: Adjustment with Growth, 1987–94.* Occasional Paper 121. Washington, DC: IMF.

Shaw, Timothy M., and E. John Inegbedion. 1994. "The Marginalization of Africa in the New World (Dis)Order" in *Political Economy and the Changing Global Order,* ed. Richard Stubbs and Geoffrey R.D. Underhill. New York: St. Martin's Press.

Shellukindo, W. N., and R. Baguma. 1993. "Ethical Standards and Behavior in African Public Services" in Rasheed and Olowu 1993.

Siddiqui, Rukhsana, ed. 1993. *Sub-Saharan Africa: A Sub-Continent in Transition.* Aldershot: Avebury.

Silverman, Jerry M. 1992. *Public Sector Decentralization: Economic Policy and Sector Investment Programs.* Technical Paper no. 188. Washington, DC: World Bank.

Sirleaf, Ellen Johnson. 1995. "Africa Must Develop Its Own Vision." *Africa Recovery* 9 (3): 3.

———. 1996. "Challenges to Africa's Leadership." Statement to the Conference of African Ministers of Planning and UNDP Resident Representatives in the Africa Region, Ouagadougou, Burkina Faso, January 30–31.

Smith, Brian, C. 1993. *Choices in the Design of Decentralization*. London: Commonwealth Secretariat.

Smith, Jim. 1996. "All Eyes on Once-Humble Stokvels as the Informal Sector Begins to Flex its Multi-Million-Rand Financial Muscles." *The Sunday Independent* (March 24): 16.

Somolekae, Gloria. 1993. "Bureaucracy and Democracy in Botswana: What Type of Relationship?" in Stedman 1993.

Sorensen, Georg. 1991. *Democracy, Dictatorship and Development: Economic Development in Selected Regimes of the Third World*. London: Macmillan.

———. 1993. *Democracy and Democratization*. Boulder, CO: Westview Press.

Southall, Aidan. 1980. "Social Disorganization in Uganda: Before, During, and After Amin." *Journal of Modern African Studies* 18 (4): 627–56.

Stedman, Stephen John, ed. 1993. *Botswana: The Political Economy of Democratic Development*. Boulder, CO: Lynne Rienner.

Stevens, Mike. 1994. "Public Expenditure and Civil Service Reform in Tanzania" in Lindauer and Nunberg 1994.

Storck, Elise, and Nicole Brown. 1992. *HIV and Development*. London: Panos Institute.

Stover, John. 1994. "The Impact of HIV/AIDS on Adult and Child Mortality in the Developing World." *Health Transition Review* 4 (Supplement): 47–63.

Strydom, P. D. F., and F. H. Fiser. 1995. "Structural Adjustment Programs." *Development Southern Africa* 12 (3): 321–32.

Summers, Lawrence H. 1992. "The Challenges of Development." *Finance and Development* 29 (1): 6–9.

Summers, Lawrence, and Shekhar Shah, eds. 1991. *Proceedings of the World Bank Annual Conference on Development Economics*. Washington, DC: World Bank.

Sunday Times: Business Times. 1996. (February 18): 2.

Svedberg, Peter. 1991. *Poverty and Undernutrition in Sub-Saharan Africa: Theory, Evidence, Policy*. Monograph Series no. 19. Stockholm: Institute for International Economic Studies, Stockholm University.

Tacon, P. 1991. *Survey on Street Children in Three Urban Centers of Namibia*. Windhoek, Namibia: Ministry of Local Government and Housing.

Tanzi, Vito. 1992. "Structural Factors and Tax Revenue in Developing Countries: A Decade of Evidence" in *Open Economies: Structural Adjustments and Agriculture*, ed. I. Goldin and L.A. Winters. Cambridge: Cambridge University Press.

———. 1996. "Corruption, Governmental Activities, and Markets." *Finance and Development* 32 (4): 24–26.

Tarp, Finn. 1993. *Stabilization and Structural Adjustment: Macroeconomic Frameworks for Analyzing the Crisis in Sub-Saharan Africa*. London: Routledge.

Taylor, D. R. Fraser. 1992. "Development from Within and Survival in Rural Africa: A Synthesis of Theory and Practice" in Taylor and MacKenzie 1992.

Taylor, D. R. Fraser, and Fiona MacKenzie, eds. 1992. *Development From Within: Survival in Rural Africa*. London: Routledge.

Testa, Graciela D. 1989. "The Invisible Entrepreneurs of South Africa." *International Health and Development* 1 (2): 22–23.

The Botswana Gazette. 1995. (May 31): 9.

The Courier. 1992. no. 134 (July-August): 77–84.

The Economist. 1990. (December 8): 71.

———. 1994. (December 17): 43.

———. 1995. "Cities Survey" (July 29): 3–18.

———. 1996a. (February 10): 40.

———. 1996b. (March 2): 44.

The Midweek Sun. 1994. (August 17): 2.

Thomas, Duncan, and Ityai Muvandi. 1994. *How Fast Is Fertility Declining in Botswana and Zimbabwe?* Discussion Paper 258. Washington, DC: World Bank.

Thomas, Neil, and Charles Mercer. 1995. "An Examination of the Fertility/Contraceptive Prevalence Anomaly in Zimbabwe." *Genus* 51 (3–4): 179–203.

Thomas, Vinod, et al., eds. 1991. *Restructuring Economies in Distress.* New York: Oxford University Press.

Tipple, A. Graham. 1994. "The Need for New Urban Housing in Sub-Saharan Africa: Problems or Opportunity." *African Affairs* 93 (373): 587–608.

Tripp, Aili Mari. 1994. "The Universe of Civil Society: The Heterogeneity of Associations in Africa." Paper presented at a USAID Workshop on Civil Society, Democracy, and Development in Africa, Washington, DC, June 9–10.

Tshishimbi, wa Bilenga, Peter Glick, and Erik Thorbecke. 1994. "Missed Opportunity for Adjustment in a Rent-Seeking Society: The Case of Zaire" in Sahn 1994.

Tsie, Balefi. 1995. *The Political Economy of Botswana in SADCC.* Harare: Sapes Books.

Turrittin, Jane. 1991. "Mali: People Topple Traoré." *Review of African Political Economy,* no. 52: 97–103.

ul Haq, Mahbub. 1995. *Reflections on Human Development.* New York: Oxford University Press.

United Nations. 1988. *World Demographic Estimates and Projections, 1950–2025.* New York: United Nations.

———. 1990. *Practical Measures Against Corruption.* New York: United Nations.

———. 1991. *The World's Women 1980–1990: Trends and Statistics.* New York: United Nations.

United Nations Children's Fund (UNICEF). 1987. *The State of the World's Children 1987.* New York: Oxford University Press.

———. 1989. *The State of the World's Children 1989.* New York: Oxford University Press.

United Nations Development Programme (UNDP). 1990. *Human Development Report 1990.* New York: Oxford University Press.

———. 1991. *Human Development Report 1991.* New York: Oxford University Press.

———. 1992. *Human Development Report 1992.* New York: Oxford University Press.

———. 1993. *Human Development Report 1993.* New York: Oxford University Press.

————. 1994. *Human Development Report 1994*. New York: Oxford University Press.

————. 1995. *Human Development Report 1995*. New York: Oxford University Press.

United States Agency for International Development (USAID). 1989. *AID Micro-Enterprise Stock Taking: Synthesis Report*. Washington, DC: USAID.

————. 1993. *Economic Reform in Africa's New Era of Political Liberalization: Proceedings of a Workshop for SPA Donors*. Washington, DC: USAID.

————. 1994. "Executive Summary." USAID Workshop on Civil Society, Democracy, and Development in Africa, Washington, DC, June 9–10.

Valleroy, L., J. Harris, and P. Way. 1990. "The Impact of HIV-1 Infection on Child Survival in the Developing World." *AIDS* 4 (7): 667–72.

Vandemoortele, Jan. 1991. "Labor Market Informalization in Sub-Saharan Africa" in *Towards Social Adjustment: Labour Market Issues in Structural Adjustment*, ed. Guy Standing and Victor Tokman. Geneva: ILO.

Van de Walle, Nicolas. 1994a. "Neopatrimonialism and Democracy in Africa, with an Illustration from Cameroon" in Widner 1994.

————. 1994b. "Review Essay: Adjustment Alternatives and Alternatives to Adjustment." *African Studies Review* 37 (3): 103–17.

Vengroff, R., and A. Johnston. 1987. "Decentralization and the Implementation of Rural Development in Senegal: The Role of Rural Councils." *Public Administration and Development* 7 (2): 273–88.

Von Braun, Joachim, et al. 1992. *Improving Food Security of the Poor: Concept, Policy, and Programs*. Washington, DC: International Food Policy Research Institute.

————. 1993. *Urban Food Insecurity and Malnutrition in Developing Countries: Trends, Policies, and Research Implications*. Washington, DC: International Food Policy Research Institute.

Wamala, A. S. 1994. "The African Public Service and Democracy." *Africa Insight* 24 (3): 206–11.

Watkins, Kevin. 1996. "Eclipsing the New Dawn of Development." *Ceres* 28 (1): 27–32.

Way, Peter O., and Karen A. Stanecki. 1994. *An Epidemiological Review of HIV/AIDS in Sub-Saharan Africa*. Washington, DC: Center for International Research, U.S. Bureau of the Census.

Wekwete, K. H. 1992. "Africa" in *Sustainable Cities: Urbanization and the Environment in International Perspective,* ed. Richard Stren, Rodney White, and Joseph Whitney. Boulder, CO: Westview Press.

Wellard, Kate, and James G. Copestake, eds. 1993. *Non-Governmental Organizations and the State in Africa: Rethinking Roles in Sustainable Agricultural Development*. London: Routledge.

Wells, Louis T., Jr. 1994. "Foreign Direct Investment" in Lindauer and Roemer 1994.

Werlin, Herbert H. 1994. "Revisiting Corruption: With a New Definition." *International Review of Administrative Sciences* 60 (4): 547–58.

West Africa. 1992. (May 18–24): 840.

————. 1993a. (September 20–26): 1683.

————. 1993b. (September 27–October 3): 1727.

———. 1995. (February 13–19): 217–19.

Westcott, Clay. 1994. "Civil Service Reform in Africa" in *Civil Service Reform in Latin America and the Caribbean,* ed. S. A. Chaudry, G. J. Reid, and W. H. Malik. Washington, DC: World Bank.

Whitaker, Jennifer S. 1988. *How Can Africa Survive?* New York: Harper and Row.

Whiteside, Alan. 1993a. *AIDS: Socio-economic Causes and Consequences.* Occasional Paper no. 29. Durban, South Africa: Economic Research Unit, University of Natal.

———. 1993b. "The Impact of AIDS on Industry in Zimbabwe" in Cross and Whiteside 1993.

Widner, Jennifer A., ed. 1994. *Economic Change and Political Liberalization in Sub-Saharan Africa.* Baltimore: Johns Hopkins University Press.

Woods, Dwayne. 1994. "The Vertical and Horizontal Dimensions to Associational Politics in Sub-Saharan Africa." Paper presented at a USAID Workshop on Civil Society, Democracy, and Development in Africa, Washington, DC, June 9–10.

World Bank. 1981. *Accelerated Development in Sub-Saharan Africa: An Agenda for Action.* Washington, DC: World Bank.

———. 1983. *World Development Report 1983.* New York: Oxford University Press.

———. 1989a. *World Development Report 1989.* New York: Oxford University Press.

———. 1989b. *Sub-Saharan Africa: From Crisis to Sustainable Growth: A Long-Term Perspective Study.* Washington, DC: World Bank.

———. 1990. *World Development Report 1990: Poverty.* New York: Oxford University Press.

———. 1991. *World Development Report 1991: The Challenge of Development.* New York: Oxford University Press.

———. 1992. *World Development Report 1992: Development and the Environment.* New York: Oxford University Press.

———. 1993a. *World Development Report 1993: Investing in Health.* New York: Oxford University Press.

———. 1993b. *The East Asian Miracle: Economic Growth and Public Policy.* New York: Oxford University Press.

———. 1994a. *Status Report on Poverty in Sub-Saharan Africa 1994: The Many Faces of Poverty.* Washington, DC: World Bank.

———. 1994b. *Adjustment in Africa: Reforms, Results, and the Road Ahead.* New York: Oxford University Press.

———. 1994c. *Trends in Developing Economies Extracts: Volume 3: Sub-Saharan Africa.* Washington, DC: World Bank.

———. 1995a. *African Development Indicators 1994–95.* Washington, DC: World Bank.

———. 1995b. *World Development Report 1995: Workers in an Integrating World.* New York: Oxford University Press.

———. 1995c. *Labor and the Growth Crisis in Sub-Saharan Africa.* Washington, DC: World Bank.

———. 1995d. *Bureaucrats in Business: The Economics and Politics of Government Ownership.* New York: Oxford University Press.

———. 1996. *Partnership for Capacity Building in Africa.* Washington, DC: World Bank.

World Health Organization (WHO). 1991. "Update on AIDS." *Weekly Epidemiological Record* (November 29): 355.

Wunsch, James, and Dele Olowu, eds. 1990. *The Failure of the Centralized State: Institutions and Self-Governance in Africa.* Boulder, CO: Westview Press.

Young, Crawford, and Thomas Turner. 1985. *The Rise and Decline of the Zairean State.* Madison: University of Wisconsin Press.

Zack-Williams, A., and Stephen Riley. 1993. "Sierra Leone: The Coup and its Consequences." *Review of African Political Economy,* no. 56: 91–98.

Zeller, M., et al. 1994. "Sources and Terms of Credit for the Rural Poor in the Gambia." *African Review of Money Finance and Banking* 1/2: 167–86.

Zuckerman, Elaine. 1991. "The Social Costs of Adjustment" in Thomas et al. 1991.

Index

About the Author

Kempe Ronald Hope Sr. is a United Nations Chief Technical Adviser to the Government of Botswana and Professor of Development Studies at the University of Botswana. His books include *Development in the Third World: From Policy Failure to Policy Reform* (1996), which was also published by M. E. Sharpe; *Development Finance and the Development Process* (1987); *Economic Development in the Caribbean* (1986); *Urbanization in the Commonwealth Caribbean* (1986); and *The Dynamics of Development and Development Administration* (1984).